T. W. (Thomas William) Webb, John Webb

Military Memoir of Colonel John Birch

T. W. (Thomas William) Webb, John Webb

Military Memoir of Colonel John Birch

ISBN/EAN: 9783337153816

Printed in Europe, USA, Canada, Australia, Japan

Cover: Foto ©ninafisch / pixelio.de

More available books at **www.hansebooks.com**

MILITARY MEMOIR

OF

COLONEL JOHN BIRCH,

SOMETIME GOVERNOR OF HEREFORD IN THE CIVIL WAR BETWEEN
CHARLES I. AND THE PARLIAMENT;

WRITTEN BY ROE, HIS SECRETARY;

WITH AN HISTORICAL AND CRITICAL COMMENTARY,
NOTES, AND APPENDIX,

BY THE LATE

REV. JOHN WEBB, M.A., F.S.A., F.R.L.S.

EDITED BY HIS SON THE

REV. T. W. WEBB, M.A., F.R.A.S.

PRINTED FOR THE CAMDEN SOCIETY.

M.DCCC.LXXIII.

COUNCIL OF THE CAMDEN SOCIETY

FOR THE YEAR 1873-74.

President,

THE RIGHT HON. THE EARL OF VERULAM, F.R.G.S.
THE RIGHT HON. LORD ACTON.
WILLIAM CHAPPELL, ESQ. F.S.A., *Treasurer.*
WILLIAM DURRANT COOPER, ESQ. F.S.A.
FREDERICK WILLIAM COSENS, ESQ.
JOHN FORSTER, ESQ. D.C.L.
JAMES GAIRDNER, ESQ.
SAMUEL RAWSON GARDINER, ESQ., *Director.*
ALFRED KINGSTON, ESQ., *Secretary.*
SIR JOHN MACLEAN, F.S.A.
FREDERIC OUVRY, ESQ. Treas. S.A.
EDWARD RIMBAULT, LL.D.
JAMES SPEDDING, ESQ.
WILLIAM JOHN THOMS, ESQ. F.S.A.
SIR WALTER CALVERLEY TREVELYAN, BART.
J. R. D. TYSSEN, ESQ.

The COUNCIL of the CAMDEN SOCIETY desire it to be understood that they are not answerable for any opinions or observations that may appear in the Society's publications; the Editors of the several Works being alone responsible for the same.

PRELIMINARY NOTICE.

THE Commentary and Notes which illustrate the following Memoir were the production of an author the greater part of whose ninety-third year was employed in their preparation. But, whatever interest may be attached to them from this cause, they are still more deserving of attention from the scrupulous fidelity as well as the unwearied diligence which they express. Such, as is well known, had been the uniform character of the earlier works of the same hand; and during this last effort of a feebler age, neither vigour of thought nor truth of discernment failed. The editorial office which had been entrusted to the Reverend John Webb by the Camden Society was, at the time of its interruption, nearly fulfilled: the latter part, however, of his manuscript had not received his final touch, and the close was left very imperfect. These deficiencies could be ill supplied even by one who best knew his revered parent's intentions, but, having been honoured by the Council of the Society with permission to complete the design, he has done it to the best of his ability. A portion of illustrative material has been reluctantly omitted, which may, however, it is hoped, find a place in the future publication of another posthumous work by the same hand—the History of the Civil War in Herefordshire.

The extent of the present writer's responsibility has been indicated by brackets. The initials J. W. are attached to certain notes which the original editor had not appended to his manuscript, but which it did not seem desirable to suppress.

PREFACE.

The document now first published contains an account of events in which the person therein described acted a more or less conspicuous part. The period it involves is comprised between the years 1642 and 1645; a time during which England became the scene of violent political and military agitation. In all cases of this nature, in which the talents and passions of men are exercised with unusual force, there will ever be some whose powers will raise them to eminence. Colonel John Birch, in the sphere in which he moved, was among the remarkable personages of the time; by no means inferior to many whose names have been better known, though not more deserving of being recorded. He attained to considerable distinction in the field and in the senate, and after a long share of personal exertion and sufferings survived the troubles and dangers of a stormy and eventful struggle, and ended his days in retirement and peace.

Considering the part that he took in this drama, it is remarkable that so little direct information respecting his earlier life has been handed down to posterity. The mention, however, of his name, traditionally or otherwise, has always been coupled with that of low origin and of very humble calling. The fullest account of him, as far as the Editor's research has extended, is given in a note on pp. 203 *et seqq.* of Newcome's Diary (Chetham Society) by a very diligent antiquary, the late Thomas Heywood, Esquire, of Hope End in the county of Hereford. In this he shows his connexion with the Birches of Lancashire, though his statements with regard to his origin are not quite so satisfactory as could be wished. He repeats the lowness of his birth; and this is indeed far from being controverted by the expression on Birch's monument, which only describes him as "of worthy parentage." Be this as it may, Heywood has by no means set the question at rest, and accepts the original notion of his first employment. The opinion of him in his life-time was that he had been a carrier. Burnet, a contemporary, who writes as though he was personally acquainted with Birch, affirms it; and argues from his manner and address that he retained proofs of it, and encouraged the impression by his mode of speaking in Parliament. The Bishop positively says he was a carrier.[a] Others have adopted the same notion: it was universally prevalent during his life; and succeeding times have concurred in it, with such enlargement as tradition might be expected to bring with it. The substance of what has been commonly reported is, that, while he was employed in driving pack-horses along the road, he so resolutely and successfully resisted the attempt of some Parliamentary soldiers under Cromwell to rob him, that he attracted the notice of that

[a] History of his Own Time, i. 546. A merchant who delivers his goods may be said to be a carrier. Birch had done so, and might thus have fastened the report upon him: he might have done nothing more. [The following passage, from Seyer's Memoirs of Bristol, ii. 351, illustrates this view of the subject. "Mr. Yeomans in all the contemporary writers is called a merchant, and the circumstance that masters of ships and sailors were found in his house on that unfortunate night confirms that he was so. Yet whereas an apprentice of his is mentioned, a youth of 15 or 16 years old, it is probable that he was also a tradesman, especially since at that time there were few tradesmen in Bristol of respectability who were not also engaged in commerce."] Lord Macaulay, in quoting Burnet, does not seem to have been aware of the difference between a *carter* and a *carrier*. [Possibly he may have been misled by the fact that Colonel Birch's kinsman Thomas, who, holding the same rank in the service of the Parliament, was alike distinguished by successful and disgraced by inhuman actions, was called, even among his own party, *the Earl of Derby's carter*, from the circumstance that "his Lordship had trailed him under a hay-cart at Manchester." (Seacome's History of the House of Stanley, 304.) This was probably the Col. Birch who is mentioned in the History of Whalley as having been imprisoned by the Parliament in 1645, notwithstanding his faithful services.]

commander, who offered him a commission in his troop.[a] It is hardly necessary to assert that a slight comparison of dates and circumstances would show the fabulous nature of this opinion. As far as Cromwell and the introduction of Birch into the army are concerned, it is impossible. Under Cromwell he fought for a while in the West, but the commencement of his soldiership is of earlier date. If it be difficult to show in what he might be employed in his earliest youth, it will be proved that while he was yet a very young man he could not but have received an education beyond that of a packhorse-driver, and that he was actually otherwise occupied when he took up arms.

Concerning Roe, the writer of this singular narrative, the Editor has been able to collect little more than his name: the post that he held under Birch has been variously described as Major, Quartermaster, or Secretary; and if he be, as is probable, the same individual, a Colonel Roe is named in the Perfect Diurnall as connected with the regiment of Birch when he was no longer at the head of it, and it was ordered to Ireland.[b] That he held a post of inferior rank when this account was written is evident from the story. Closely attached to the person of his Colonel, and holding him in respect and admiration when their common term of service had ceased, in gratitude for past favours he felt it his duty to record the achievements of his superior officer, having been for the most part an eye and ear witness of what he has related. This is his own representation of the matter. The tone and expression are highly in

[a] History of Leominster, by the Rev. G. F. Townsend, 109.
[b] Sept. 14, 1646. [This may perhaps require a slight modification. Further research has shown that Birch was succeeded by Humphreys in the command of the regiment, and that it never, after all, left the shores of England. Roe may, nevertheless, have obtained the command of some other body of troops; and from the internal evidence afforded by Birch's corrections it may be surmised that the two were separated after the completion of the memoir.]

character with that of the party in which they were both engaged: but the peculiarity of this attempt at biography is the general employment of the second person throughout the whole, and the reduction of it into the semblance of an epistolary form.

If it be worth inquiry why this should have been adopted (as there must have been a motive for so singular a mode of expression,) in what the inferior officer wrote and his superior approved, it may seem that out of compliment to the latter an opportunity was afforded not only of avoiding egotism, but of introducing circumstantial traits of character in a way that modesty would hardly have allowed Birch to use in speaking of his own exploits. To some it may appear that the Colonel might perhaps himself have suggested this description of his own doings and sayings: at any rate he gave it his sanction by correcting it, as is evident to the Editor, with his own hand. It must be admitted that Roe in his zeal to exalt the Colonel has attributed to him the springs and results of certain successes unnoticed in this way by others; but, whatever may be thought of this, the reader will probably be amused by the earnest deference, amounting almost to flattery, oddly mixed with the frankness of the soldier and the pious exhortations and licence of a friend; while he calls his grateful attention in the language of the time to what the Colonel had been permitted to do, as well as to the perils that he had escaped, and reminds him of what he might have forgotten.

In an abridgment that has been subsequently made from the MS. by an unknown hand, and which refers the authorship to Birch's Quartermaster, the second person has been changed to the third. This MS., which, singularly enough, contains corrections of its own, has been collated with the original; the variations will be found in their places, but the alterations by Birch in Roe's MS. are alone of any importance.

PREFACE. vii

The Editor cannot but here record those obligations which have attended the origin and progress of the publication of this volume, too numerous now to be minutely expressed: some of those to whom he has been indebted have long passed beyond the reach of grateful acknowledgment. Among these he may be allowed to name the former possessor of the MS., to whose kindness he was first indebted for a transcript of it, the late Samuel Peploe, Esq.; the late Thomas Bird, Esq., sometime Town Clerk of Hereford, the owner of the abridged copy; the late Lord Liverpool, for the inspection of the Ottley Papers at Pytchford; the late Sir Robert Peel, for permission to examine the State Paper Office; Sir Henry Ellis, Sir Frederic Madden, and the officials of the British Museum; with many other official and private departed and living friends, particularly the Reverend John Hopton of Canon Frome; the Reverend Thomas Powell Symonds of Pengethly, in the county of Hereford; and two ladies, Mrs. Acton of Acton Scott, in the county of Salop, and Lady F. V. Harcourt of The Homme, in the county of Hereford, to whom he owes his best thanks for zealous assistance and valuable information.[a] It would be tedious to specify the various collections to which he has had recourse for printed pamphlets of the period, the chief of which have been in the Bodleian Library, that of the British Museum, and of the London Institution.

The object of this attempt being in the course of illustration to communicate a variety of information from sources not easily accessible, such miscellaneous matter will be found distributed according to convenience between the Commentary and the Notes. It may be best at once to premise that the Commentary sets up no pretension to rivalry with the information in the Text, but is

[a] [To these must be added the names of Major Peploe of Garnstone, the present proprietor of the MS.; R. W. Banks, Esq.; J. Stone, Esq.; A. C. Ranyard, Esq.; and the Revs. H. Hubbard, O. A. Hodgson, T. Woodhouse, H. W. Phillott, C. J. Robinson.]

intended chiefly to be so far explanatory as to show its connection with the events, characters, and manners of the time. Some things will be added, and others corrected, as occasion may require. With reference to the Title of this narrative, nothing more has been attempted than here and there a commonly pictorial representation, where they occur, of the incidents of war. Whatever endeavours may have been employed towards a military history of the age, it may be fairly considered as a desideratum; and the writer may be excused if he should appear to give any other than an unprofessional view on the subject of warlike operations. Indeed the original affects no more. When Bishop Burnet was writing his History, he is said to have received a hint from Marshal Schomberg not to interfere with military affairs, and the caution might not have been unnecessary. The modesty of Hampden had already anticipated this point: when requested to give his opinion upon such matters his expression was, " Refer that to soldiers—they understand it."

As the MS. opens somewhat abruptly, and leaves us in the dark concerning Birch's previous occupation, it will be useful to premise a short review of public and private affairs at the city of Bristol, at which place the Memoir discovers him to us when the curtain rises.

HISTORICAL INTRODUCTION.

No sooner had the war broken out between the King and the Parliament but its influence was felt along the whole line of the River Severn, through its adjoining counties, and the places situated on its banks from Shrewsbury to the sea. Other places had their share in the effects of the disturbance, and much internal distress ensued.

Before the battle of Edge-hill Charles I. had secured Shrewsbury, and selected Colonel, afterwards Sir Francis, Ottley,[a] governor. Considerable intercourse that had long existed by water between this town and Bristol began to be interrupted by the state of affairs. Ottley had hardly been invested with his appointment when the following letter reached him : [b]

S^r

Uppon a letter rec: from Richard Reeve which is confirm'd P' word of mouth P' Young Henry Reeves ; I have P$^\text{rt}$ly in Regard of myself and P$^\text{rt}$ly for the love I bear to free trade made bould to Trouble you with these few Lines which by Order I write unto y^r Hon^r it appears that whereas I sent to Shrewsbury by Richard Reeve fower butts of Sack you have made seasure or at least stop of them in Shrosbury as my self being one of the malignant P^t that have taken up Arms against the King

---

[a] When Charles I. in October, 1642, withdrew from York to Shrewsbury, he was attended there by Sir Francis Ottley, of Pitchford, in the county of Salop, a gentleman of devoted loyalty, who had been declared a delinquent, Aug. 6, 1642, and to whom, by warrant dated Oct. 11, he gave command not to remove out of that county: "he could not think of sparing him," was his expression, "till the present great distractions should be better settled." He was then about to draw out his forces from the place and county. Jan. 16 or 17, he was appointed Governor of Shrewsbury. Nichols, Collectanea, v.

[b] Ottley MSS.

which God forbid and I P'sume you are misinform'd in that. now so it is that there being a free trade intended between Shrowsbury and Bristoll the May^r my good frend and the Collonell Essex do desire by no means the least Jarr or Occasion of breach and therefore by the same rule though they might have made stopag of the Goods and Trow of Shrowsbury yet neither they nor myself desire it, but they have engaged themselves to me to make good the 4 butts at 16^l a butt only it was thought good I should write unto you to know your pleasure and if you wou'd be pleased to lett my wines be disposed off According as I shall Ord^r and according to free Trade which they are confident off (and young Henry Reeves Afirms it) then that y^r Hon^r would be pleased the next Spring to answer this my letter and to declare if I shall give Order for the dispose of the Wines aforesaid which will make it to Appear that yor Hon^r desires a free trade as we also desire and for myself shall be ready to do you any Resonable service and so rest desireing that this great breach and misunderstanding may be made up

So prays y^r Lo Frend
Though unknown
Jo: Birch

I desire to send my Bro: to Shrewsbury to dispose of the Sack there and some other Goods I shall send up next Spring If y^r Hon^r please to give way.

Bristoll: 28th Jan: 1642

To the Hon^{rable} Sr Francis Oatly Govern^r of the
Town of Sallop these P'sent P" a Frend whom
God P'serve.

We have here at once the future Colonel Birch in a new light, together with a brother, subsequently an officer in the Parliament's service.[a] They are both resident at Bristol, and engaged in commercial enterprise. It appears that, according to the common usage then existing, the brothers were general merchants, and, if not in partnership, were acting together. John, in suitable language, speaks of "my wines," as a principal in the house, and that these had been stopped in Shrewsbury: he mentions also other goods that he intends should be sent up and disposed of by his brother if

---

[a] [John Birch had two brothers, Samuel and Thomas, the latter of whom became Rector of Hampton Bishop, in the county of Hereford. Samuel must therefore be the one here referred to. He reappears as Major, commanding at Hereford in his brother's absence in 1647-8.]

matters could be arranged. The letter is an attempt, accompanied by an awkward apology, to save certain articles of property which existing hostilities had placed in danger; and what he dwells upon most particularly, the free trade, is an allusion to the setting aside of those monopolies that had given so much public offence, and were in part the cause of the existing dispute. He wishes at the same time that it should be distinctly understood that he is not one of those who entertain hostile opposition to the Royal cause: Parliamentarians would not allow that they were doing so. The mayor for that year was Richard Aldworth,[a] and the governor (both of whom seem to have ordered him to write) was Colonel Essex. This latter had been commanded by the Lord General the Earl of Essex to proceed to that city and seize it into his hands for the Parliament. He did so: he gained an entrance by stealth,[b] and contrived for the time being to suppress the Royalists. Colonel Essex, however, in the end, proved more of the Cavalier than the Roundhead, to the neglect of his duties: he was fond of merry-making, feasting, and dancing; he behaved capriciously to Birch, quarrelled with him over night, and arrested and released him on the following morning.[c] There is unquestionable evidence that Birch at that time was captain of a company of volunteers that had been raised on the part of the Parliament for the defence of Bristol.[d] The

[a] Aldworth was a merchant who had accepted, conjointly with Richard Wollaston of London, a contract for shirts for the soldiers in Ireland.—Commons' Journals, July 13, 1642. A proof of the commercial relation between the two towns.

[b] Owing to the interference of the mayoress and other ladies, whose entreaties threw the mayor and corporation off their guard.—Barrett, Hist. of Bristol, 216.

[c] His temper was equally ungovernable towards his own men. He acted with such despotic power, says Barrett, that, "offended with one of the soldiers for modestly asking for his pay, he instantly shot him through the head."—Hist. ut supra, 227; Merc. Aulicus, Feb. 10, 1642.

[d] Hargrave's State Trials, i. 796.

irregularities of the governor were reported by letters to Parliament, and all was soon changed. A successor was found for him in Colonel Nathaniel Fiennes, the eldest son of Lord Saye and Sele, who proceeded to Bristol, arrested Essex at one of his festive meetings, confined him in Berkeley Castle, and took his place.[a] Then immediately commenced a reign of severity and restraint: and the troubles of the divided citizens increased to a fearful height. As to the place itself, it has been universally agreed that, though but a city of the second class, it was one of great importance to whichever party could occupy it; the storehouse of merchandize, ammunition, and arms; the key of the River Severn: but internally it had then become a theatre of distraction and confusion. Trade was at a stand; lists of the names of the Royalist opponents were framed; their houses were searched for arms; it was dangerous for them to walk abroad; they were forbidden to go beyond the walls under pain of imprisonment. The populace took advantage of the disorder, and broke loose, as was the case in many other places, according as either side held the ascendancy over those that had adopted the contrary part. The temper of the place, private and public, was that of a general wrangle. They openly reviled each other, and the King's party complained that their

[a] [A remarkable passage occurs in a letter from the new governor, apparently to his father, given by Seyer, Memoirs, ii. 326. He complains of Essex as " being himself familiar and intimate with the chief malignants, and siding with them against the good partie, and that in so high a degree, that even after I came to the town he imprisoned Capt. Birche, who is and always was the most active man in the town for the Parliament, and swore that neither he nor any of his men, nor any of the Bridge-men (who are known to be the honestest men in the town, and who only appeared in their arms for us when Prince Rupert came before the town) should have any arms or any command in the city; and this I can testifie myself, for he swore it deeply in my presence." Fiennes, it appears, disarmed some of the citizens who had been armed by Essex.—The Earl of Stamford had said, in a letter to the Speaker of the House of Lords, Dec. 19, 1642, " I find this city infinitely well affected to the good cause."]

adversaries spat upon them in the streets, and treated them contemptuously:—Baxter [a] and others have made the same complaint in Worcestershire and elsewhere. In Hereford it was past endurance.[b] Such proceedings could not consist with a sound condition of society. The King by proclamation forbad all seamen to enter into the service of the Parliament: that portion of the population were strongly attached to him. The new governor published a counter-proclamation, and ordered the former to be burned in the market-place. He came in state in his coach, escorted by a troop of horse, and held a brace of pistols to the breast of the common crier, whom he compelled to read his own proclamation while the former was thrown into the flames.

Tidings of these and other violent proceedings reached the King at Oxford, and he resolved at the request of the Royalists to send them relief. His friends were accordingly encouraged in secret to expect that Prince Rupert was coming to their assistance. They had held close meetings, and communication had been made to Oxford with regard to the day and hour when the Prince should be received by throwing open the gates for his admission. It was to be in the early morning of the 8th of March; a signal was to be given by ringing the bells of St. John's and St. Michael's churches,[c] when the guards were to be seized at Frome-gate and New-gate, and the King's troops admitted into the city. True to his appointment, the Prince had appeared on Durdham Down with about 7,500 men. Throughout the night his fires at the bivouac enlightened the horizon. He waited till the morning, but all had

[a] Life, i. 40.
[b] Lady Brilliana Harley's Letters, Camden Society, 18, 202, *et al.*
[c] [In a letter, apparently by Aldworth, it is stated that the bells of three churches were to be tolled. "St. Nicholas' bell for the butchers, St. John's bell for the sailors, and St. Michael's bell to bring down the cavaliers."—Seyer, Memoirs, ii. 354.]

Memoirs of some Actions in which Collonel John Birch was engaged. Written by his Secretary.[a]

THE MANUSCRIPT.

[The text is given with the corrections, additions, and alterations of Colonel Birch, printed in italic type: the original reading being subjoined at the foot of the page. Where there is no mark of reference, the italic word or passage is inserted by him.

There seems reason to surmise that the MS. now printed is not the autograph of Roe, and that it may possibly have been transcribed after his departure for Ireland. Blanks occur from time to time, as though the copyist had failed to decipher the original—perhaps very illegibly written—and had no opportunity of referring to the author; and mistakes may be found in punctuation, which could hardly have arisen except in the process of somewhat unintelligent transcription. The more remarkable of these have been indicated in the foot-notes.]

HONERED SIR,—

All men in the world haue one maine and principall worke to doe, which is to advance the glory of God, that being the very end of their creation, about which they ought to spend their cheifest time, whole tresure, and, if need bee, not to bee spareing of their dearest blood. And to the end that God may loose noe glorie, nor such as hee hath made instrumentall in an extraordinary way may neither bee themselues forgotten, nor forget what the Lord hath done for them, I haue collected these passages of God's providence, though weakly yet truely, every passage thereof being of my owne knowledge ; which though I haue noe reason to question but that God's hand therein was by you well remembred, yet I could not doe less then present you with [b] short notes, which haue been taken

---

[a] On fly-leaf, in a later hand.   [b] "my" cancelled.

by mee in your service; wherein soe much of God is seen, that I should haue looked vpon my selfe as an eclipser of his glory, if I should not haue comitted the same to paper. And in the first place I cannot omitt God's great goodnes to you at Bristoll, when Prince Rupert came before it, haueing with him about 7500 men, Anno 1642,[a] hee haueing assurance from Mr. Yeomans, Mr. Bowcher, and others in that cittie, that it should bee deliverd to him, the gaurds surprised, with diverse principall persons; and [b] I supose you will never forget [c] the message deliverd you on the bridge in that cittie, that night about 8 of the clocke (vizt.) : that before the next morneing you should bee a dead man; and that, in stead of ffeare and flyeing as divers others, whose presence was very necessary, and profession should haue taught them otherwise, you addrest your selfe presently to finde out where those parties were gathered together, whoe within a few howers were to act that treachery; which indeavor the Lord was pleased soe to order, that before eleaven a clocke, you had about one hundred cheife men in your *custody*,[d] whereof most *had*[e] been leaders in that worke; for which some of them afterwards deservedly suffered; and the Prince himselfe the next morneing returned toward Oxford *with shame;* the which *work*[f] God particulerly honord you in.[g]

After which *about 7 monthes*[h] the said Prince comeing againe before that cittie with an army on the north side, and Prince Maurice, his brother, with Sir Ralph Hopton, and that Western army on the south side, against whom you were to act your part, God inabling you soe to doe. And although the place offended was weake, and *Prince Morris and the Cornish forces*[i] there stormed

[[a] This was in the beginning of March; and therefore 1642 in contemporaneous, 1643 in modern reckoning: a discrepancy requiring careful attention in the study of the times. The date is underlined in the original.]
[b] " that word " cancelled.   [c] " vizt " cancelled.
[d] castle.   [e] haue.   [f] time.
[g] " at his " cancelled, with a blank space following.
[h] Underlined, orig.   [i] the Prince.

vs often, yett neere 100 persons of honner *weare slaine in the last storme*,ᵃ and more private soldiers *fiue times ouer then weare slaine*ᵇ in all other parts of *the city*.ᶜ Notwithstanding which, on the otherside the cittie, neere Windmill Fort, the line was vnhappily *entred*,ᵈ for I cannot call it *stormed*,ᵈ because at that entrance there was not a man slaine on either part. And here I might envy ᵉ against men; but I shall forbeare: it would but weary you to heare them named. Thus was that famous cittie taken and spoyled, contrary to articles, to the eternall shame of him whoc had the conduct of that army; which though noe man but your selfe stayed to see, yet is notoriously knowne. And here miraculously the Lord preserved you those three dayes, in the midest of those lyons, when soe many messengers of death were sent vnto you, your selfe well remembers: and his hand was noe less seen in bringing you to London, thorowe them all; which I hope you will never forget. Whither being come, contrary to the practice of many at that time, both great and small, some runing to Oxford, others getting pardons, and the best saveing what they had beyond sea, God caried you beyond these to raise a foote regiment, by the assistance and vnder the comand ofᶠ Sir Arthur Haslerig, (though vnder your own whole management) and the truely honerd Sir William Waller as generall. And before I do proceed further I

ᵃ Inserted in a space left purposely blank.
ᵇ Inserted in a space left purposely blank; "then" cancelled.   ᶜ that storme.
ᵈ Underlined, orig.—[Seyer says (Memoirs, ii. 404) that the line was entered by Colonel Washington, making a breach in it near a barn, at or before sunrising; and that he had heard old persons call the place Washington's bridge, *i.e.* breach.]
ᵉ The writer obviously means "inveigh," and the allusion is to Fiennes [and, perhaps, also to Major Langrish, who failed to charge the storming party on their entering the line].
ᶠ "that honerd preserver of his country," orig. cancelled by Birch. This serves to show that the MS. had been revised some time after it was written. How much soever Colonel Birch and his secretary might originally have admired Sir A. H· there can be no doubt that the latter, who acted under Cromwell's usurpation, and Birch, who retired and was set aside, were not at last upon terms. [The cancelled word appears to have been "patron," or more probably "patroit" (*sic*).]

cannot chuse but put you in minde of God's great worke, that from the day you marcht out with that *foote* regiment *and when afterwards you had a regiment of horse also*, to the day you had the additionall honner to sitt in the House of Commons, never any, whither horse or ffoote, vnder your comand, came away with the worst, as I shall take the bouldnes more particulerly to put you in minde. And in the first place at Farnum about three of the clocke in the afternoone, the Lord Hopton's army and Sir William Waller's *being drawen into* ᵃ batalia, soe soone as ever your regiment *of foote* came into the ffeild and engaged, *the Lord*ᵇ Hopton's army *in halfe an houre* retreate*d* in disorder: which I cannot attribute to the strength of your regiment, but God's hand then sheweing you what you haue never failed since to finde; (vizt.) that none of his enimies should ever stand before you. Presently vpon this, your great hazard in lyeing at *Crundale twoo miles from Farnum*,ᶜ the *enemy*ᵈ at Alton, their head quarters, but 4 miles of, and Sir William Waller's head quarters at Farnum; which though your quarters was hazardos, yett God there made you the instrument for the sending out spies and discovering their fortification soe well, that though you were never at Alton, yet when you had made all ready, you did aswell knowe where there trench was deepe and wheare shallowe, and where to enter, as if your selfe had ordered the worke. Nay, lett mee never forgett, and I hope you never will, that deliverence God gaue you on the hills short of the towne that morneing goeing out; where 6 of those enimies scouts, *though*ᵉ they had *you*ᶠ amongst them, were not able to carry you prisoner to the towne, but, contrarywise, sufferd you to bring the comander of them away *prisoner back to our owne army, haueing but the helpe of twoo more, God giueing*ᵍ you that as an earnest of that great mercy he gaue you a few houres after; where hee made you the

---

ᵃ were draweing in. ᵇ did not then.
ᶜ Inserted in a space left purposely blank. ᵈ evening.
ᵉ thought. ᶠ gon. ᵍ prisoners. God gave.

leader, first to enter that towne, then the church-yard, where, a man would haue assuredly thought, must haue been your burieing place. Nay, at the entring of that church, *dreadful to see the enemy opening the doore when ready to receue you with their pikes and muskets,* the horses slaine in the allies,[a] of which the enimy made brestworks, *the churchyard as well as the church being couered with dead and wounded, amongst whom you long strugled,* witnesseth the Lord's wonderfull protection: from which dayes service you escaped with a few dry blowes with the musket stockes of those whoe afterwards, soe many as were liveing and able, were caried prisoners to Farnum; the choicest men, for soe many, that were taken since the beginning of theis warrs. And long you rested not, after this story, before your generall Sir William Waller attempted further, which was his march towards Arundell, begun from Farnham the four*teenth*[b] day of December, 1643;[c] which was prosecuted with such speed that the 16. day at night followeing the head quarters was in Arundell parke, where your lodgeing with many others was vnder the best spred trees. In the morneing at the breaking of the day the enimy and some partie of ours begun to skirmish, which continued vntill about *eight*[d] of the clocke, at which time Maior Generall Potley comanded your selfe with about *1400*[e] men to storme the *enemis rampier, within which thear army was drawne vp;*[f] which was conceived, by more then my selfe, hee did on purpose to haue you cutt off, for your being too active a few dayes before at Alton, there being double[g] the number *of infantry of the enemy, besides a great body of horse,*[h] to those you stormed with, and noe horse *of ours could get order to*[i] assist you. But God orderd it otherwise by his owne ffinger, though it cost you good store of your blood. I question not but that

[a aisles? See Historical Notices, N. Wallington, i. 44, 70.]
b th.   c 42.
d seaven.   e 700.
f towne.   g " of " cancelled.
h in the towne.   i did.

deliverance you will remember, yet give mee leave to present to you what I remember to helpe your memory loaden with sundry things. At the same instant and to my best remembrance that the *faleing on*[a] was thus: (vizt.) Sir William Waller's leiftennant collonel was marching vp the narrow lane, with about three hundred *musketeers;*[b] which your selfe perceaveing, and being nere ready your selfe to ffall on, not likeing his rash attempt, you vnhorsed the London scoute master whoe at that instant stood by where you were draweing the men into divisions, and speedily ridd that horse to the van of that partie of ffoot, and turned *again*[c] the leiftenant-collonel and his partie, and drew them into the hollowe of the lane out of the enimies shott, which tooke place on 7 or 8 of that partie, *as you weare spekinge*, before they could bee secured, which retreat caused a great shout from the enimy, not feareing your comeing on againe. About a quarter of an hower after this, you were ready with your men in 3 divisions; on the left hand marched the aforesaid leiftennant collonel with about 200 muscateers; on the right hand your owne maior Cotsforth[d] and twoe hundred muscateeres; in the body your selfe, 40 paces backe, with *the rest*,[e] pikes and muskets. Thus marching on, the *enemy*[f] letting ffly very thicke, you not likeing your maior's pace whoe was marching before you *on the right hand*, but indeed more softly then you vsed to doe in such a shoure, you comanded the captens where you were to come on speedily, and you ran vp to the maior's partie then about 40 paces short of the enimy's line; where they being almost at a stand your example drew them on instantly to enter that line, vnto which your selfe first entred, though it was intricate to gett over that steep line; but one assisting another, instantly there was neere 200 entred; in which instant of time, before the rest could enter, (and

[a] storme.   [b] muscateers.   [c] against.
[d] This may have been the Cotsforth who had been a captain in Lord Brook's regiment. Lord Brook was slain at Lichfield March 2, 1642. Peacock, Parliamentary Army List, 33.
[e] three or at the most 400.   [f] evening.

the great ffishpond lieing between *our* [a] army and the place where you entred, soe that the enimy sawe you could not quickly bee *releived*,) *on* [b] came they with about 100 gentlemen reformadoes on horseback besides ffoot *and other troups of horse*, and gave your disorderd foote at that very instant of entry such a charge, that they layd many flat to the ground, *as well as your selfe*. The rest went backe over the line with great speed; and I think I may say truly not one man stayed within the line, except those that were slaine, wounded, or prisoners, but your selfe; whoe leaning on the line with one hand, and your halbard in the other, the enimies horse could not fall vpon you but to their great loss, bestoweing some few pistolls on you: but God would not haue you then hitt; and indeed you had never escaped soe, had it not been for those musketeers, who lieing neare you on the topp of the line kept of the horse at present, and made some ffew to ffall; soe that they were forced to drawe *further of*,[c] and there stand: in which place (neither could they indeed long continue; for the rest of the musketeers) followeing the example of those by you, got on top of the line and from thence fir(c)ed [d] soe hott on the enimies horse, that they were gladd to withdrawe. Thus God gaue you possession of the enimies *ground* [e] the second time: which efected, your great care was to make way for *some* [f] honest *captaines* [g] of horse and *their* [h] traine, which voluntarily came vp to your assistance: which being done, imediatly whilest you were putting those horse and foote in order, whose number were both about eigh*teen* hundred, the enimy looked vpon them contemptably; and there vpon drew forth [i] to fall on you *neere the towne walle*, where you were between the enimies twoe lines. And their horse and foote *doeing their vtmost*,[k] at this instant was *that* [l] gallant Scott slaine,

[a] the. [b] received) out. [c] vnder there inner line.
[d] forced. [e] first line.
[f] an. [g] captaine. [h] his.
[i] "of Mariegate" cancelled. [k] but not without danger of shott.
[l] alsoe.

whoe had vowed that day, afore hee went on, that hee would never flee further from you then the length of your halberd, saying hee would sticke to you whilest you lived, but hee would be neer to the intent hee might examine your pockets when you fell; which God called him vnto first. At this instant, *the enemy spending their shot at too great a distance,* your order was to horse and foote instantly to assault the enimy; your selfe with cherefull speech assureing they would not stand, which proved accordinglie. For the enimy, *feeling the force of the shott poured on them*[a] with three ranks at a time, *after short time gaue grond, and* your selfe entred the towne with them, scarce knoweing freind from foe; the enimy as much as they could betakeing themselues to the castle; into which place your comand was to enter with them. At which instant Sir William Waller's leiftennant collonel, whoe but then you incouraged by clapping your hand on his shoulder, your hand noe sooner of but hee was shott dead; and your selfe not gone aboue 20 paces further received that *wonder*[b] of God's mercy, the shott in your belly, which deliverance to you was soe great that I cannot speake of it without admiration; and the more at the hand of God soe assisting, that though you kept in your gutts, stoping the hole with your finger, yet none knew it vntill you had slaine or taken prisoners the enimy then about you, and orderd your men to drawe into a body on one side the street, where the shott had not such power: and then pretending you must turne to the wall, giveing a capten by you private notice, you went towards the Parke house, as if noe such shott had been, vntill your spirritts yeilded and your selfe sunke, and were then caried to the lodghouse aforesaid with life in you, but suposed by all to bee past cure, this being about 9 in the morneing; *when*[c] you *weare* laid with many others on the ffloore, groveling, and to the chirurgeons not soe much probabilitie of life *apeared* as to bestowe a dressing.[d]

[a] faceing about the maine volley of shott which you poured on them.
[b] wound.   [c] and.   [d] " you lay " cancelled.

Thus *you laye* vntill about 6 at night; at which time being as you were in the morneing, the chirurgeons thought to adventure a dressing, and to bestowe soe much paines as to carry you vp vnto a bed. Thus haue I presented you with Gods great worke, much of *it carryed on by* [a] your hand that day, and the great mercy in your deliverance, which I hope will never bee worne out of your minde. I beseech you, remember the 17. day of December 1643. That castle in a few dayes after being yeilded, therein was ffound twelue hundred men, besides those that were slaine, *fled* and taken prisoners at the entry of the towne: which number I the rather mention, to make more plainly appear Gods hand, that these should bee driven into the castle by *so smale a nomber*.[b] This done, the army quartered in Sussex the remainder of that winter; and your selfe in London, to bee cured; which was soe blest of God that you went backe perfectly whole to Arundell, the 6th day of March followeing: within 5 dayes of which time the army rose out of there winter quarters, the wether being very faire, and marched towards *Alsford*,[c] wheare Sir Ralph Hopton was at the heade of an army *of great strength* ;[d] which army on the 25. of March followeing you had sight of marching on the plaine towards you in batalia: vpon which you drew vp by Sir William Waller and Sir William Belfores comand, and faced one another most part of twoe dayes at cannonshott distance. While the army was at that posture a councell of warr was called, at which it was resolued, as I haue heard (vpon the defeat of the Parliaments forces at Newarke and in the North,) to make fiers and retreat; which being sore against your minde, whoe then was capten of the watch, you vsed these words *to Sir Arthur Haselrieg*,[e] that surely wee did feare whither that were Gods cause wee had in hand: for did wee assuredly beleeue it, when hee called vs to 'fight with his eneimies; wee should not run from them; for mans extremitie

[a] Inserted in a space purposely left blank.   [b] eight hundred.   [c] Alford.
[d] for the King. About 5,000 foot and 3,000 horse.—Clarendon, ii.
[e] publiquely.

is Gods oppertunitie. Yet, notwithstanding that order of the councell of warr, you disposed it *so, being then captain of the watche*, that the parties on both sides were in the night soe engaged that there was noe marching off without a palpable discovery. Therefore, according to your desire, the army kept their ground, and the next morneing, by breake of the day, drew into batalia, your place being with your regiment in the maine battle. And presently 1000 muskateeres were drawne out, to make good the wood on the right wing; and, contrary to your desire, put vnder the comand of Leiftennant Collonel Layton, whome you said did sweare too hard to haue God with him. However, hee went and tooke possession of the wood : but stayed not aboue halfe an hower before the enemies foot, *vnder Collonel Appleyard*, beat them clearly out, and tooke possession, pursueing our men, whose *heells* ᵃ then were their best weapon, to the amazement of our whole army. One passage then I cannot omitt. It fell from Sir Arthur Haslerig, which was thus: seeing our men put to soe shamefull a route,ᵇ turned to your selfe saying, " Now, Collonel, haue you ffighting enough?" Your answere instantly given was, " Sir, this is but a rub; wee shall yet winn the cast:" ᶜ and you further added that, whereas your selfe and regiment were now in the maine body, might you haue order to march with your regiment to make good the right wing, you would quickly set all right againe: which comand imediatly by Sir William Waller was given you, and by your selfe instantly executed; and the enemy soe turned in his pursute that hee thought it best to saue himselfe by speedy draweing off, leaveing the wood to your pleasure to the great comfort of our army. This brought on the engagement *of seuerall bodys of foote vnder Sir*

ᵃ hearts.   ᵇ retreat, altered by Roe.

ᶜ The cheerful allusion to bowls tells us that Roundheads as well as Cavaliers amused themselves with this favourite game. The King himself indulged in it while he was in his confinement at Carisbrooke Castle; and his son during his escape was nearly detected by a party that were playing at it when he arrived among them at Bristol.—J.W.

Richard Browne and others, whoe did exceeding well, and also of the horse, which with great violence and various success continued vntill about 4 in the afternoone; at which time twoe thousand muskateeres were drawne out at your request; one thousand whereof on the left wing were comanded by Collonel Rea, whoe did very gallantly, the rest by your selfe on the right wing; all the rest of the army being to second them. Those twoe great parties went on with such success, that in one houre the enimies army was between them, all our horse and foote comeing on in the front of them. The first thing that I could perceive, they puld of their collours, thrust them in their breeches, throw downe their arms, and fled confused. Your selfe and others hot in pursute had not followed them above 100 paces into their owne ground, before one, whome I shall not name, overtooke you, comanded you to stand: but for what end I never yet could tell, except it was to give the enimy leave to runn away, and carry away there cannon; sure I am you stood there 3 quarters of an houre, vntill the enimy was far enough. The reason is too deepe for mee to give: only this I am sure of; had the enimies comander in cheife been there, hee could not haue comanded any thing more advantagious to them. Thus was that dayes victory gayned; vnto which I make bould to add, that it was indeed a victory, but the worst prosecuted of any I ever sawe. After this battle, fought the 28.[a] of March 1644, noe great matters were done the begining of that summer, but marching vp and downe: only Winchester cittie surprised ; in which your guide might well haue caused you to miscarry : whoe being to guide you to a lowe place in the wall, your selfe being a stranger, when hee came about on(e) hundred paces short, and the enimy fireing a few muskets, (as hee said) hee was soe hastily taken hee must needs presently vntruss, leaueing you to finde the lowest place in the wall your selfe ; which God soe directed you vnto,

---

[a] 29th, Symonds, Rushworth, Dugdale, Clarendon; who calls it "a very doleful entering into the beginning of the year 1644."

that with the helpe of your ladders you were in before the enimy could make any head. After this your march was after a few dayes backe to Farnum; and shortly after by order of the Parliament to meet his Excellency the Earle of Essex *neere*[a] Oxford to keepe in the King with that army hee had there: notwithstanding which, the King marched out and speedily went towards Worcester. I would bee loth to say what pass hee had: only it is strange hee could march ffrom twoe armyes both stronger then hee; and yet hee received noe considerable loss: nay, hardly any thing attempted vpon him. Vpon this his Excellence was pleased to comand Sir William Waller to ffollowe the King, and himselfe would march into the West, which was done. His journey into the West I sawe not; but many more then my selfe heard of it. For our followeing the King, it was very tedious for about 6 weeks; at last hee was gott to Oxford, and there draweing out what ffoot hee could, marched out northward, as was supposed to meet Prince Rupert neere Banbury. Our army came within veiwe of him, and both were drawne vpp supposeing an engagement. A forlorne hope of fifteen hundred muscateers was drawne out to fall on with the horse; which notwithstanding was not done that day, neither on the second day. The third day the King drewe of on the north[b] side the river. Sir William Waller marcht speedily after[c] on the south side; and although the Kings army was in our veiw before vs, yett that gallant bodie of musketeeres must bee drawne to secure the reare. These are pollicies in warr far beyond my reason: yet this was occasioned thereby: the regiments that had the van were, Sir William Wallers, Maior Generall Potleies and Collonel *Weams*,[d] and the 5 companies from Farnham: these regiments at their best would not all make 1200 men; but all this time many of their choice men were in that bodie of musketeers vsually called

[a] at.
[b] [Roe has here, as in a subsequent passage, mistaken the points of the compass. For N. and S. we must read E. and W.]
[c] "him" cancelled. [d] Wemies.

a forlorne hope,ᵃ were vsed for a reare gaurd.ᵇ Soe the regiments aforesaid, *contrary to your desire afirmeing the Kings army desired to drawe vs ouer Croperdy bridge,* went over the bridge,ᶜ and with the horse fell into the midle of the Kings army ᵈ on the other side the bridge; which at the first promised a glorious victory. But when there begun to bee need of shott, and that the Kings army began to drawe vp, then it was found there was in these regiments, cullers, pikes, lether guns; but our shott was in the reare,ᵉ as aforesaid; which the enimy findeing, suddenly fell on, the bridge being narrowe, that those regiments that were strong could not speedily get over to their releife: soe that the enimy tooke all their guns, in number twelue, divers of their cullers, and about *fiue hundred*ᶠ men, the rest looseing their arms, comeing of through the river: and had not the regiment of Tower Hamblets, whoe were then marching over the bridge in the reare of the other regiment, *at your earnest request* stoutly made good the bridge, our whole army ᵍ had been in great danger. This was the substance, I doe humbly conceive, of that ingagement, which by your selfe for the manner was soe publiquly spoken against both before and after. Imediately vpon this the Kings army drew vpp on the North side the river, ours on the South side the bridge.ʰ They made as though they would attempt the pass that day,ⁱ and sundry times the next day: but the second night they made many great fires, by the light of which they marched towards Oxford; soe that in the morneing, when wee expected an ingagement, there was noe enimy within eight miles of vs. Soe they marcht to Oxford, and thence after the Lord Generall into the West; wee to Northampton, and thence to Abbington; where for very vexation your selfe impaired your health, *and left the army; your regiment theare being turned to*

ᵃ " but nowe when the King was in the van, they " cancelled.
ᵇ " such pollicie was vsed " cancelled.   ᶜ " called Croperdy " cancelled.
ᵈ " just " cancelled.   ᵉ " there " cancelled.   ᶠ 250 ?
ᵍ " else " cancelled.   ʰ " kept by vs " cancelled.
ⁱ Clarendon gives the date June 29 ; Dugdale, June 30, 1644.

dragoons: your selfe was[*] sent for to take comand of the Kentish regiment; soe that I heere obserue that the same day you had your comission for Leiftennant Collonel to Sir Arthur Haslerig, (whoc notwithstanding would never doe any thing as collonel of foote, delighting all in horse,) I say, the very day twelue month, you had your comission for collonel of the Kentish regiment aforesaid, with which from Knole in Kent you marcht out the 2d day of September 1644. You had noe sooner received that regiment, which indeed was gallantly sett out by the gentlemen of Kent, but you were comanded by Sir William Waller to march westward, which you did without one dayes rest vntill you came to Weymoth. Before which time that great defeate was given to my Lord Generall in the West, which occasioned you forthwith to bee comanded for to take shipp, and goe for the securing of Plimouth, then in bad condition, haueing lost most of their men in Cornwall: in which voyadge to Plymouth God soe blest you that the next day you ariued there: and a fewe dayes after the King seing noe hopes to gaine that place, left the westerne forces before it, and marcht eastward. It would bee tedious to count the many stormes made by the enimy dureing the sixe monthes of your aboad there: I shall only put you in minde of one, wherein the Lord was greatly seen on your behalfe; which was the storme by them made in January 1644, about ii. at night. The shott then begining to thunder, your regiment, 8 companies of them, the rest being then on the gaurds, made good hast to your lodging, and thence, in as good order as that blacke and darke night would admitt, hyed towards that part of the line, where the maine busines was. At which place your comeing sooner then was expected found the enimy entred, but disorderd; there cheife ayme being to take the 2 works on the line: the greater whereof they being then hott about, which was that night kept by one of your captaines and 46 men, and well defended; for which his gallant defence hee received a peece of plate:

[*] and from thence were.

you quickly sett them thence, leaueing behinde them about 60 [a]
slaine in the place. The next worke to this being quiett as if it
had nothing concerned them, you presently comanded your men to
ffollowe you thither; which being done, as fast as men could rune
in soe darke a night, when you came within a pike's length, they
in the fort bid "Stand; whoe are you for?" you answereing "For
the Parliament," they fired to purpose. Your selfe then percciveing
it was taken by the enimy said it was safer to goe on then retreat:
vpon which all run on: the fort was taken, and 66 alive and
dead of the enimy taken therein; and Collonel Arundell the
comander of that partie there taken, whose sword you yet weare.
This was one amongst many of those great deliverances and
successes God gave you there.[b] The enimy at last being weary of
their seidge, and draweing of within 14 daies after, you by the
comand of Sir Thomas Fairfaxe were called thence. But before I
proceed with what past after you were with your regiment called
thence, give mee leaue to remember you how you spent the
monthes time in which you were absent from Plymouth, being
part of the monthes of September and October, 1644, at which
time for want of suplies for your regiment you were forced to take
a journy to London. And there in a few dayes receaveing your
dispach, in your way backe you *came vnto*[c] Bazing Stoake,
where his Excellency the Earle of Essex, Sir William Waller, with
the Earle of Manchester then lay with *the armys*[d] vnder their
comand; the King with his army lieing about 8 miles of, towards
Reading. Wherevpon tendring your service to those generalls,
and letting them knowe you were goeing to your charge, the Earle
of Essex desired you to stay a day or twoe, afirmeing that in that
time sure there would bee some action; and at present desired you
to ride to Reading, and doe your endeavor to keepe that towne,

[a] 40.
[b] [A sally in which he took many prisoners is mentioned in "Perfect Occurrences," Jan. 15, 1644.]
[c] tooke.   [d] their army.

wherein Collonel Barksted and a regiment of the London foot lay: his Excellency letting you knowe hee was very doubtfull, if the King should march vpon that towne, it would bee in hazard, being weakly manned, and then not well fortified. Wherevpon that night you went to Reading; but the next day the King turned aside to Newberry with his army, and his Excellency drew up between Reading and Newberry. Wherevpon you then made your address to the Earle of Manchester, the generall being sicke at *Basingstoake*;[a] desired of him that forasmuch as the danger of that place was past, and nowe an ingagement like to bee, his honner would give you leaue to wayte vpon him till that the *euent of that present action was seene*;[b] which hee easily graunted. And the next day neere the evening, the Lord gaue a great victory; though the evill prosecution of it vexed you more then the other cheared you. However, with a few other gentlemen that were there with you, *and suche as you could gather vp*, the pursute was followed by you.[c] And after noone you being well wearied in the twoe nights and dayes (before), you dismissed your partie, and your selfe wayted on by Maior Ashley, your regiment quartermaster at that time,[d] and my selfe, returned late at night towards Newberry, where the head quarters were. And rideing easily 2 miles short of Newberry in [e] the way from Hungerford, my selfe being before you, I heard a noise of horse and coaches comeing downe the way towards vs. Wherevpon I giveing you notice you stood a little, and presently affirmed it was the enimy; for wee had neither horse nor coaches at the head quarters. And they comeing on ffast, you had noe more time but only to vtter these words, "What ever you see mee doe, lett the like bee don by you:" This was about *eight*[f] of the clocke at night the 30th day of October, 1644, the moone shineing pretty light: and instantly therevpon you turnd your

[a] Reading.   [b] enimy were seen.
[c] "vnto Hungerford, and 4 or 5 miles beyond," cancelled.
[d] This looks as though Roe might *afterwards* have been his quartermaster.—J.W.
[e] "the comeing downe" cancelled.   [f] 10.

horse in at a broad cart way into the feilds on your right hand *out of the comon road to Hungerford.* And instantly after vs about three pikes length they come into the feild the same way; and comeing on fast some of them were got vp even with us: but your face being towards the west, and the moone being in the east-south-east, your face was soe shadowed thereby that they could not easily discover you; but, as I suppose, takeing you to bee of their owne company, passed on with their whole partie, consisting of 96 mounted men, three coaches and a coach-wagon, with 30 led horse; as you presently tould your quartermaster, saying you had counted them, which I was at that time in too great a feare to doe. And soe soon as the last of this company was done, you turned backe your horse and wee likewise: and haueing gon backe about 40 paces, you mett on(e) of their company, to whome clapping your pistoll you bid him hold his peace, and turne backe with you, else hee was a dead man; which hee did; and carrieing him backe into the lane hee conffesed hee was one belonged to the Kings Lord Generall, the Earle of Forth, whoe then past by; and those with him are his gaurd; and in the coaches his ladie and some other ladies; and the coach wagon was full of his bagadge, hee being come out of Dorington castle, into which hee was forced to fly the night before in the battaile. Vpon this relation you instantly turned for vs, and said, " I knowe not in what way God will bring it about; but I am very confident that all these coaches, horses and men will bee mine: nay, they *are*[*] mine. Come, therefore; lett's vse the meanes." And vpon that rid sharply with your prisoner towards Newberry; and comeing there gaue this account to the Lord Manchester of what you had seen, and what danger you had escaped, desireing of him a partie of horse, and you would give him a good account of that company. But hee, haueing long watched was soe extreame heavy with sleepe, you could not haue one ready

[*] Underlined, orig.

word from him. Wherevpon you thought of another course; and that was, to goe to the[a] houses where souldiers lay, and see if you could gett vp a partie by your perswasion, and for hopes of prize, which you failed not to promise them, as was afterwards well performed. By this meanes you had got vp 47 resolued horse, *wherof foure weare trumpeters;* and away you marched: and vpon the way Leiftennant Calthorp asked you howe many you judged the enimy to bee: to which you replyed, " They are 30;" and then turned to your quartermaster and said, " If my heart faile mee not, noe bodies else shall for the number;" and soe went on, your selfe being still a distance before to discover any noyse, and likewise to finde the way they were gon; which you did at every turneing with your bare hands, feelling in the darke which way the coach wheeles turned; it being now about 2 of the clocke and somewhat darke. Thus wee went on about 16 miles; your selfe still before; and being at a turneing and feeling for the way the wheeles had gon, one standing neere by you, at a gate, as you after informed vs, vsed these words, " What rouge is that there?" for then it was neere breake of the day and very darke. You doubting, as indeed it was, that the wyly generall might haue left a rearegaurd, and hee might bee a centry, and you had better goe to him: possibly you might make good the gate till wee came vp (*whoe weare eleuen score yards behind,*) rather then lett him and his ffellowes come out vpon you; which assuredly they would doe if they were souldiers. Therevpon you takeing out your raper and holding the point of it downeward vnder your rocket, went to the gate to him with your horse as hee was then in your hand; your pretence being to aske him the way: but another *coming out to* [b] him clapt his face over the gate close to you, and though darke yet discoverd you, and pulling out his sword, with *an oathe* [c] not to bee named, as you after informed vs, said you were a Roundhead: but you being more readye then hee beleeued

[a] their.   [b] standing by.
[c] another (?)

made such a hole in his skinn as brought a groane from him. The other starting, but not seeing the danger, you said with soé loud a voice that wee heard, whoe were then *a good way*ᵃ short, " What's the matter, gentlemen, doe you meane to abuse a man travelling on his way?" and with that more of them comeing to the gate and indeavoring to fforce it, you made it good with your rapier, vntill instantly the trumpet (*whoe had charge what to doe some hours before,*) *comeing vp*, and finding you ingaged, sounded a charge. Wherevpon the partie rushing upon ᵇ that rearegaurd, being twelue, were quickly dispatched; and from some of them that were then alive you did learne that the Earle of Forth was then refreshing himselfe in that village: which soe soone as you herd, you guest, as indeed it was, that the enimy would take the alarum and drawe into a body, and then the busines might bee hazarded. And therevpon instantly, the lane being pretty broad, and day appearing at the very instant, God was soe good to direct the timeing of that busines, you *orderd the former deuision being neere*ᶜ thirty prime men and horse *to go on with you*:ᵈ the rest of the partie being almost tired were to march on 3 score paces after, and one trumpeter with them sounding a march, and another trumpeter 3 score paces behinde them sounding a march; and soe to continue till they had ffurther order from youι In this posture marching a good trott, the first partie, where your selfe was, entring into a little *comon*ᵉ in the midle of the village, there, close by you, was the Lord Ruthen drawing his men together: and at that very instant the trumpets that were behinde sounded a march, and you cried aloud, " Gentlemen, letts not stay for the bodie of horse but fall on them instantly;" which at a high trott was done, and they presently routed, haueing not drawne 40 together. This was noe sooner done, but, musket shot

ᵃ 40 paces.

ᵇ [Interlined à primá manu, or by some one who may be thought to have mistaken Roe's meaning.]

ᶜ drew out.   ᵈ for a forlorne; and.

ᵉ towne.

distance, as many more, whoe had then taken the alarum, were then gott together. Some of your partie seing them said, "Looke, Sir, backe yonder is a partie more." You replied, "The same are rallied againe; downe with them:" and imediatly vpon a full gallop you charged them. Dureing theis 2 charges all the coaches and wagon were runne away.[a] This busines being pretty well over, and all that were in those twoe parties fallen or taken, with the generalls armes in his trumpet;[b] none escaped but the Earle himselfe, Collonel Feilding, and three more, whoe by reason of the goodness of their horse, after they had mett with some blowes, leapt of the comon into the closes, you being between them and the lanes end; by which meanes they escaped. Your selfe presently, and about *twelue*[c] more whoe were able, pursued after the coaches;[d] and haueing gon at a great speed four *or fiue* miles you were close at them in a village, where God was wonderfully seen for you. For *a considerable part of* the Queens regiment of horse quarterd then there,[e] who could not come time enough to *the* flight: which you discovering *by seeing souldiers stirr hastily about*, presently cried to the people as you were vpon a hard speed after the coaches, "Gentlemen, lay out quarters in this towne presently for my Lord Manchesters regiment of horse;" and further called loud to your quartermaster, whoe then was most gallantly as hee had been all the morneing at your backe, sayeing, "Quartermaster, in the next village let Sir William Wallers regiment quarter." Vpon this, and heareing the trumpets, whoe were then farr beehinde, *sound*, all the *souldiers*[f] there, three times the number of your partie, runn away; and before our faces, some ridd out backe wayes; most footed it into the woods; and you had an opertunity to ffall on the partie with the coaches, whoe never offerd to strike, but cried for mercy; not one man of them escaped; coaches and coach

---

[a] " and a partie with them " cancelled.
[c] 20.
[e] " a part of them " cancelled.
[b] *i.e.* the flag attached to the trumpet.
[d] " and a partie with them " cancelled.
[f] sadles (corrected à primâ manu).

wagon and all the ladies taken, with 57 men brought prisoners; and of their whole partie but the 5 aforesaid escaped. Of horses of theirs, and those tooke from the Queens regiment flieing as aforesaid, you brought away 107, besides twenty one horse that were in the coaches and wagon. And now being 20 [a] miles from Newberry, and in the enimies country, yet it pleased God soe to bless you that you brought safe away that day all the prisoners to your quarters neere Nuberry; although your partie was soe small that you were forced sometimes to put one man to gaurd 3 prisoners. This mercy of God, though I doubt not but you haue it in perfect memory, yet his hand being soe plainely discoverd in it, I could not omitt it, and hope the time you spend in reading of it will not seem long. Which that it may not, I shall proceed on where I left; (viz[t].) at your marching from Plymouth towards his Excellency Sir Thomas Fairefaxe, and meeting him nere vnto Bridgewater; and within a few dayes had your poast given you on the west side of that towne, wheare your devise of fireing severall parts of the towne [b] was soe successful, that whilest it was in burneing they hanged out a white flagg, desireing only their lives. Thus was that strong towne deliverd, *after a smale storme on one part;* whereof you were 14 dayes governor. But being soon weary of a comand soe ffarr from the enimy, vpon your desire the generall removed you to Bath, a towne little defenceable, and nere Bristoll, wherein was *Prince Rupert and* at least 4000 of the King's *armie*,[c] and therefore noe want of employment. By that time you had bin there sixe weeks, the generall Sir Thomas Fairefaxe and the army drew towards Bristoll; hee sending to you to joine with some of his horse, and goe before and keep them from burneing the villages in Gloucestershire; which you did with 1000 horse and 700 of your owne foote. The army comeing vp, many

---

[a] [Considerably more, no doubt, according to modern computation; probably nearer 30. Skippon's dispatch gives seven or eight miles.]

[b] By putting red-hott bullets rapt in leather into the mouths of their musketts, and then fireing upon the thatched houses.—Bird's MS.

[c] broaken armies.

great disputes arose, not without some discontent towards yourselfe, lookt vpon as the instrument that drew them on that hapless service, as then it was done.[a] But after many councells of warr and great debates, with great perswasion to a storme, and particulerly by your selfe, after it was caried by question, you said thus to the generall, " May it please your Excellency, you haue now resolued of a storme, wherevnto I haue vsed my best arguments; and because it may not bee thought by any that I am the earnester to perswade to storme, because my owne person is not like to bee hazarded, I doe now voluntarily offer, that what place of the line your Exelency please to appoint I will, God willing, enter it, or lay my body there to shewe my reality and goodwill to the service." This was received with acclamation,[b] and Harnell gate appointed you; and the comand of Maior Generall Skippons regiment given you, hee lyeing then wounded; with which regiment and your owne you made ready for the storme. And although by the runing a way of one of your owne men into the towne the enimy stood ready cockt, and the gunners by their gunns, *thee fight*[c] whereof at the first goeing on made it soe light[d] a man might perfectly see all the men about him and horse, which continued for about a quarter of an houre, the night otherwaies being as darke as ever I sawe;[e] yet God soe blessed you there that you entred in that very place; and about 90 were kild or taken that kept that place: but not without some hazard; whole volleys dischargeing when you were but the breadth of the trench of, and many case shot. But God went with you then, and inabled you, when you were inn, to keepe it; though you were forthwith charged with 500 horse appointed to scoure that line. Thus was that cittie by God's blessing entred, which some yeares before you defended on one side to the great cost of Prince Maurice

[a] as it then seemed.—Bird's MS.
[b] with an huzza.—Bird's MS.   [c] [this ? sight ? qu. originally "light"?]
[d] the light of whose fire at the beginning of the attack was so great.—Bird's MS.
[e] The storm on Prior's Hill Fort began before break of day. Sprigge's account of it (107) is striking.

and Sir Ralph Hoptons army, whoe came on vpon that side (but that I haue already put you in minde of). I therefore proceed to Gods further manifestation of his presence with you. For returneing to your government at Bath, and Bristoll alsoe being vnder your charge, you begun againe quickly to bee weary of being out of imployment. Wherevpon you went vp to London, November the 10th, 1645, and adrest your selfe to your freinds there, either to put you in some more active place, or to give you leaue to lay *downe.* Wherevpon it was considered by the Comittee of both Kingdomes, and they appointed you to drawe out 1000 foote and your horse, the 5th of December, and to march to Herefordshire ; and to endeavour with that force and some *from Worcestershire and others*[a] belonging to Collonel Morgan, Governor of Gloucester, whoe were to joine with you, *in all about 1800 horse and foote,* to endeavour to distress the cittie of Hereford, and vse all meanes to take it in ; giveing you in hand one weeks pay for your horse and foote, and promiseing you a months pay more if you were succesfull. Herevpon you went on that hopeless designe ; marcht of from Bath and Bristoll the 6th of December, which day it pleased God to begin a great frost, without which it had bin impossible to haue marcht at that time of the yeare in those countries of Gloucester and Herefordshire. Comeing to Gloucester you were to conferr with Collonel Morgan, Sir John Bridges, and Mr. Hodges, whoe were to assist you, and advise you howe things stood at Hereford: vnto whome when you came, your incouragement was soe small that their earnest desire was that you would march backe to your garisons, it being vaine to thinke of attempting Hereford. Wherevpon you desired they would give your men 3 or 4 dayes quarters where they now lay nere Gloucester ; and dureing that time you would goe into Herefordshire in a disguise, and see if there could bee any hopes of Hereford, or Matchfeild ; you then saying that being you were marcht soe farr in soe cold a time, you would beat or bee beaten

[a] A space with two asterisks in orig.

before you returne. Vpon[a] this they were content to allowe your men quarters for three or 4 dayes. Wherevpon your selfe, with Sir John Bridges, whoe in that busines was both very helpfull and serviceable, went along with you, both private, first to Ledbury, after to a country house, one *Sissells*,[b] nere therevnto, and from thence sent privately to twoe officers of the Kings, whoe vpon some discontent had lately laid downe their comand, and then were greatly enraged against the governor; suposeing, as indeed it prooued, that those men to bee revenged would give their best assistance and advise. The next night those men came from there houses, 2 miles from Hereford, where they recided, *at Nunington*,[c] and vpon discourse with them, it was by you quickly found that they earnestly longed to bee revenged; and you promised them that, if they would assist, and the designe should take, you would give them *100l.*[d] a peece; and soe enquired what possibillitie there was of a surprize; how there gaurds were kept? whither there were any houses nere any of their gates? what cariages vsed comonly to goe into the cittie? and if there were any hollowe ground where a bodie of men could lye nere the gate? and what number was in the garison? To which the reply was: the number of men in armes in the garison, of horse and foote, was about 1500; that their gaurds by night were strict kept vntill the gates were open; but after the towne mayor[e] was gone the souldiers went to gett their morneings draught, and many times left not aboue tenn on the gaurd; that the officers in the towne vsually dranke and gamed all night, and lay in bedd the fore part of the next day; that there was within less then musket shott of the gate an ould building called the Priory, where 500 men might lye close;

[a] [MS. "returne vp, on this." This punctuation seems to show that it was copied by a transcriber, who mistook Roe's meaning, as in other places.]
[b] Cissells [or Cirels?]
[c] Bunnington.—Bird's MS.   [d] 500.
[e] city Mayor.—Bird's MS.; but, query, might it not be the Town Major, who visited and set the guard?

that every morneing sundry carts came in loaden with wood and
strawe; and that at this time, the frost still very strong, the
governor sent out warrants to the constables in the country to send
him soe many men every morneing to breake the ice on the mote
and river; and that there was a hollow ground behinde the Priory *on
the other side a smale hill neere the city and* about *twoo* [a] musket
shott *from the Priory,* where 1000 men might bee drawne into
batalia. Vpon this discourse, and further findeing most of their
horse weare at that time *within the* [b] walls by night, you begun to
bee confident the towne would easily bee surprised; and your way
was, 6 carts; 4 with wood, and 2 with strawe, which were to bee
laden hollowe, that in the bodie of every cart 6 men might lye with
swords and pistolls; and when they came just within the gate, there
being only a bundle of strawe in the hinder end of the cart, they
were to through that out, and presently fall on the gaurd; and that
you would lay firelocks in that ould priory in the night to second
those in the carts, when the gate should bee open, and they haue
possession; which would assuredly bee done without suspicion. Thus
that designe layd, it pleased God, that hee might the more bee seen,
to send that night soe great a snowe that carts could not travell;
therefore there must bee a new proiect; which you instantly thought
vpon to bee this. The governor, as before, every day sent out men
vnto the country to breake the ice, the ffrost houlding strong.
Wherevpon you resolued to provide a man to goe to the towne
pretending to bee a cunstable, and to carrie sixe men with him,
with spades and pickaxes, great breeches and country habbitt,
and *a* [c] warrant you writt to carry in his hand to avoid suspicion when hee came neere the gate, and a hedg bill vnder his
arme, a vsuall thing for constables to carry in their hand. The
designe was to bee put on; and you went [d] presently to Cannon

[a] another.
[b] with Sir William Wallers horse-gaurds without the. (The writer must have un-
doubtedly meant Sir William Vaughan, who was much in Herefordshire.)
[c] that. [d] sent.—Bird's MS.

froom, then a garison for the Parliament, where were many stout fforrest men; out of whome for their habit and countenance sake, being soe like labouring men, you resolued to choose your constable and his men. And at last you found one *Berow*,[a] whose face and *bodie*[b] promised, when fitly clad, to bee noe other but a constable; and vpon conference with him found his resolution answereable *and yet his vnderstanding not so pearceing as to afright him with the enterprise:* and withall sixe men there fitt for your turne. Wherevpon you hasted backe to Gloucester, the third day after your departure, and came to Collonel Morgan, telling him you were resolued on a designe into Herefordshire: which hee was soe willing to imbrace that though hee was then sicke of an ague, yet hee would march with you, *though vnder great distemper,* which hee did the day followeing[c] to Ledbury, and all the night afterwards towards Heriford in the deep snowe, where *some*[d] of your men ended there dayes in the ext(r)emity of the ffrost and snowe. You thus marching on slowly, your designe being not to doe your busines that night, but only to make the enimy the more secure by your returne, day broke when you were foure miles short of Heriford. Wherevpon you gaue it out to your officers, *after they weare all called together,*[e] not one of them *knowing*[f] any thing of that designe, that you would now lett them knowe your intentions, which were these: Sir William Brierton then blockt up Chester; Sir Jacob Ashley and Sir William Vaughun were gon towards him; and you were comanded speedily to march to their releife: and you hoped all your officers would beare you witness that the extremity of the wether was such you could not march, and therefore hoped you should well answere it if you went backe to your garisons; to which they all agreed, and

[a] Beiroe. [b] countenance.—Bird's MS.
[c] [Monday, Dec. 15, according to Vicars, Burning Bush, 330; from Morgan and Birch's Letters to the Speaker, &c.]
[d] 4 or 5; [three, Birch and Morgan's Letter, Lords' Journals, Dec. 22, 1645.]
[e] whoe.   [f] knew.

the souldiers gladly accepted; and then presently you gaue order the soul(d)iers should get some meate and drinke at the next villages, on purpose to give out what you had said of your march thither; only one body of horse to stand ready if the enimy should haue marcht out of Heriford. And the greate designe alsoe tooke well: for the country people desirous to knowe whither the souldiers were goeing, they were as ready to tell the whole matter: and the governor of Hereford not wanting freinds in the country presently was advised of the whole busines. Yet *hee* for more sureness that day sent out horse, whoe found it true; and that the forces were indeed marching backe *towards Ledbury and so towards Glocester :* which designe did worke soe that the garison *of Hereford* was exceeding secure. And yett to make them the more secure, you findeing out whoe gaue the governor vsuall notice from Ledbury, chose to quarter your selfe at his house; and theire called some of the towne togeather, informeing them of your hard march, and desireing they would give your men good quarters that *night*,ᵃ and you would bee gon next day; for the wether was soe bad you could not march as you had intended. This they willingly agreed vnto; and quickly the governor of Hereford had notice from his freind at Ledbury. The day past; *and it now beeing*ᵇ about 9ᶜ of the clocke *at night the 16th of December 1645*, all haueing well supped, you called hastily to one of your officers, and caused him to beat vp an alarum; which imediatly hee did; and from him tooke all the rest of the drumers: which made not only your owne officers, but some of the townsmen hastily to run to your lodgeing. Where pressing to knowe the matter, you told them that you had advise the governor of Hereford and some others joyned with him were marching *towards you;*ᵈ and desired to advise with the officers to knowe whether wee should stay there vntill hee came, or rather to goe and meet him, if happily wee might finde them in a hasty

---

ᵃ day.   ᵇ and the enimy comeing. [Qu. evening in Roe's autograph copy ?]
ᶜ 8.   ᵈ within five miles.

disorderly march, and soe breake their bodies. They, willing to concur with you, said, there was noe way but to goe and meete him, the snowe and moone both giveing light enough. By this meanes you gott out all your men presently without suspicion either to themselues or the towne, *whoe weare charged on payn of death to keepe their houses;* whoe else would surely haue advised the governor of Hereford. And thus marched you *almost to Heriford which was from Ledbury tenn*[a] miles, without speaking one word, still expecting to bee engaged; which thoughts kept the souldiers warme that terrible night of frost and snowe: which had it been any other way, you could never haue compassed your designe. When you had marched soe far, the officers cam to you wondring they heard of noe enimy; to which you replyed, they are retreated, and if they did thinke it fitt you would march on, with all probabillity before they gott into Hereford you might doe some considerable service on them, they suspecting nothing. Wherevpon they every one returned to his place, marching on speedily, but soe silently that a dog scarce barked all the night, though wee marched through three or 4 villages; but in deed that was not strange, for if a dog had bin without doores that night hee would haue been starved to death. Your selfe in the meane time ridd to Cannon ffroom the Parliament garison, *sixe*[c] *miles from Heriford,* and there made ready your constable and his sixe men, gaue him his warrant, appointed him his bill, and to them their pickaxes and shovells, bound *up for*[d] them very black *rie*[e] bread and cheese in course table napkins, soe that to see them goe a man would haue ventred his life they had bin country labourers[f] indeed. Thus you went on till you were within a mile of Hereford; at which time the officers againe repaired to you, and heareing of noe enemy, begun to say vnto you, sure

[a] on sixe.   [b] [Fifteen of modern measure.]
[c] [Nine of modern measure.]
[d] [Interlined, like some other corrections, by an unknown hand.]
[e] browe (corrected à primâ manu).
[f] ["labourers, Indeed thus." A punctuation showing probably the hand of a copyist.]

you had some other busines there; to which you did them answere, you had indeed, and if they would keepe close and silent at their charge they should, by and by, see what it was; which they willingly agreed vnto. Wherevpon, being marched neere the cittie, you laid your maine bodie in a hollowe ground which you ffound as you were advised fitt for your turne; thence drew 150 firelocks into that old *priory which lay just by the roade leading to Bysters gate*.[a] Then you tooke the constable and the sixe men, and laid him with them in [b] the priory, giveing this order to the constable; that when you put of your hatt where you lay aboue him a good distance that you might see when the gate oppened, and the towne mayor gone, and the gaurd did growe thinn, then hee should goe on; and to the firelocks comanded by Leiftennant Collonel Raymond and Capten Browne gave this order, that when the constable was just at the drawbridge they should rush out; and to the maine body, that when they sawe the firelocks run on they should hasten. Things thus laid, you tooke a speciall care, the officers whoe first you advised with liveing neere Hereford should bee soe lookt vnto that they should give noe intelligence, which you had reason to ffeare, they expressing some discontent; which caused you to keepe them honerably close for the three dayes your designe was acting, and soe at this present time.[c] Thus the severall parties lay close in the snowe twoe full howers, noe man soe much as stirring, hope keepeing them warme. At last the gate was opeined;[d] and within a quarter of an hower after few souldiers you could see about it; and you supposed, as it proved, that that terrible cold morneing of ffrost and snowe had sent them to a fire. Wherevpon you gave

[a] highway goeing by the Priory. (The Priory of St. Guthlac, in ruins, founded by Hugh de Lacy in 1101, lying without the walls of the city. The gaol is built on the site of it.)
[b] " a ditch neere " cancelled.
[c] [Captain Alderne was with the reserve of foot.—Vicars, 332.]
[d] " [Upon the first letting-downe of the draw-bridge, three men came out of the city, not discerning anybody."—Vicars, 332.]

notice to the constable, whoe in respect of his cold, which made him and his sixe men goe as if they were almost starved, and alsoe by reason of their broad hatts, great breeches, spades, pickaxes, and bundles of bread and cheese, they might well haue deceived a wise man and vigilent comander. Thus went hee on peaceably to the gate; which when hee came close vnto, and goeing to shew the officers and souldiers that were with the centry his warrant to bring those men to worke that day, the firelocks rush fourth, and were run almost halfe way before the guard (then busie with the constable) discoverd them. Wherevpon the gaurd began to crye "Arme." The constable with his bill knocks downe one: the rest with their spades and pickaxes fell vpon others: this held not one minute, but the firelocks and your selfe fell inn; and presently the remainder of your bodie, with Collonell Morgan;[a] and after halfe an howers dispute in the street, and the loss of about tenn of your men, that great and strong garison, which soe long held out a great army, was taken, and in it abundance of gentry and souldiers; the governor Barronet Scudamore with some fiftie others escapeing over the river Wye on the ice, which that night was ffrozen soe hard that they were able to goe over. Thus did the Lord worke for you: the like hath not been heard: and I am confident you will never forgett to honner God, whoe soe honerd you in this admired service. Vpon notice of this great worke to the Parliament, they forthwith appointed you Governor of that cittie, which was almost as difficult to keepe as take, lieing surounded with enimies garisons; Sir Jacob Ashley at Worcester 20[b] miles of, Sir William Vaughun at Ludlowe with a force; and others at Gutheridge, Ragland and Matchfeild; all the strong garrisons lyeing round. Yet God soe enabled you to manage his worke in your hand, that you kept your horse alwais[c] quartered in the country, (though the enimy dureing all that tyme durst never quarter but in their garisons,) and never

[a] [Morgan commanded the horse.—Vicars, 332.]
[b] [Thirty of modern measure.]   [c] alwaise.

lost (saueing 13 Sh(r)opshire horse that came vnder your protection) one horse to the enimy. And although within the cittie of Hereford was 1100 townsmen whoe had taken vp armes for the King, yet by your speedy ffortifieing the castle you secured that cittie for the Parliament with a few men, soe that though you tooke that place but the 24th day of December, 1645, yet in the beginning of March followeing you had soe strengthened the castle that with the helpe thereof 460 men kept that citty, that the 6th of March you were able to drawe out three hundred horse, and leaue a horse gaurd for the cittie; with which 300 horse and 600 foot you then tooke the ffeild, notwithstanding the enimy all round about. But in an especiall manner you were molested from Gutheridge with Sir Henry Lingen, whoe had about 90 horse belonging to that garrison, 9* miles from Hereford; with which and the knowledge and resolution of the riders they made roades every way into (the) country: soe that although on the 5 of March you were desired to drawe out what force you could, and to joine with Collonel Morgan to engage with Sir Jacob Ashley, then intending with the fforces of Worcester and Ludlowe, and his owne, being about 1000 more, to march to Oxford to the King to joine with his army, there to take the ffeild that summer, yett this could not possibly bee done without vtter ruine to the country, except you could some way breake and destroy the forces vnder Sir Henry Lingen; but especially the horse, whoe vndoubtedly when you were gon soe ffarr of would bring all the contry to subiection, and come to the gates of Hereford it selfe.. Wherefore you tooke vp such a resolution as seldome hath been heard of : yett your God wrought for you: vizt. theis horse stood in one great stable, within the outward wall of Gutheridge Castle; the backe of the stable being it selfe part of the wall; a gaurd lay in this stable, and another gaurd about a pistoll shott behinde the stable, being as neere the castle wall that only a carte loaden could pass between the castle it selfe and this outer counter scarfe. Yet

* [About sixteen of modern measure.]

you did resolue this stable must bee entred in some fowle night, when the horse were sure in it; it being the stable wherein they lay all their sadles, corne, and hay; and this must bee done, else you could not doe your busines. Therefore you tooke a time 4 nights after, and marcht silently all night; devided your bodie into three parts; one to fall on the out gaurd[a] silently with their swords; and another to storme the wall with ladders of 13 rounds, which by intelligence you found to bee as a sufficient length; and when they were gott in that counterscafe to fforce the gaurd, and enter that stable: but neither of theis to give any fire vntill they were fired vpon againe and againe; hopeing that might somewhat alay the mistrust of any danger thear. The other partie were to goe directly to the gate, both horse and foote, and there to fire with great noyse; and it pleased the Lord soe to prosper you there, that they in the outgaurd supposed those whoe first came on to bee some of the castle or stable gaurds; therefore they tooke not the allarum, it being very darke, vntill they were gott in soe close, that they were taken or slaine every man, being 2 maiors, 2 captaines and 30 souldiers. At the same instant they on the counterscarfe, soe soone as they perceived the partie came towards them, thought it it had been some of those from the outgaurd; and soe was not hastie to give the alarum, till they had sett and mounted their ladders and were presently entred the maine force of the castle. The castle it selfe, heareing soe great a noyse about the gate, suposed the danger there, therefore applied all their force thither. In the meane time the stable was entred, a hole beaten through the backe of the wall according to order, and then ledd out by the partie 76 horse: 12 were left in that would not come out; wherevpon instantly that great stable being full of hey, strawe, and cumbustable matter was fired and burnt to the ground, with

---

[a] [According to Birch's Letter to the Speaker, published by Vicars (Burning Bush, 396, 397), this out-guard was in the boat-house by the river-side. It "held out two houres untill it was digged thorow."]

the horses, sadles, and all things else for the enimies vse.ᵃ Thus their force being subdued you were in a condition to march to meet Sir Jacob Ashley, which you delayd not long; but the very next day, haueing designed your force to come after, you went your selfe with Collonel Kirle, fower of your servants, your trompets and twoe choice troupers in your company ᵇ towards Gloucester, to lay the designe and to conferr with Collonel Morgan about the management thereof. But whither they at Gutheridge had advice of your goeing soe ill attended or it was casuall I am not able to say, but suspect the first; but soe it was that Sir Henry Lingen had a partie of 14 choice horse were out on a party the night the stable was burnt, and his horse taken: which horse by that meanes escapeing lay at Ould Goare, just in your way ready to catch you as you went for Gloucester, the place being twoe ᶜ miles from the enimies garison; you presumeing to goe soe neare with that small partie, suposeing you had left them neare a horse; yet these 14 were ready for you there: where you rideing without suspicion hapt to spye a coites cast before you: wherevpon they standing in a little hollowe, and findeing them to bee the enimy, all that you said was, " Doe as I doe,"ᵈ and with that on a full speed roade through the very midle of them. The fury of your horse overthrew one, and dismounting one or 2 more, the comander of them turneing about his horse to clap his pistoll to you, I was soe neare you that my pistoll touched his side; where I shott him, his scarfe was fired with the powder, and downe hee ffell. By that time you and Collonel Kirle had feld,

ᵃ March 16, 1645. We had likewise by letters from Hereford, that a party of Colonell Birches from Hereford and Colonell Kirles from Monmouth went against Gotheridge Castle in Munmouthshire, surprized 60 horse in the stables, and other provisions, fired downe the stables, and have close besieged the castle. Colonell Kirle besides this snapt another party of the enemy from Ragland, and took a lieutenant, a quarter-master, 12 firelocks, and six case of pistols.—Perfect Diurnall, No. 138, 1104.

[ᵇ Qu. Is Roe to be included in this enumeration? if so, in what capacity?]

ᶜ Eight of modern measure.

ᵈ If we can believe Colonel Birch to have been sufficiently collected at the moment, he might have alluded mentally to the passage in Judges, vii. 17.

with the other sixe with you, 7 or 8 of them; the rest began to face about, but were all killed or taken, except twoe whose horses weare too swift. Thus were you strangely deliverd at that time alsoe; and on you went towards Gloucester as if this had bin only a rub in your cast, haueing lost noe mans life on your part. This was the Lords owne worke. At Gloucester agreeing with Collonel Morgan of the place and time of rendevouz, you mett accordingly with about 1060 men; hee with about 1100; and the garison of Esam with about 600. With this little army of about 2700, you marcht to meet Sir Jacob Ashley, whose army consisted of about 3000 men, halfe of them being reformads, men of vndoubted resolution. On the 5th day after your rendvouz, Sir Jacob Ashley came marching with his army in veiw; wee lyeing on the topp of the hill nere Cambdin sawe him march at least sixe miles together. And I well remember your councell was, being wee had sent for Sir William Brereton, and that hee had provided to come with a force that day, not to tempt God by fighting overmuch, when it may bee hee would afoard vs more meanes; but if noe helpe came before such time that the enemy would bee out of our reach towards Oxford, then wee would ffight them, and trust God to beat them with the fforce wee hadd: in the meane time to vexe them with 500 good horse and some ffew foote, to make them spend the time and tire them; and in the meane time the rest of our army to ffeed and refresh themselues abundantly, which they did from Cambdin. By which meanes the enimy disputed it till eight at night, before they could get vp that hill, and had then 7 miles to Stowe; they not desireing to fight with vs but to march vnto the King, which they did very quietly: for you comanding that none should ffollowe them in the reare, they tooke it for graunted they should not bee molested. But, about tenn or eleaven of the clocke, you said to Collonel Morgan, "Come, Sir, God will give vs noe more meanes: yett I am confident hee will deliver them into our hands:" and to your souldiers about you said, you had a strong confidence you should haue Sir Jacob Ashley in custodie. Wherevpon all resolued to march; and did at the very instant, with that resolution and willingnes as if they had gone to a ffeast: and about three in the morneing were gott close vp to the enimy then drawne vp in the ffeild neere Stowe; it being very darke; yet you resolued to fight presently, "because," said you, " wee haue the disadvantage of ground, yet they cannot see it; besides wee being the assailants, they will conceive Sir William Brereton is come vp to vs, and that wee are many more then they." At this very instant comes vp tenn or twelue troops of horse vnder Sir William Brereton; and to worke wee went, the forlornes being ingaged before. Hott it was for a while; their reformadoes standing stoutly to it; insoemuch that you had 32 horse shott in your owne regiment, beside your owne that you ridd on alsoe shott: but at length God gaue you the victory, 1600 prisoners and vpwards, besides the slaine: and in the midle of the heate a souldier had taken Sir Jacob Ashley, brought him to you; whoe according to your promise, deliverd him to your souldiers. And here, certainely, was a more then ordinary hand of God, which could not pass by without observance, being the last battle fought in England.[a] Nowe only remaynd to take in the garisons. Wherevpon you marcht backe; first to Worcester; where at the first comeing on, your horse with a pistoll was shott soe vnder you that hee fell downe

[a] We shall conclude this weeke with the further welcome newes of the routing of Sir Jacob (or the new made Lord) Ashley's forces, the only remaining party the King had left him to make a new army, and to carry the King from Oxford; which rout was on Satterday the 21, upon the edge of Gloucestershire, and the newes brought here to the Speaker of the House of Commons by Major Temple on the Lord's Day early in the morning, the said Major having been in the fight. And after him came another messenger to the Speaker with a letter of the perticulers so far as could on the sudden be gathered, and is to the effect as followeth:—

SIR,—
This morning, Saterday, 21 of March, Colonel Morgan, governour of Glouster, and the forces under him, having also the forces of Sir William Brereton the night before joyned with him, did fall upon Sir Jacob Ashley and all his forces intending for Oxford, to joine with the King and to disturbe the siege at Banbury Castle, at

never stirring, but died presently; which was another remarkeable deliverance. Leaveing Collonel Morgan neare Worcester, you marcht by order of the Parliament to Ludlowe, and God soe blesst you that you tooke in that towne and castle within 33 dayes; though not without great envy from the Shropshire men, in whose countie I was gon.[a] Thence to Gutheridge you marcht, a place of wonderfull strength; yet God soe blesst you that with mineing, battery, and morterpeeces soe well bestowed that your selfe shott into the castle 19 of 22 granadoes, which much shooke it, and by reason of a great morterpeece you made there (the biggest in England),[b] the enimy was terified, much of the inner part of the castle ffallen downe, and the roofe spoyled. Yet the enimy resolued to hold out, and by countermine drew neere to your mine, which went heavily on for tenn yards at least through ffirme rocke yett there to bee seen: but by your battry vnexpectedly planted in the night you beat downe a tower of the castle into the mouth of their countermine; the tower ffalling soe furiously that they could noe wayes defend their mine. By which meanes you gott vnder them;

Stow-in-the-(W)old upon the edge of Glocestershiere, and, after a sore conflict on both sides, Sir Jacob Ashley was totally routed, himself taken prisoner, and 1100 more horse and men at the least taken, and all their cariages, great store of armes, bag and baggage taken. Our word given to Col. Morgan was "God be our guide;" the word of the enemy was "Patrick and George."—Perfect Diurnall, No. 138, 1110.

[a This resembles a transcriber's error. It might possibly have originally stood "it was done," or "won."]

[b It carried a 200 lb. shell, according to Birch's own account when he requested 80 barrels of powder from the Houses for the bombardment. (Perfect Diurnall, June 22, 1646.) An ancient mortar, called "Roaring Meg," and measuring 15 inches across the muzzle, which at one time was set up as a post in Bridge Street, Hereford, but has since been removed to the Castle Green, may be the piece in question, notwithstanding the local tradition that "it saved the Cathedral." Nothing of the kind is mentioned in the accounts of the defence against the Scots; and it seems very probable that Birch would preserve and remove to his own residence the instrument of the reduction of Goodrich Castle. His "mortar pieces" were transferred to Raglan. (Cary's Memorials, i. 142.) "Roaring Megs" were sent for from London to the siege of Reading.]

and they findeing the same, and sawe themselues lost, desired only their lives: Sir Henry Lingen and all the rest being your prisoners, whereof 60 were officers and gentlemen. This was the end of your martiall imployment, wherein I thinke as much of God was seen as most can recite: and although I doubt, not of your ffaithfull and gratefull memory hereof towards God, yet I conceaue my selfe bound to present you with this breife collection, being all I haue to tender to you in answere for all your ffavours towards mee: therevnto adding my prayers, that, *beeing*[a] God hath called you to bee a Member of Parliament, hee will continue his goodness to you,[b] and make you *very* instrumentall *theare*, as you haue been elsewhere, for the glorie of his name, and good of his people. Amen.[c]

[a] nowe.   [b] "there" cancelled.
[c] Colonel Birch was chosen a Member of Parliament for the borough of Leominster in the year 1646.

COMMENTARY.

1643.
[State of Bristol.]

Confusion prevailed in the city of Bristol on March 7, 1643.[a] The appearance of so many armed men in the neighbourhood of course excited great ferment among the population. Fiennes, who had openly declared himself by other actions, kept his counsel and was not unprepared. He had been opposed to the Cavaliers in fight at Powick Bridge, Edgehill, and elsewhere, and now took his stand, in defiance of Royal authority, as governor for the Parliament. He had under him sufficient force to suppress a rising: his own regiment of cavalry at least, with such soldiers as Essex had left behind him, and volunteers[b] who had placed themselves under him. We have seen Birch as their captain. From the beginning of October many of the youths of the place, under the Parliamentary plea of acting for the King, were already expert in arms, the defences had been made up, and evidently there was no access but by the gates. Fiennes was therefore ready: and, as he had secret instructions from the Parliament, he skilfully anticipated the place and the time. Five in the morning was the appointed hour. There was an ancient bridge[c] over the Avon, connecting the northern and southern parts; it stood upon four arches, and, like that at London over the Thames, was covered with houses. It formed a quarter for the Parliamentarians, who were called by their opponents

---

[a] [1642 in the MS., the year then ending on March 25.]
[b] Note 1.
[c] This bridge was only 19 feet in width, and had a chapel of the Virgin upon it 25 yards long and 7 wide, built in the reign of Edward III. The whole was demolished, and a new one erected, in 1768.

COLONEL JOHN BIRCH. 39

Bridgemen and Roundheads.[a] Both parties were aware of its importance; but the Parliamentarians had already secured it. Here then at the hour of 8 P.M. in the month of March stood Birch upon his guard as captain of volunteers, when he was privately informed of his danger: "some poore body or other," says a writer[b] who selects his account from the numerous pamphlets relating to this transaction, "(some say twas a poore boy[c]) came to that company which guarded the bridge that night, and acquainted them that they

1643.
March.

[a] Among many papers found in the house of Robert Yeomans was one to the following effect: "All inhabitants of the Bridge, the High Street, and Corn Street, keep within your doores upon perill of your lives." (Vicars, God in the Mount, 280.) The Bridgemen were the strongest Parliamentarians in the city. (A Full Declaration, &c. London, 1643.) We have no idea where Birch's residence might be, but it may be fairly inferred that his abode, or at least his store, was not there, as that was entirely plundered, which Roe would not have omitted to mention.—J. W.

[b] Vicars, God in the Mount, 278.

[c] According to Barrett (History of Bristol, 227) the disclosure was attributed to "some tattling females." Roe has not said that the search and arrest were personally conducted by Birch, only that he had them in his custody within a short time after he received the information. The real actor was Captain Jeremie Buck, who made oath before the council of war of having seized Yeomans and twenty-three others at his house on 7th March at ten at night. The discrepancy of hours between this information, the statement of Vicars, and that of our narrative, is of little importance. ("The severall examinations of the treacherous conspirators," &c. Husbands, May 25, 1643, King's pamphlets, Brit. Mus.) The character of Buck for wanton severity and cowardice well qualified him for such an undertaking. Mercurius Rusticus, xvii. 156, "a busie mercer of Hampton-rode." Bibl. Gloucestrensis, cl. 164. [A letter published in Seyer's Memoirs states that intelligence of the meeting at Yeomans's was given to the governor in council of war, where the writer was, about 1 (qu. 10?) o'clock; and that they sent Buck and 40 musketeers. Langrish says in a letter, "At ten at night we had intelligence that the malignants of the city had meetings in several houses thereof, namely, at one Yeoman's house : whereupon our Capt. Buck with some foot, and I with a party of horse, were sent thither; where we found 24 persons that stood upon their guards at the said Captain's entrance thereunto; but when they saw my party and said (*sic*) that I had sent for a canon to batter the house, they yielded, and laying down their arms I conveyed them all to the castle." He also, and Capt. Goodier's soldiers, made the subsequent seizure at Boucher's house. No mention occurs of Birch, who may have been ordered to the castle to receive the prisoners.]

1643.
March.

saw some men go into Mr. Yeomans house at 10 or neer 11 of the clock that night. Wherupon halfe that company (the Lord being pleased to make the matter serious to them in the first and bare relation,) with a troop of horse went presently to the house, and there found many men (as had been related to them) with many pistols and muskets ready charged: All these men were presently apprehended and sent away to the castle to be kept safe; and the same night also the company at Bowchers house, being suspected because they had not hung out light as they should have done, were in the like manner apprehended, and so happily hindered the tolling of that fatall knell."

[Suppression of Royalist plot.]

Encouraged by ordinance of Parliament, the governor proceeded with rapidity in his career: the press and the pulpit lent their ready aid: a thanksgiving was appointed without delay.[a] John Tombs, a Puritan divine of great celebrity, had recently arrived with the Earl of Stamford, when, after spoiling Hereford and the neighbourhood, he passed through on his journey to raise the West. Tombs had been hooted at in the streets and expelled from his parish of Leominster, and there he was, a refugee, prepared by suffering and temper for the occasion. He stood up in the pulpit of All Saints, from which George Williamson had been ejected to the regret of the people, and preached to the civil and military authorities two sermons, which were published by order of Parliament. A short preparatory narrative of the affair seems to have been read by him. In the epistle dedicatory he mentions the deliverance of the city as a very remarkable and memorable thing, and thus alludes to his own sufferings as the cause of his appearance among them. "In commemoration and acclamation thereof it pleased God that by the appointment of one of you I should have a part, having by God's providence bin driven hither for shelter against the unreasonable and impetuous violence of superstitious

[a] The Parliament ordered a thanksgiving throughout the kingdom, to be held March 19. (Commons' Journals, March 14, 1642.)

people, enraged by the instigation of bloody-minded Papists, corrupt priests, and loose libertines." Such is his account of those from whom he fled. Happy in his escape from Herefordshire, and seeing nothing but what was right in his new friends, he justified their proceedings; endeavouring to make it appear that their ends were to protect the city for his Majesty, and to remove all scruples and prejudices by labouring to prove that sometimes it might not be rebellion to resist the personal will and command of the King.[a] In other similar publications this unsuccessful attempt made with the King's approval was branded with terms that the Royalists considered could only be applied with his Majesty's authority and for his defence. It was called a plot, a conspiracy, an attempt at wholesale murder: but what chiefly annoyed them was the latter assertion. Though much allowance must be made for exasperation in such an unnatural contest, candour will be ready to admit that the intention of massacring their opponents was urged against the unfortunate Royalists for party purposes, and as a justification for the severities that ensued. It is far from being improbable that death might have been occasioned in the struggle, for arms were in the hands of either party; but those on the King's side upon their examination utterly denied any intention of bloodshed. The King himself denied it. The sufferers themselves denied it with their dying breath. Colonel Essex had in the first instance got possession by stratagem when no resistance had been made; and again, when Fiennes took his place, his entrance was conducted with equal success. But those who had just now failed were traitors, con-

1643.
March.

[a] Howell has described how those who really desired peace were affected amidst the confusion introduced by the cross-application of terms. "Never such an amphibious quarrel, both parties declaring themselves for the King and making use of his name in all their remonstrances to justifie their actions. The affections and understandings of the people were never so confounded and puzzled, not knowing where to acquiesce by reason of such counter-commands. One side calls the resisting of royall commands *Loyalty*: the other terms *loyalty* the opposing of Parliamentary orders and ordinances." England's Teares; Dodona's Grove, 161.

1643.
March.

spirators, and had intended to massacre man, woman, and child. Robert and William Yeomans and George Boucher with Edward Dacres were eminent citizens; the first had been sheriff of the city the previous year. Roe has only specified two of the leaders, and passes briefly over the tragedy of the story. A commission was sent down for holding a court martial, of which Fiennes was the president: the trial of the party ensued, and Yeomans the elder and Boucher were sentenced to die as traitors. Great efforts were made by the King to save them: a letter was written by the Earl of Forth at his Majesty's command containing a threat that if sentence should be executed several prisoners whom he had in his hands should be put to death. He endeavoured to stay the proceedings by addressing the civil authorities; Fiennes in his turn threw out a menace of retaliation upon certain prisoners of consequence left in his power by Sir William Waller after his expedition into Herefordshire; but such barbarities had not then been as they afterwards were practised at a still more savage period of the war, and the King humanely forbore. Happy had it been if all in this dispute who had the power of retaliation in their hands had followed this noble example. To such even the heathen could assign his paradise or heaven:—

> Quisquis est placide potens,
> Dominusque vitæ, servat innocuas manus,
> Et incruentum mitis imperium regit,
> Animoque parcit; longa permensus diu
> Felicis ævi spatia, vel cœlum petit,
> Vel læta felix nemoris Elysii loca.[a]

The governor had now got the upper hand, and proceeded to put the sentence into execution. Robert Yeomans and George Boucher were to die the death of traitors. Much interest in Bristol was employed to save them. The mayor and corporation endeavoured to intercede for them, for they were highly respected; the former had eight, the latter seven, children; but the governor was inflexible, and

[a] Seneca, Hercules Furens, iii. 739, *et seqq.*

the execution took place under great humiliation and cruelty. These circumstances, though omitted by Roe, are not unfit to be dealt with, and might have been much enlarged, as characteristic of the heat and temper of the times.[a]

1643. March.

Things being in the state that has been described, we are not informed what the merchant-soldier continued to do at Bristol. We may be prepared to find that he had not at once laid aside his sword, though from his letter it may be fairly inferred that he remained in the occupation described by it. The inference is fair, though conjecture is not history. This however is certain from the tide of events, that the proceedings of commerce were everywhere greatly impeded; the connection between London and Bristol was hampered by the Cavaliers; Gloucester was in possession of the Parliament; Worcester and Shrewsbury were in the hands of the King; and the passage of the river was still infetsed by the operations of war.

[Birch at Bristol.]

Fiennes, satisfied with the course that he had taken,[b] had strengthened the garrison to 2,000 foot, 200 volunteers, and 300 horse and dragoons at least,[c] had repaired the fortifications, and had been complimented by the Parliament for having placed so important a city in security for them.[d] But the hour of reverse was at hand, and it is not to be wondered at that the Royalists should have considered it as a retribution, though the extent of it could have been

[Proceedings of Fiennes. Capture of Bristol.]

---

[a] See Bristol Tracts, *passim*. Vicars represents the population at Bristol as having acquiesced in their sufferings and execution, i. 284. Compare the account with that in Mercurius Rusticus, i. 174, *et seqq.* for both sides of the question.

[b] He justified it by the command of his superiors, His Excellency the Lord General and the two Houses, from whom he had received thanks.—J. W.

[c] Trial, 796.

[d] In confidence of heart he was proved to have boasted at times that, should it be assailed, he would dispute every foot of ground with the enemy to the utmost; that it should be won from him by inches; that his flag should be his winding-sheet; that he would keep the city or it should keep him, or he would lay his bones there. (Trial of N. Fiennes.)—J. W.

1643.
July.

little foreseen. The indefinite period of seven months mentioned by Roe must be reduced to that which is comprised between March 7 and July 26. In the course of this interval the Royalists and Parliamentarians had been struggling for superiority in the West with a variety of fortune, inclining at length to the former, who were looking towards Bristol with regret and indignation. It was a prize to either party. Sir William Waller, the Parliamentarian general, to whom we shall have occasion to advert more particularly hereafter, had lately received a severe check. On the evening of his memorable defeat at Roundway Down,[a] July 13, 1643, to the astonishment of the governor, he entered the gates of Bristol, accompanied by the shattered remains of the horse under Hesilrige that had suffered heavy discomfiture in that battle. This omen of ill fortune was succeeded by another, and Fiennes must have accepted it as a warning to prepare for the worst, for Bristol was in imminent danger. Hopton, recovered from his personal disaster at Lansdown[b] (July 5), with his own Cornish and other forces commanded by the best officers in his Majesty's service, was close at hand, and Rupert, with a considerable body of men, came there to direct the operations. The details of the ensuing capture are unnecessary to be given: the line was not entered on the side where Birch was posted to defend it: he was in a quarter opposite to the Cornish forces, where the most successful resistance was

---

[a] Young Edward Harley, the eldest son of Sir Robert Harley, was, with a younger brother, in this battle in the regiment of Sir Arthur Hesilrige: he lost the horse that his anxious mother Lady Brilliana had given him, and narrowly escaped there with his life. In a subsequent engagement on the Parliamentary side he received a ball in his body which he carried to his dying day. He was a much valued and respected friend of Colonel Birch; and is here mentioned as one to whom he looked up with no common reverence, and as a neighbour to whom he was greatly indebted when the Colonel settled in the county of Hereford in after years.—Lady B. Harley's Letters, ccii.

[b] [He had been shot through the arm, and on the following morning dangerously hurt by the explosion of an ammunition-wagon.]

made; and the number of principal officers killed on the King's part, though not equal to what Roe ᵃ has stated in a general way, was yet very considerable; among them some of the flower of that army. This was a loss that Roe might well allude to, for it was a disaster that, as in the case of the loyalist officers, Grandison, Slanning, and Trevanion, could not be repaired.ᵇ Yet he admits that the conduct of the defence was far from satisfactory, by treating it with a delicacy that checks from indulging in the language of merited censure. Of course in his cautious expressions he is alluding to Fiennes and other officers of the garrison. Fiennes, a better orator than swordsman, afterwards challenged inquiry into his conduct, was brought to trial before a court-martial at St. Alban's, Dec. 14, 1643, and received sentence of death in his turn. More fortunate than the wretched victims who fell under his lash at Bristol, he was sheltered by the interest of his father with the Lord General. Mortified by his disgrace, he passed over to the Continent, whence, after a residence of two years, he returned, but not to war. It could hardly escape notice, as a singular circumstance connected with his own reverse, that he had himself persecuted the family of Yeomans to such extremity that the eldest son had been driven into exile.ᶜ

That Birch was of some consequence with the governor may be inferred from the evidence he gave upon the trial of Fiennes. He is mentioned more than once: for instance, as being well acquainted with the arsenal and the quantity of powder contained in it at the surrender, and as being a member of the council of war held previous to the parley. He was also of the party who met the King's commissioners on behalf of the city, and treated expressly with them. The 5th article in the surrender ᵈ specially provided that

[Surrender of Bristol.]

ᵃ [Or rather Birch; for this is one of the passages where a vacant space in Roe's MS. has been filled in by him.]
ᵇ Clarendon, vii.   ᶜ The Two State Martyrs, 19.
ᵈ Trial, 787, 794.

1643.
July 26.

"all the gentlemen and other persons shall have liberty to reside here 3 days, or depart with their goods, which they please;" and this article was introduced at his express suggestion. Such being the extreme limit allowed, he appears to have availed himself of it, and to have stayed to the last to witness the behaviour of the soldiery. The 6th article of the capitulation contains a pledge that " all the inhabitants of the city shall be secured in their persons, families, and estates from plundering and all other violence and wrong whatsoever."[a] It is upon the violation of this to a certain extent that Roe has attributed "eternal shame" to him who permitted it. That the writer has here indulged in an expression of indignation against the Prince, when the war was over, is no wonder. Rupert was throughout the whole of it a butt for a Parliamentarian to shoot at. It should however be remembered that the Governor Fiennes himself acquitted both the German princes of connivance at any excesses, for some indeed there were, that were directed both against the soldiers that retired and the citizens that remained. " I must do this right to the princes," says Fiennes, in his relation made to the House of Commons a few days after the event, " that they were so far from sitting on their horses triumphing and rejoicing at these disorders, that they did ride among the plunderers with their swords, hacking and slashing them, and that Prince Rupert did excuse it to me in a very fair way, and with expressions as if he were much troubled at it."[b] But Fiennes could only have spoken to what he had himself observed when he marched out with the garrison in the morning: the evening and the two following days exhibited scenes of a different character. The spoil of Reading that could not be prevented by the Parliamentarian general had already set the example. Every town within the theatre of con-

[a] E. Warburton's Pr. Rupert, ii. 260.

[b] Warburton, ii. 267. " Prince Rupert (as the governor saith) was very noble in doing his endeavour to prevent disorder, but could not prevail with the common soldiers."—Kingdom's Weekly Intelligencer, Aug. 1 to 8, 1643.

tention had its sufferings:[a] those of Bristol, from its consequence, stood high upon the list. Throughout, it endured the miseries of a divided population, and, though not exposed to the horrors of a lengthened siege, was twice subjected to those of a surrender after a storm.

1643. July.

Birch at the time of the capture showed himself a brave and a prudent man. Having by his personal interference [b] secured an extension of three days to all who desired to withdraw themselves, their families and property, and having himself taken advantage of this to the last, he is represented as waiting so long after the garrison and others had marched out towards Warminster as to compromise his personal safety. The volunteers were unnoticed in the capitulation, but of course as a citizen he had liberty under the agreement to retire. Of this, or of the fate of his property, it is only intimated that his personal escape was attended with danger; in the recollection of it, and of the many obstacles in the way, he is reminded in general of that superhuman Power, by which, amounting almost to a miracle, he was conducted and sheltered through them all. He quitted the place, never to return till he entered the line a victor, sword in hand, when it was stormed by Fairfax in 1645.[c] In noting his escape, and the language in which it is described, the reader who is acquainted with the reverses of this fatal story will hardly forget that the same expression is applied to him that was long after employed towards the King, when, subsequent to the

[Birch quits Bristol.]

---

[a] The royal visit after this calamity is thus noticed in the Court Mercury.—The King was received at Bristol with great joy and triumph and acclamations. The town seemed on fire with bonfires, and the streets could hardly be passed for the throng of the people. The mayor and his brethren were commanded to keep to their houses till they had answered for the murder of the two martyred citizens. Merc. Aulicus, July 30.

[b] Trial, *ut antea.*

[c] [It appears from Seyer (Memoirs, ii. 298) that he gave an account of what he had witnessed in a tract entitled " The Tragedy of Bristol ; published by Captain Birch, Mr. Powell, and other citizens of Bristol, friends to the Parliament."]

48   MILITARY MEMOIR OF

1643.
July-October.

loss of his last great battle he was wandering through the wilds of Herefordshire, encompassed by enemies; *leo in itinere* was a favourite phrase of the time.^a

[Alarm of the Parliament.]

The lions to whom Roe alludes had indeed struck terror into the hearts of the Parliamentarians, and this, it has been confidently affirmed, had it been immediately followed up, might have decided the question in favour of the King, though there is yet sufficient evidence to excite a reasonable doubt whether the delay at the siege of Gloucester, through which Charles ultimately lost his cause and his life, was altogether at the moment a blunder.^b

[Defection from the Parliament.]

In touching upon the confusion and hesitation of many of the Parliamentary party, the writer has censured the conduct of those noblemen, the Earls of Bedford, Clare, Holland, and others, who left their quarters ^c to repair to those of the King at Oxford, with a view of seeking reconciliation and pardon. Enough had occurred to shake the public and private confidence. Bloody battles had been fought, strong-holds had been lost and won, cities had been stormed and sacked or laid under contribution, more than enough indeed to create alarm either in remaining at home or going abroad. Many of all ranks, gentlemen and others,^d who had just after the capture obtained passes to visit their friends, contributed by their accounts to inspire a dread of the Cavaliers wherever they were to be met with. Birch had no other alternative than that of taking his journey, and by the account must have run considerable risk on his way.

[Difficulty of travelling.]

Though the dangers of travelling are here only alluded to, they may easily be understood. Trade had continued to languish, for

^a Iter Carol. Sept. 15, 1645. Waller's Vindication, 45. The Scots used it; Clarendon, vi.

^b It is not generally known how strongly the King was urged and tempted by intelligence on which he thought he could depend. Rapin is of opinion that he was in the right to set about it. Rupert was earnestly pressed by communications from the City itself. MS. Correspondence, Brit. Mus. i. 85, 100, 106.

^c Note 2.   ^d Clarendon, viii.

overland communication was interrupted by serious embarrassments. The Houses had endeavoured to secure all intercourse for themselves upon the high seas; the Earl of Warwick had been made High Admiral of the fleet, and such of the Parliamentarians as in despair had resolved to emigrate could at any time have put their trunks on board at the Thames, and bid farewell to their native country; for the process of voluntary exile with removal of property was still going on.[a] The mouths of the Thames and the larger rivers, and most of the ports, were open to them. But though the Parliament were dominant by the sea-board, there were too many difficulties by land or river conveyance to allow free trade, once the object of Birch's desire, to be as yet anything more than a wish and a matter of contention. If the attempt at treaty that took place at Oxford during the spring of 1643 was attended for a short time with the opening of communication with the metropolis, it could not control what was taking place in other parts. It entered indeed into the discussions there, but transit was grievously hampered elsewhere; neither goods nor persons attending upon them, such carriers as Birch was reported to have been, were by any means secure from pillage. Much of the traffic was managed on packhorses; but these might be the bearers of ammunition; when the packages were stopped and opened on the road,[b] they became the booty of the greedy soldiers. The King had openly professed to have redressed this grievance on his part wherever it had happened; he affirmed [c] that " no complaint concerning the robbing of carriers by his soldiers had been made to him, which he had not received to

1643.
July–October.

[a] Hampden and his friends were not the only parties that made the attempt. Sir Edward Nicholas, writing to Thos. Bushell, esq., Dec. 21, 1642, says: "there are 200 trunks sent aboarde shippes belowe London bridge, with warrant and order from Parliament that they shall not be opened or searched." Nichols's Collectanea Topogr. et Genealogica, vol. v. p. 299.

[b] The Parliament had long previous to this time given strict orders for searching carriers before they started from their inns in London. C. J. July 4, 19, 1642, *et alibi*.   [c] April 4, Rapin, II. xxi. 473.

the relief and reparation of the sufferers;" but the state of the country where the Cavaliers prevailed had become increasingly worse; and those who ventured to travel for commercial purposes might hazard their property or their lives.[a] Experience had shown that neither the road, the inn, nor the walled town were sufficiently secure. Instances had occurred in several places. When Colonel Hastings, younger son of the Earl of Huntingdon, was abroad with his troopers from Ashby-de-la-Zouch, he had infested the passages within his reach, and gained the unenviable distinction of "Rob-Carrier." It was believed that he had plundered upon one occasion, about the beginning of May, 60 packhorses with their packs. A month after his soldiers dragged a Blackwell-Hall factor from his lodging at Daventry, plundered him with violence, beat him, burned his papers, and trampled him in the mire.[b] At Reading in the month of December Mr. Boys, a citizen of London, an eminent dealer in strong waters, was arrested on his journey to receive such moneys as were due to him, brought to a court martial, and hanged as a spy by Sir Arthur Aston the governor.[c] Through all existing and ensuing difficulties, however, Birch escaped, in Roe's opinion as by a miracle; and it is evident that, though still a man of business, he became a merchant no more.

The rout and ruin at Roundway Down had been nothing short of complete.[d] Several hundred of the best troops from the garrison

---

[a] [The city of Worcester presented a petition to his Majesty that their trade consisted chiefly of clothing, but being unable to come to London they could not sell their goods or pay their assessments; thereupon they intreated permission to trade, which being granted, the clothiers and chapmen sent out their commodities, but were met by the King's forces, who robbed them of their goods on the road. Weekly Accompt, June 26, 1644.]

[b] Certaine Informations, May 29 to June 5, 1643. He was thus furnished and attired:—He rode with a cloke-bag, containing his books, &c., had a riding coat, hanger, cane, and buckskin gloves, and was distinguished by a gold ring.

[c] Speciall Passages, Dec. 1642.

[d] Corbet, who was military chaplain to Massey, the governor of Gloucester, affirms that Waller had not "the reliques of an army." Military Government, in Bibl.

of Bristol had shared the fate of that battle, and by their loss contributed towards the surrender of the city. Hurrying in utmost confusion by way of Warwick with a scanty company of horsemen, Waller and Hesilrige had reached the metropolis. Fiennes and Birch had also arrived there, and the latter, as already shewn, was summoned to give evidence on the trial of the former for cowardice in his late command at Bristol. The Parliament wisely caressed their beaten general, received him as though he had been triumphant,[a] gave him a more ample command, and strained every effort to supply him with another army. According to the proverb then in use, they saw that there was no alternative, but that they must "either win the horse or lose the saddle."[b] At this juncture Birch met with Sir Arthur Hesilrige, whom, it is fair to believe, he might have seen at Bristol: they became personally acquainted, and the captain availed himself of the experience the colonel had acquired in raising volunteers. He had been a frequenter of the Artillery Garden and the musterings in Moorfields,[c] and understood well the art of enlisting. He could go into Smithfield, as he once did, to buy a hundred horses for his regiment when occasion required.[d] He was also the very man to instruct and help him in the work of levying a foot-regiment. While Essex was complaining of neglect,

1643.
July–October.

Glouc. 54. He came to London with about 100 men: Hesilrige with about 20. Parl. Scout, July 20–27, 1643. Second Intelligence.—How Hesilrige contrived his personal escape is a mystery that is unnecessary to look into. He had received a wound in the arm and a hurt in the ear, and been publicly prayed for in the metropolitan churches. True Relation, &c. Bibl. Glouc. 202.

[a] [The following entries in Dugdale's Diary afford an amusing comparison: "July 13, Waller defeated at Roundway downe. — 25, Waller enters London triumphantly."]

[b] Speciall Passages, Aug. 27, 1643.

[c] Vicars, God in the Mount, 93, 213. Places selected for general musterings of horse on different occasions were Tothill Fields, Moorfields, and the New Artillery Ground. C. J. July 5, 22, Nov. 14, 1642. In his eagerness to obtain recruits Waller himself did not disdain to go among the butchers of Newgate Market. Merc. Civicus, Aug. 8, 1643.

[d] Ludlow's Memoirs, i. 112, 8vo edit.

52   MILITARY MEMOIR OF

1643.
July-October.

[Character of Hesilrige.]

of ranks thinned by disease, and desertion for want of pay,ᵃ recruiting still went on in London. The operation of enlisting could not, it is presumed, have been performed without some means on the part of Birch; who, whether his misfortunes might have arisen from plunder of stock, destruction of premises, abandonment of good-will in business, or of debts from customers, appears far from having been ruined by the pillage of Bristol,ᵇ and literally, according to the expression of Shakspeare, to have embarked in "the trade of war." Whence could he expect to be remunerated? He was himself well acquainted with profit and loss, and was coupled with a good adviser. By the act of disbursing money on such an account, he enrolled himself among the patriots, and rendered himself a creditor to the State.ᶜ

Though there were points in carrying on this business on which these partners would agree, the manner in which Hesilrige is treated in the MS. shews how careful Birch had afterwards been to retouch it with his own hands. The lines drawn across the commendation of this his old comrade are significant of a very different opinion subsequently entertained of him from that suggested by Roe:ᵈ the caution of Birch thus provided that his own character should never be so far committed for the time to come, as to be identified with that of Hesilrige, and that no such expression as that originally

---

ᵃ Appendix I.
ᵇ [It appears by the Perfect Diurnall, Oct. 16, 1644, that he estimated his loss on that occasion at " many thousands."]
ᶜ Scobell, 40. Ordinance, May 6, 1643.
ᵈ The manner in which he was set forth by his admirers is thus expressed by Vicars, *ut supra*. " Sir Arthur Haslerig, a most pious patriot of his countrey, and a most worthie member of the House of Commons, and a most valiant and couragious commander in the late famous battell at Keinton."—Vicars, in spite of his religious abuse, incorrectness of numbers, and other absurdities of party, is very valuable and useful in the features, tone, and temper of the metropolis.—J. W. [The expression employed by this writer renders it probable that *patroit* (in Roe's uncouth spelling) was the word so diligently obliterated by Birch in the original.]

used should stand before a future eye. This striking erasure seems to need some further observation. Here had been an acquaintance formed with one of the most extraordinary persons of this tumultuous age: the manuscript shows it to have been so, but how far they ever approached towards the "idem velle atque idem nolle" of a firm friendship must remain unknown. Truth must be told. Sir Arthur Hesilrige must have met with hard measure indeed from his contemporaries, if he could have been supposed to have acquired consequence in any other than such a period as this. His temper and actions seem to have been repulsive to the intercourses of friendship. Hardly any of those who knew him have been found who more than tolerated him: and the greater part of them have looked upon him with an unfavourable eye.[a] Clarendon in one place describes him as a "bold, absurd man:" elsewhere as "of a rude and stubborn nature, and of a weak understanding."[b] Ludlow, who knew him well and acted with him, is perhaps the only one who has cast the shield of honest purpose over his grievous defects. "He was a man of a disobliging carriage, sour, and morose of temper, liable to be transported with passion, and to whom liberality seemed to be a vice. Yet, to do him justice, I must acknowledge that I am under no manner of doubt concerning the rectitude and sincerity of his intentions."[c] Lilly, who had a quarrel with him, calls him "furious." His constituents had been warned on his election that they "had chosen a knight who had more will than wit:" his life gave ample proof of it; and his transports of passion were as extravagant as his blunders. He represented the county of Leicester, and had been one of those five members whom Charles had attempted to arrest in the House of Commons. Forward in offering his personal services,

1643.
July-October.

[a] [Instances, however, might be cited of generous feeling towards fallen adversaries. One, relating to Lord Brudenell, and specified in the petition of that nobleman to the Parliament, July 8, 1651, was originally intended for insertion in this Commentary; another connected with an allowance to the Countess of Nottingham appears in Whitelocke, May 21, 1649.]
[b] Clarendon, i. iii. [c] Memoirs, ii. 718.

1643.
July-October.

[Birch obtains his command.]

and leaving his beautiful house at Noseley, near Leicester,[a] to go out "a colonelling," he exchanged it for the strifes of the great senate and the perils of the field.[b] Extremes of political feeling, and a common interest, like misery in the proverb, bring together those who might otherwise have stood at a distance. The acquaintance of Birch and Hesilrige soon ripened into co-operation. Hesilrige, in spite of the late disaster, attributed in great measure to his own imprudence,[c] had still considerable influence with Waller and the Houses of Parliament; and great ability was granted to him in the use of the resources which the latter employed. The general had strong reasons for dissatisfaction with the conduct of his officers in the late annihilated army; and was resolved to correct it in the new appointments. To effect this he proved that he placed great confidence in his commander of horse. "The Parliament," he tells us, "required persons qualified with piety and ability, such faithful centurions as knew how to command * * * though they were not otherwise such refined men as I could wish. * * * I ap-

[a] "A sweet place," says a Royalist officer who passed by and saw his deserted home.
[b] If these statements should be thought to have borne too hardly on the character of this prominent actor in the drama, its singularity is certainly not contradicted by the expressions of his epitaph in the church of Noseley:—

Here lyes Sir Arthur Hesilrige, Baronet,
Who injoyed his portion of this life
In y[e] times of greatest civill troubles
Y[t] ever this nation had.
He was a lover of liberty,
And faithfull to his country.
He delighted in sober company;
And departed this life 7th of January,
In England's peaceable year,
Anno Dom' 1660.

Nichols, from whom little escapes that can be learned by diligent investigation, will amply satisfy the inquirer. (History and Antiquities of the County of Leicester, 2, ii. 743–753.)
[c] Holles, Memoirs, 11.

pointed a council of warr, whereof Sir Arthur Hesilrigg was president, to examine the merits of every man that should stand to bear any office in that army."[a] From this circumstance may be dated the result of the connection between these men; all applicants that did not upon examination and inquiry come under this description were to be crossed out, as unfit or unworthy to be employed: and Birch, being such an one as was approved, obtained to his credit a command. Their intimacy or friendship, if such it should be called at this or any other time, is proved by the narrative; and the estimation in which Birch was held is justified by his appointment. Selection as regarded him might be further advanced through the interest he might have had in this joint undertaking; and the way, already hinted at, in which he might have contributed to their joint success. Some better instructed pen might be able to show how in the negotiations that attended the choice made of this officer he secured no higher rank than that of captain, and yet was admitted to the privileges of colonel. As yet there are no traces of his being styled colonel of a regiment, though in courtesy he is set down as such, and has by himself been allowed to have been at this time endued with the authority of that command.[b]

1643.
July-October.

But to pass on to the General himself:—

[Character of Waller.]
The denial of patriotism to Hesilrige on Birch's part does not extend obliteration to the just praises of the " truely honerd " Sir William Waller. The terms applied in the MS. to Sir William Waller, and permitted to stand as opposed to the erasure of the attributes of his companion, of whom Birch appears to have been afterwards most justly ashamed, may admit of a short notice. Waller was a gentleman of honourable descent, that had learned the art of war in foreign service, and possessed some of the best

[a] Vindication, 14, 15.
[b] [His commission as Lieutenant-Colonel under Hesilrige bears date September 2: yet he is repeatedly styled Captain in the Commons' Journals during October 1643.]

1643.
July-October.

qualities of the soldier; for he was pious,[a] generous, and brave. If he chose his side, as has been said, through pique, he gained nothing by it ultimately but hard blows, personal suffering, obloquy in character, and ruin in estate. In spite of his late reverse he had well earned the epithet of "truely honerd" here assigned to him. Whatever may have been his other merits or defects as a leader, the chief point in his strategy seems to have been that of partizan celerity and surprise. Through these he had obtained from his friends the fond title of " William the Conqueror; " from his adversaries that of the "Night Owl." For military purposes winter or summer, night or day, were to him alike. It was thus that he had annihilated the force of Lord Herbert at Gloucester, and captured Hereford almost without a shot. He was a kind and it might be too lenient disciplinarian to his own soldiers, and ever disposed to give quarter to a submitting enemy. His lively courage and cheerful disposition (the Cavaliers called it *gaieté de cœur*) might sometimes have drawn him beyond his judgement, but they seem to have contributed towards softening the stern asperities of war. His well-known letter to his ancient comrade Hopton, before they crossed their swords in this unnatural dispute, is beyond all praise.[b] Such in brief was the general under whom Birch was now about to hold a subordinate command. It was the misfortune of Essex and Waller, and those that composed their respective armies, that they were of an entirely different temperament, that disagreement had taken root between them, and they soon showed that they could not accord.[c]

[Parliamentary levies.]

As to the new levy with which either Parliamentarian general was craving to be supplied, the exertions of Waller's agents would naturally and in a great measure be directed towards the capital

---

[a] Note 3.   [b] Appendix III.
[c] Though Essex, or as he was called " Old Robin," was the first of the leaders employed in this cause, Waller seems to have more thoroughly gained the affection of the new levies; and, indeed, on many accounts he deserved it.—J. W.

where he was on the immediate personal look-out, and from which so much assistance had previously been drawn; and this, by the subsequent account of his measures, is shown to have been the case. Soldiership had still the ascendancy of citizenship in London, and was fostered in the most eager manner by all the energy of the two Houses. The city was still a vast hive of armed men. A multitude of these had previously issued forth to fight the battle of Edge-hill[a] and had returned to that of Brentford, and were still on foot for the protection of London. There were the militia and trained bands, there were volunteers still to be picked up among apprentices freed from their indentures,[b] clerks released from their offices, and others from less respectable quarters; for there is an unknown rabble in the dark parts of every large city. Some of these were to form the ranks of hastily raised regiments. But besides volunteers formed from various parts of London and its environs, the associated counties engaged to send out and maintain under Waller, by different contingents, 3,000 foot and 500 horse; so that without exactly specifying numbers the general must have had sufficient to repair his loss and retrieve his military character. By this reinforcement added to the wreck of his former strength, some of which would be reimbodied after the dispersion, he lost little time in getting together what might be called a new army. The name of Birch may be searched for in vain as colonel in command of any of the regular city regiments that accompanied Waller into the West. Waiving the question of the composition of either opposing army,

1643.
July--October.

[a] The rage for fighting among the Londoners was shown by the calculation that was made of enlisting 10,000 volunteers in the levy of 1642. C. J. July 9.—In 1647 the City had at their command no less than 18 regiments of foot, some of them 1,800 and 2,000 strong, "all compounded of as gallant men and as well provided for the field as any in the Christian world;" and might have had between 4 and 5 thousand horse, all mounted by reformado officers and gentlemen of quality. Waller's Vindication, 188.—J. W.

[b] [An ordinance had been passed, Nov. 9, 1642, encouraging apprentices to enlist, securing them against their masters, and commanding the latter to receive them again without punishment for their absence after their public service should be ended.]

1643.
July--October.

as they respectively differed or agreed in character, or the preponderance of misery that either of them inflicted upon an unarmed population, it is clear that the Parliamentarian might unfortunately claim a large share of unenviable fame. Nehemiah Wharton,[a] a subaltern under Essex in the first campaign, and one of that sort that the writers of the time often affectionately call "the London boys," draws a lively portrait of the temper and behaviour of himself and his comrades, a frightful mixture of religious talk and immoral outrage, of love of mischief and rage for levelling. Yet he was an officer, and more than disapproved [b] of the conduct of the private under him; "the ruder sort of soldier, whose society," he says, "I hate and avoid." When out of materials such as these Birch was to form his regiment, and Waller his new army, the outcry of the country as to their conduct could hardly be ill-founded. The recently-appointed captain claims the entire responsibility of the regiment under him. It might be hoped, rather than expected, that they were not identified with such as have been here described. The character of the army has yet to be written. On an impartial view of the subject there can be little doubt that, as to the common men, the war let loose all the needy and disreputable part of the population, particularly of London and the great towns; such as necessity compelled, or those whose disposition led them, to plunder and fight. Essex and Waller, but particularly the latter, who was now coming a second time upon his levies, enrolled, under the name of defenders of a reformed policy and a purer religion, much of the offscouring of the metropolis. It is certain as to the former that wherever they came they left traces that defaced England like an enemy's country; the deer were slaughtered in all the parks of the Royalists; their mansions

---

[a] Letters of a Subaltern Officer, Archæologia, xxxv. 311.

[b] Trevor, a Royalist, who passed through Worcester and saw it in the state in which they left it prior to the battle of Edge-hill, states the little power their officers had to repress their enormities. "In all this hurly-burly their general or officers durst manage no other instrument of correction in their hands but their hats." Carte, Letters, i. 15.

were plundered or destroyed by fire. Bad as they were, those that were commanded by the Earl of Essex were more popular than those that followed Waller. The sequel will tell us how, when well directed, and under proper leading, they were able to fight. {1643. July--October.}

Nothing can furnish a clearer insight into the motives of Birch, and the plan he steadily pursued throughout of seeking recovery from his losses, than the transactions now to be revealed. Of course they would not fall within the scope of Roe's purpose, which is but to exhibit his military doings and sayings to the best and fairest advantage consistent with truth. Although the information here supplied is little more than given in outline, it may be fairly thus enlarged. Settled, as we have seen him, originally in commercial pursuits, in one of the most flourishing cities of the kingdom, as soon as the place was agitated by civil discord, this adventurer had cast in his lot on the side of the Parliament. When he became a volunteer it was for a while the best safeguard of his property: the loss of that place involved to a certain extent his own loss, and, as he had chosen his side, he adhered to it with all his heart, as the only future means of obtaining restitution. With this view he once more took up arms, and having observed, and, it may be, acted, in compelling confiscations, had seen the advantage, and kept his eye steadily upon the first opportunity that presented itself in his own case. Meantime he was too discreet to interfere without the authority under which he was serving, that it might appear as a mere attempt at reprisal, and not as wanton spoil. {October. [Motives of Birch.]}

About this time the Houses had brought into play their system of sequestration upon the Royalists, whom they stigmatized as "delinquents,"[a] and on whose property, real and personal, of what kind soever, they laid their hands, under rules and circumstances enacted in ordinances stringent and severe. Committees were formed for this purpose at different times and different places, wherever they could employ their power. The practice had been {[Commencement of Sequestration.]}

[a] Scobell, 39, 40.

1643.
October.

already put in execution at Bristol, under the government of Fiennes, and was extending itself in all directions. By warrants from these committees, the property of all, rich or poor, who had voluntarily declared or acted in the most trivial manner on behalf of the King, became liable to be seized upon and confiscated. In case of resistance the agents employed were to be effectually supported by military force. It will be readily understood that this would ultimately open a door to abuse: for though the commission was placed in the first instance and for the most part in respectable hands, it fell in the course of time into those of the most crafty and unworthy, whose sole object was plunder, and occasioned results the most calamitous and unjust. The measure, both in its origin and the method of carrying it out, has not been without its apologists.[a] But partizanship alone can forbear to weigh its acts of wanton tyranny and oppression against the alike indefensible measures of the ill-educated, misguided, unfortunate Charles.[b] This machinery being already set on foot, and on the increase, though not absolutely perfected, our attention is caught by the following entry in the proceedings of the House of Commons:

"Monday, Oct. 9, 1643. Ordered, that the petition of Elizabeth Clement and Ann Clement, daughters and administrators of the goods and chattels of Anne Goffe their mother, late of Bristoll, deceased, and the petition of Walter Sendy, merchant, of Bristoll, and the petition of Mary Hooke, the widow of Thomas Hooke of Bristoll deceased, and the petition of Richard Vickeres of Bristoll, merchant, be referred to the Committee of the Navy."

Here is a question of grievance that calls for investigation. The transaction, whatever it may be, occurs with reference to a place with which Birch had been so deeply concerned, though now in the hands of the Royalists: and hence it might at first sight be difficult

[a] Godwin, History of Commonwealth, iii. 491. Retrospective Review, ix. 1, 6; xii. 2, 1.

[b] The King's, Queen's, and Prince's revenues were ordered to be sequestered and collected by ordinance precisely at this time. Lords' Journals, Sept. 21.

to understand why any appeal at all should be made to a Parliamentary committee, seeing that the present interests and authorities of that city had passed over to the servants of the King. It will, however, perhaps be discovered, in the absence of other proof, that some explanation may fairly be obtained from an entry in the same journal on the ensuing day:

1643. October.

" October 10. Ordered, that Captain John Birche be forthwith sent for in safe custody, and that he bring with him such warrant as he hath to seize any man's goods."

Should it admit of a doubt, whether or not this has any immediate connection with the preceding complaint, the article is closely linked to a string of entries exhibiting some striking points in the character and conduct of Birch before he repaired to the army. He has not yet set out, and the date points to the period at which he was resident in London. The scene that now takes place is curious and instructive, and, if actually witnessed by Hesilrige and Waller, for both of them were frequenters of that assembly, might convince them of the drift of his intention. It will be recollected that the Speaker Lenthall is in the chair, and the several members are in their places: then

[Birch as sequestrator.]

" Oct. 11. Captain Birche was called in, who produced to the House the warrants from the Committee for Safety for seizing of goods, &c.

" After he had withdrawn, the warrants were read, and Captain Birch was called in again and informed the House in particular of his proceedings therein, and of the good services he had formerly done for the Parliament, and the many thousands of pounds he hath lost in their service.

" Mr. Speaker, by command of the House, told him (after he had withdrawn and come in the third time) that the House did take notice of the special services he had done, and of his discreet carriage in the execution of these warrants, which gave too great a latitude of power, and have ordered he be discharged without fees, and that the warrants do remain here.

1643.
October.

"Ordered, that the goods stayed by Captain Birche do remain undisposed of in those hands they were stayed until this House give farther order.

"Ordered, that the House do take into consideration to-morrow morning the two warrants granted to Captain Birch.

"Ordered, that the House do take care in due time to give satisfaction to Captain Birch for the monies he hath disbursed to the Parliament.

"Oct. 11. Ordered, that it be referred to the Committee concerning the clothiers' petition in Gloucestershire to examine the business concerning Captain Birch, and to whom those goods or monies seized or stayed by him do belong."

At the end of a week the whole of this ludicrous business was concluded by a final order: "Oct. 18. That the warrant given by the Close Committee unto Captain Birch, to seize the monies and goods going to Bristoll and Worcester, &c., and the monies and goods of the malignants of Bristoll and Worcester, &c., be recalled and taken up, and the forty-three pounds ten shillings taken by the said Captain from William Coles the factor be restored again."

Such was, to all appearance, the first and singular introduction of this remarkable man within those walls where he was afterwards to act so conspicuous a part, and has been described by one who knew him well as one of the best speakers to carry a popular assembly before him.*

ndiscretion Birch.]

The disclosure of these incidents from another quarter thus throws a light upon the motives and proceedings of Birch, while he continued to adhere to his resolution of remaining in the service of the Parliament. Of course, as already observed, if Roe knew of them, it cannot be expected that they should be found in what is merely a narrative of the courage and conduct of his superior officer as a soldier in the field. Rightly intentioned as Birch seems to have been, according to the views sanctioned by his own party, his discretion, though in part flattered and commended by the Speaker,

* Burnet, i. 547.

had not been allowed to temper the boldness with which he had too hastily acted in pursuit of his remuneration;[a] for it will be manifest that he kept this constantly in mind. So far, however, he had been exonerated from blame. If a blunder had been committed, it was not entirely with him. His part was rather to submit to restitution in a case in which he had thought to have made a successful seizure for himself. The practice here exhibited was not put an end to by having in this instance been checked. All parties concerned therein had, however, received a lesson of caution. Waller would more than ever be confirmed as to the necessity of scrutiny in the choice of officers; and Birch himself might see the uncertainty respecting the success of that scrutiny, and the obligation of looking well to the future behaviour of his own regimental comrades, and that in more than one respect.

1643.
December.

For that there had been already sundry offences against their laws of war, among those to whom the Parliament had confided the leading and example of their army, cannot be denied. The fact is couched adroitly in the expressions of their records that allude to it, but nevertheless appears to be a fact. Whether it were only mutiny, or gross and unwarrantable seizure of the property of delinquents, or both, has been left to the judgment of those under whose eyes the evidence might hereafter fall.

[Misconduct in Waller's army.]

" Dec. 9. Ordered, That Mr. Trenchard [b] do write to Sir Wm Waller to send for Colonel Potleyes [c] men; and that he desire Sir

---

[a] His share of the sequestered property as discoverer, according to the ordinance (Scobell, 50), would have amounted to one shilling in the pound, besides such gratuity for extraordinary service as the Parliament might think fit to allow him.

[b] Trenchard was treasurer. Of the difficulties with which Waller had to contend, and the expense of his and other armaments, some notion may be formed from his own words of complaint against the Parliament: "In what condition I was maintained may be demonstrated by the treasurer Mr. John Trenchard his accompts, where it will appear that from the time of my setting forth unto my disbanding I never received full one hundred thousand pounds (an inconsiderable summe compared with what others had), and yet out of that stock I was fain to play the good husband, and to be at the charge to pay for part of my arms and ammunition." Vindication, 16, 17.   [c] Note 4.

1643.
December.

Wm Waller to pay them a fortnight's pay at their coming to his forces; and that if any refuse to march, that they be proceeded against according to the law martial: And that Colonel Potley cashier those two captains of his regiment that Mr. Trenchard informed of, not to be worthy of their command."[a]

From these hints may be formed some estimate of the officers of the Parliamentary army assembled at the rendezvous in and near Farnham.

[Farnham.] The castle of this place was of great importance in a military view. Built upon an eminence commanding the town, it had been famous in early history as the seat of the Bishops of Winchester. It was of noble extent and magnificence, and contained ample accommodation for cavalry and infantry. Its existing state, as to strength and measurement, according to the survey of an officer in this army, Lieutenant-Colonel Baines, long quartered there, in the possession of the writer,[b] shows it to have been very formidable. The seal of the town has adopted it as an emblem of consequence.[c] Besides a principal tower, called Jeyes Tower, it had a first, second, and third turret, a court-yard with a pigeon-house and stables, with several high basket batteries, and, except perhaps Basing, it seems to have been one of the best fortified houses in those parts. It had too easily fallen into Waller's hands, after Winchester and its cathedral had been rifled, in the early part of December in the campaign of 1642. According to Vicars[d] it was taken by surprise,

---

[a] C. J. *loco*. [" It is little knowne amongst us in the army that Sir W. Waller, being to march upon a hopefull designe, some of his commanders would not march without pay; whereupon such as refused, being 7 or 8 in number, he called them in, one by one, cashired them, and gave their commissions to their lieutenants, and put some of them in the gaole, and the rest were earnest suitors to be entertained againe, but could not prevaile." Kingdome's Weekly Intelligencer, May 9 to 15, 1643. But as late as Feb. 13, 1644-5, Whitelocke informs us that " letters from Sir W. Waller intimated disobedience in some of the soldiers to march into the West, and desired further power," which was granted: as the army had then received their pay, this writer considers that " here began their first unruliness."]

[b] Baines' MSS.   [c] Lewis's Topograph. Dict. *sub v.* Farnham.

[d] God in the Mount, i. 223.

for Sir John Denham the poet, who had been made governor of it by the King, surrendered it after a few hours' resistance.ᵃ At this place occurred one of those hazards in war that Waller has recorded in his "Experiences." He escaped a very near shot from one of his own men, as he followed him in a narrow passage after he was entered.ᵇ The castle subsequently formed the Parliamentary headquarters in this district. Here they held their courts martial, occasionally deposited their prisoners, and formed a magazine. Thence they issued, and thither they retreated for security. After the loss of his army Waller still retained possession of it, and to return to it was the first object of his march. The Parliament always had an eye to it. Essex had been charged of old to observe it,ᶜ for they were very sensible of its worth. It looked towards Winchester, and the advance of the Royalist force from that quarter, where Hopton, with a reinforcement under Sir Jacob Astley from the garrisons of Oxford, Wallingford, and Reading, was about to move forward for the opening of the next strife in arms. He had recovered from his hurt received at Lansdown, and was very desirous to try his fortune against his ancient comrade, who was not loth to meet him in his turn. Indeed Hopton, by orders from the King, anticipated his adversary, for while part of the new-raised regiments were drawing nigh to Farnham, he had himself led a party to Arundel, the castle of which he seized, and left in it a garrison under command of Sir Edward Ford, sheriff of the county, to encourage the Royalists there. Scarcely had he returned, when he found that Waller was

1643.
December.

ᵃ Waller forced the gate with a petard, and it surrendered. Sir John Denham in return for this mortification thus lampooned him for his rout at Roundway Down :—

        Great William the Con——
        So fast did he run
        That he left half his name behind him.

It had been as unfortunate on the King's side to entrust the government of Farnham to Sir John Denham, the poet, as it was on the other side to confide Bristol to Nathaniel Fiennes, the lawyer. Neither of them proved fit to be trusted with important command.—J. W.

ᵇ Experiences, MS.   ᶜ C. J. Nov. 23, 1642.

1643.
December.

[Military operations at Farnham.]

in and around Farnham, whither he hastened, to bring him to action.

The arrival at this place of new levies from London was soon followed by petty encounters on the debateable ground near Waller's head-quarters. According to Clarendon and Whitelocke these bickerings for a day or two were attended with no greater result to either except that Waller's horse were driven into the castle: but an event occurred that, according to his own admission, might have been attended with a most serious issue. The Royalist drew out and formally offered his adversary battle.[a] Thus they stood for some time opposed to each other in the field, and Birch's regiment advanced to take up its ground, when both parties separated without a stroke. His eulogist insinuates that the strength of his regiment might have had an effect upon the fortune of the day, and that a Providence interfered in his favour; whereas the armies never seriously engaged: the same, but with the real reason and extent of the danger, is candidly admitted by Waller himself, who reckons it among his hazards, and congratulates himself upon his own escape from ruin. Let the reader judge for himself. " Att Farnham God appeared wonderfully for me, when the Lord Hopton drew upp his whole army within demy culverin shott of me, being (with the forces of Sir Jacob Ashley, who was then joyned with him,) att the least eight thousand horse and foot, and (thorough the mistake or neglect of my adiutant generall, and the slackness of my men in drawing to the rendevous,) I was not able to face him with two thousand, in that extremity the Lord tooke opportunity [b] to shew himself for me, by sending so thick a mist all the morning, that, by reason thereof, the ennemy durst not give on, but, without attempting further, drew off again. I was that day delivered from an imminent destruction." [c]

[Strength of regiments.]

There can be no doubt that the regiment in which Birch was to serve was, through his own efforts, and those of Hesilrige, complete; and that after what had happened to correct and improve it, when

[a] Note 5.   [b] See Note 17.   [c] Experiences, MS.

the hour of its active duties arrived, it was as well appointed as circumstances would allow. As to the drill, there were Low Country soldiers and Scotch officers to be found in London; there was Potley also, a superior officer, to have helped them. He himself had a regiment, and was a disciplinarian expert in military matters. As to the strength and maintenance of a regiment in the maturer Oliverian times, a statement in the Antiquarian Repertory[a] will sufficiently inform the reader. It never consisted of less than 1,000 privates, though sometimes a few more. But respecting the sort under immediate observation nothing need be required beyond the satisfactory account of Lieutenant Colonel Baines[b] in a pocket-book that he kept during his sojourn at Farnham, where he occasionally acted as muster-master, and seems to have been thoroughly acquainted with their established usages according to the art of war then in vogue. When Captain Birch led his men to Farnham, a perfect regiment of infantry stood thus as to numbers and daily pay:—

"The pay of a regiment of 1,000 ffoote in 10 companies, & staffe officers.

Colonell	2	5	0	Chapleine & man	0	8	8
Lieut. Colonell	1	10	0				
Major	1	04	0	Chirurgion & 2 mates	0	9	0
7 Captains	5	05	0				
10 Leuitenants	2	00	0	Marshall & his man	0	4	8
10 Ensignes	1	10	0				
21 Sergeants	1	11	6	Quartermaster & man	0	4	8
1 Drum major	0	01	6				
20 Drums	1	00	0	p daye . . .	1	7	00
10 Gentlemen[c]	0	10	0		18	7	00
30 Corporalls	1	10	0	p daye . .	19	14	00
p daye .	18	07	0	p all			

[a] Ant. Rep. ii. 5.   [b] Note 6.
[c] [In the Earl of Essex's army, a " Gentleman of the Arms " was allowed in every

1643.
December.

	£ s. d.
All officers p diem	19 14 00
1,000 soldiers p diem	33 06 08
The Regiment compleate p diem	53 00 08
The Regiment compleate p weeke	371 04 08
The Regiment compleate p month	1,484 18 08 "[a]

The pay of a troop of cavalry officers and men in Sir Thomas Fairfax's army was as follows, for one week:

	£	s.	d.
Captain	9	9	0
Lieutenant	5	0	0
Cornet	4	6	6
Quarter Master	3	3	0
8 Corporals	8	8	0
2 Trumpeters	2	2	0
9 Gentlemen	9	0	0
91 Common Troopers (14s. each)	63	14	0
	£105	2	6 [b]

It has been seen that while Waller was gathering strength more effectually to meet Hopton, and skirmishes had been going on

company of the foot, at 4d. extra per diem; and sixteen "Gentlemen of the Ordnance" for the whole of that branch of the service.—C. J. May 1 and 6, 1644.]

Who they were receives no explanation; they were perhaps intended as supernumeraries to fill up vacancies in the officers.—J. W.

[a] [During the Protectorate, somewhat differently officered, 1,512l. Ant. Rep. ii. 5.]

[b] Major Papers, I. British Museum.—[A cavalry regiment consisted usually of three or four troops. Cruso, Castrametation (1642), 10.—On the Royalist side, it was proposed, in May 1644, to allow the troopers in garrison at Woodstock Manor 7s. per week, "which is but a little more than a third part of their pay." Sir E. Walker's Papers, MSS. Harl. 6802, 147.—An estimate by Col. T. Blagge allowed 3s. 6d. for each soldier, hay and oats each 3s. per week. Ibid. 6804, 185.—The Earl of Manchester received 34,000l. per month for 14,000 men; the new modelled army of 21,000 was allowed 44,955l. The exactions of Fairfax on the city of Bath and hundred of Bathforum are shown by the records of the corporation to have been 90,000l. for six months, in addition to twelve months pay (amount not specified) granted previously!—Such is war.]

between them,[a] the Royalist had stolen a march down to Arundel, and formed an imperfect settlement there. This was the initiative that had broken off their mutual observation of each other's motions, and had become a prelude to more serious occurrences. About this time also he had pushed forward a detachment to Alton, a rural town between Winchester and Farnham. By these means he thought to have strengthened himself and impeded the progress of the enemy in those parts, while he pursued his object of an immediate encounter. Just as he had returned from the expedition to Arundel, Waller, who saw that no time was to be lost, began to thwart his measures. He, on his part, had established an outpost at a village called Crondall, dangerous as exposed to attack from Alton, but within retreat to his head-quarters: there he set Birch in command. Waller, who had occupied Alton[b] personally in his former campaign, could not but have been acquainted with its condition as he left it; but it had now changed hands; and Captain Birch (for so for the present he must continue to be called), to whom it was new, took care, during his short stay at Crondall, to obtain exact information of every part of its existing state by spies.[c] The Royalists there under the Earl of Craford[d] had constructed defences, now wholly slighted and undistinguishable, consisting of outworks with double trenches and a half-moon near the church. As these were open to assault, Waller's determination was to carry them by a surprise, in which Birch was to bear his part. As the account of what ensues in the MS. is chiefly occupied with his personal share in the transaction, it may admit of the introduction of a few accompanying features. On the evening of Dec. 12 a rendezvous was held of about 5,000 horse and foot in Farnham Park. Marching first towards Basing to elude suspicion, they turned soon after mid-

1643.
December.

[Waller surprises Alton.]

[a] Whitelocke, 74.
[b] Carte, MSS. Letters, Bibl. Bodl. EEEE, 36.
[c] Note 7.
[d] [This nobleman had served in the wars between the Poles and Turks: but if he brought away any military reputation, it was not increased by his achievements nearer home.]

1643.
Dec. 13.

night more immediately towards Alton, taking Birch with them. They came in sight of the place about nine in the morning, Birch having captured a scout-master on the way, whose comrades escaped to apprise Craford of his danger. As the Parliamentarians stole along the slopes that commanded the whole town and adjacent country, they were amused by his irresolute efforts to escape; they saw how he was headed and turned back by a party of their own cavalry, how he passed again through the town towards Winchester, and ultimately succeeded. They raised such a shout of derision as made the neighbouring woodlands ring. Thence they descended, taking the outworks, planting their colours, closing with horse every avenue, and proceeding up the street. Colonel Richard Boles, a brave officer with a regiment of great reputation recently arrived from Wallingford, being left to the result, retired with these and some horse to the church and churchyard, and resisting in hope of receiving succour awaited his fate. Shut up and surrounded they threw wide the door, met the assault and sustained it, not a man surrendering till the Colonel was slain.[a] The particulars of this encounter are described in the MS., in which Birch has the credit of being the first who entered the street, and has, by the publication of this narrative, at length so far obtained it; though neither in an official statement published by the Parliament, nor in a letter apparently from an eye-witness abounding with particulars, does his name occur. The death of Boles, unnamed by Roe, was owing to his own refusal to surrender or accept of life at their hands; for the subject of quarter had been settled between Waller and the Marquis of Hertford before. " On Saturday a messenger came to Sir W. Waller from the Earl of Hertford desiring Sir William that in any future action between the armies, his men might give quarter; Waller replied that if any of his men should refuse to give quarter, so barbarously did he conceive of that action that he would quarter him and make him an example to others."[b] One little circumstance may wind up the story. Craford, the fugitive, had left behind him

[a] Note 8.   [b] Parl. Scout, Thursday, July 6, 1643.

COLONEL JOHN BIRCH. 71

a butt of sack that the courtesy of Waller had sent him;[a] the Parliamentary soldiers took a malicious pleasure in disappointing the chivalry of their general towards an enemy; they drank the wine with exultation, and the joke was thought so good as to find a special place at the end of the narrative authorised by Parliament. Such were the incidents that first familiarised Birch with scenes of bloodshed, so far as is recorded in the MS.; and it is afterwards more than hinted that his conduct excited the jealousy of one superior officer, who kept an eye upon his brave behaviour, and brought him into jeopardy.

1643.
Dec. 13.

Many colours were found concealed in the church at the surrender: the prisoners,[b] "some of the choicest men since the war began," tied in pairs with match, were brought to Farnham, and afterwards to London, where with certain of the city regiments they were met and paraded in procession by the Lord Mayor and authorities.[c] This seemed to give proof of an actual advantage gained over the enemy. Captors and captives, by this display they

[Prisoners removed to London.]

---

[a] [A somewhat similar instance of courtesy occurred when Prince Rupert drew off from Bristol on the failure of Yeomans's plot. The writer of a letter, who signs himself J. H., says that when the Prince sent to demand the bodies of two of his men killed by a shot from the town, "the trumpeter enquired for me, and said my Lord of Cleveland desired me to send him a pound of tobacco; but I being out of the way, Colonell Fines sent him one pound and Colonell Popham another." (Seyer's Memoirs, ii. 367.) Lloyd tells us that he would take a hundred pipes a day, "first used to it in leagures."]

[b] Note 9.

[c] It appears they were part of a picked, or what in modern times would be called a *crack*, regiment. The traces of its being repaired by enlistment or exchange are to be seen in the account of the night-march of Charles I. by the Rev. Vaughan Thomas (Oxford, 8vo.), where, at p. 25, are entries from the register of Yarnton, Jan. 14, 1643, to Jan. 31, 1644, of the burial of several of that regiment. It is also mentioned in Symonds's Diary, p. 160, as kept up under the name of Boles, and commanded by Sir George Lisle, whose lamented death at Colchester in 1648 nearly closed the military sufferings of the Cavaliers. Boles had been in Reading during the siege, and one of the party appointed to treat of the surrender.—Vicars, God in the Mount, 312. Several of the officers taken at Alton were retained prisoners till the April following, when they procured liberty to solicit an exchange. MSS. Papers of Sir Edw. Walker: MSS. Harl. 6802, 71.

1643.
Dec. 13.

helped to elevate the tone of the public mind. Birch and his volunteers were still left behind with the army. His military character continues to expand, and acquires strength as we advance. This became more and more evident to those into whose society he was cast, or who envied his talent, that though he might be a novice, he had given full proof of his valour, and was under no necessity of concealing his appetite for fighting.

Dec. 14.
[Waller's march to Arundel.]

The next step in the campaign is the march to Arundel. This is another specimen of the mode in which Waller carried on hostilities, or, in the refined sarcasm of Clarendon, " the masterpiece of his generalship." He had lately succeeded so well by rapidity of movement and surprise that the experiment must be repeated. After only a few hours of repose he led his men against another of Hopton's assailable positions. Hopton had, as we have related, recently (Dec. 4 [a]) taken Arundel Castle, and left in it an insufficient and refractory garrison composed of ill-assorted individuals, whom the governor, Sir Edward Ford, had been unable to reduce to military obedience. He had also failed to victual the place; and he was besides himself unequal to the duties required of him. The season, though nearly mid-winter, was favourable, open though severe; and the frost had dried up and hardened the roads. Accordingly, without suffering their excitement to be interrupted, Waller carried his men without delay over the distance between Farnham and Arundel, where he arrived on the evening of the second day, leaving Hopton to regret his loss.[b] It will be recollected that the greater part of Waller's army were youths, and there is no hint of their being immediately hampered by any convoy, even of guns. A leading feature of this occurrence, memorable on many accounts, evidently made a lasting impression upon Roe and his superior

[a] [Dugdale says the town was gained Dec. 5, the castle Dec. 9. He fixes the surprise at Alton Dec. 14, a day later than Roe and the " Narration " published by the Parliament.]

[b] [Clarendon observes that " the Lord Hopton sustained the loss of that regiment with extraordinary trouble of mind, and as a wound that would bleed inward." History, viii.]

officer, namely, the comfort derivable in a winter's morning from the outspread arms of the noble·leafless trees in the park, while in suggesting this he picturesquely describes the different groups of armed men, taking up their ground as they arrived, and passing their bivouac in the open air.

1643.
Dec. 17.

Eager to hasten to the encounter, Waller's skirmishers took immediate advantage. The veteran Potley, who had seen hard winter service with the Lion of the North, gave command for the assault on that winter's morning. About sunrise, with a force of less than a regiment and a half, composed partly of Sir William Waller's regiment, partly·of his own, with musketeers and pikes,[a] for cavalry at first he had none, Birch was ordered to attack the work protecting the castle and the town. Behind it stood the Cavaliers, double in number, with horse and foot ready to receive him. His exposure to a service of so much hazard is attributed to jealousy on the part of Potley, in consequence of his forward bravery at Alton. However this may be, he proved himself at any rate equal to the emergency, fearless and active, fit to direct, and add example to his command. It is his second and perhaps hitherto most arduous trial. His order is, to force his entry into the castle. After a short and imperfect movement in advance, he made an improved disposition of his inferior force, and for their better security, under the fire of the enemy, who derided him. In a second movement, still leading the way, he surmounts the rampart. Struck down and abandoned when all the assailants are driven out, he stands alone, still exposed to fire, pike in hand, with his face towards the enemy in a picturesque attitude, ready once more to receive the support of his men. Once more the attempt is made; the rampart is again surmounted, and he moves forward, some cavalry coming to his assistance. A body of reformados sally; accompanied by the ill-regulated mass that Hopton had left behind as a garrison, but at length they give way. A rush of mingled combatants towards the castle ensues; it is a dense and struggling

[Birch assaults Arundel.]

[a] Note 10.

CAMD. SOC.   L

crowd, intent upon mutual destruction. The gates are shut, but they enter the street together fighting. In the course of this confusion, while Birch is cheerfully encouraging those about him, the shot are flying thick; Waller's lieutenant-colonel and a brave Scot are slain close to him. He draws his men on one side of the street, is himself struck by a bullet in the act, and, while attempting to retire unobserved, faints in the moment of victory. This picture of an assault needs little to heighten its graphic lineaments, though some things may be added to illustrate and explain.

[Soldier-like conduct of Birch.] The coolness and impetuosity of the principal personage, his contempt of danger, and his self-possession when evil had overtaken him, and in the last extremity, give additional proofs of his soldier-like qualities. Amidst this hurricane of missiles and slaughter, the chief damage appears to have been done by the employment of fire-arms—pistols and muskets; though the latter are mixed with pikes, according to the tactics then in vogue. The sudden seizure of the scout-master's horse expresses Birch's forwardness in using his license of management, and claiming his position as lieutenant-colonel, for as captain he does not seem to have been entitled to one.[a] But the general was weak in that important arm of the service. This failure of horse will be often noticed; for it was a leading object of Hesilrige and the Houses to repair it, and it had great influence on the success of the campaign.

["Honest men and rogues."] Another point is the introduction of the "gallant Scot;"[b] that nation being the favourites of the hour. As to the epithet of "honest" captains, it must be received in its own Parliamentary sense; but it is employed on either side, and the interpretation must be rather political than moral. The remark of Clarendon, that the King's troops were "ill-officered," has too much evidence to support it; but whether he who gave an account were Royalist or Roundhead, those who acted with him would all be "honest," those who acted against him all "rogues."

[Birch wounded.] With Captain Birch all is now apparently over. His wound is

[a] Young Soldier, 1642.   [b] Note 11.

so severe, and attended with such loss of blood, that the surgeons abandon at first sight any hope of relieving him; and he is cast aside on the floor weltering among the dying and the dead. But it was not to be so; and the "deliverance," apparently owing to the same cause, was not without a parallel during this war. Hemorrhage and cold had, in a case [a] still more remarkable, proved remedial; the sufferer had been restored, and survived many years. The weather was now extremely severe, and the blood, unexpectedly retarded in its circulation, by coagulating gradually ceased to flow. The conduct of the army-surgeons [b] in this instance appeared to advantage. They had been occupied nine hours in endeavouring to afford relief to the various calls of the miserable. It was dark, the watch would be set, the agitated crowd withdrawn from the strife—

1643.
Dec. 17.

The weary to rest, and the wounded to die.[c]

It tells well for them that once more after their labours they visited the individual sufferer, almost forgotten as he had been during the whole of the day; him whom they had left as dead, they found still breathing; they dressed him, and put him into a condition of safety.

In the account of these troubles, too little credit has perhaps been given to the professors of the healing art. The regiments on both sides were furnished with this essential help. As to the Parliament, they took care that every regiment should be supplied with a staff both medical and surgical in all its departments, provided with every appliance to meet and relieve the disasters of battle. Their help in the case of Birch was most opportune; but never man had better reason to admire the deliverance, or remember the Divine mercy exhibited to him on that eventful day.

[Surgical staff.]

[a] That of Sir Gervase Scroop, who received seventeen wounds at the battle of Edgehill, and lay two days and two nights among the slain, till discovered by the filial piety of his son.—Bulstrode, Memoirs, 85.
[b] Note 12.
[c] Campbell's Soldier's Dream.

1643.
Dec. 17.

[Capture of Arundel.]

Clarendon[a] will help to fill up the account of operations at this place. He makes the surrender an affair of quarter after the alarms of three or four days. The castle was all but taken at the first rush, when they entered pell-mell into the town; but Waller, ever too sanguine, was so confident of success that he wrote to the House of Lords that he had defeated the enemy on his advance from Farnham, and had entered the town with horse and foot, and, notwithstanding a brave sally made by them, had beaten them into the castle, and entered the first gate with them: "the second," he says, "they made good and barricadoed," and adds, in his lively style, "there they are welcome. Truly, my Lords, I am very weak in foot, and my horse so hackneyed that they are ready to lie down under us."[b]

[Death of Chillingworth.]

Among the prisoners taken in this castle, may be incidentally mentioned the celebrated Chillingworth, whose case is sadly descriptive of the temper of the time. He had been at Gloucester siege, took refuge in sickness at Arundel, and was brought with the officers to Chichester. Here his life was, by the Royalists, reported to have been put an end to among controversial disputes, and his grave was certainly closed over with passionate indignity.[c]

[Birch goes to London.]

Unwilling or unable to trust to the care of a rural practitioner, Birch got conveyed to London,[d] doubtless the best place to obtain skilful attendance and opportunity of resort to his adviser when able to move. Vast numbers of sick and disabled from the beginning had pressed into the shelter of walled towns for security and repose. The streets of the metropolis had too often presented sad spectacles of the miseries of warfare. Homeless objects, wounded and maimed, begging their bread; Royalists among them and prisoners, appealing to the compassion or provoking the irritated feelings of their adversaries. To meet this discouraging sight, an

[a] Book viii.
[b] L. J. Dec. 23, 1643.
[c] Biographical Dictionary, article *Cheynell*.
[d] Note 13.

ordinance had been passed for the relief of their own poor privates and their families.   1643. December.

The removal of the captain to a place of rest and safety answered its end sooner than could have been expected. His men, too, while this was going on, indulged in a temporary pause; they went into "winter quarters." The expression is ominous. Quarters might be quarters paid for by those who had the means, and were not too rudely dishonest to withhold them, or the quarters might be free. Far from being well mannered or well flushed with pay, it is a fact that the soldiers of Waller gave special rise to the country's complaint of free quarter; but whether most in the winter of 1642-3, or that of 1643-4, on this score, cannot be fairly insisted upon; yet it is too well confirmed not to bear a strong allusion. Essex, who was everywhere indulgent to his men, and yet cautious of disgusting the country, had been forced to try the experiment for seventeen weeks with little success, or rather with intolerable annoyance to the public. It produced a remonstrance and petition of the committee and inhabitants of Hertfordshire in behalf of all classes for redress from such a nuisance and destruction of property.[a] The satirist in the Devonshire Ditty,[b] and Taylor the water-poet of Oxford,[c] prove the feelings of those who were exposed to it; which are elsewhere described by a contemporary in a few pungent sentences: "We call it free quarter. What a grief! to be made servile to provide for such guests, when the family knew that it was Judas that dipped his hand with him in the dish. What an expense it was to bring out all their stores, laid up for a year, and to waste it in a week, sometimes upon a hundred of these orgeglioes!" (haughty ones). "These horse-leeches seldom left an house till they had threshed the barn empty, and drunk the cellar dry."[d]   [Winter Quarters.]

[a] L. J. Feb. 26, 1643-4.   [b] Appendix VIII.
[c] Appendix IX.
[d] Hacket, Life of Williams, ii. 206. [The Commissioners of the county of Monmouth stipulated that there should be no free quarter allowed to the King's soldiers but for a night or two, marching: if the garrisons infringed this agreement, the contribution was to suffer abatement. July 18, 1645.—MSS. Harl. 6852.]

1643.
December.
[Birch returns to the army.]

The memoirs of John Birch are descriptive of a truly active body and a vigorous mind; for such he has already shown himself. During his stay in London and attention to his cure, his reflections were of course much occupied with his future prospects and intentions; and, if it may be thought admissible in the commentator, his condition may be thus described:—His wound has been dangerous, but the immediate danger was passed when he left Arundel. He had never before been hurt but by a few "dry blows" at Alton. He had the entire use of his limbs. What if he had been in the condition of those wretches that haunted the public streets, provoking the pity or scorn of the passenger! Though for the present invalided, he was captain of a company, with the entire command of a regiment. Though labouring under heavy losses, he had made himself an acknowledged creditor of the Commonwealth. The obvious road to reparation was for him as soon as possible to return to his men, who were only waiting for him. It may be believed that some reflections such as these passed through his mind: they are justified by his former and subsequent actions. He resolved to return to the army.

1643-4.
[Military operations during the winter.]

By his successes at Alton and Arundel, the general had obtained a power of acting over an extensive surface in Surrey, Sussex, and Hampshire, and a few features of its effects may be brought in view. At Chichester was established a committee to order, and a garrison to enforce, sequestrations. Parties could rove about from Farnham, and vex those that opposed them. At Odiham they burst into the church during the performance of the service, interrupted it by the discharge of fire-arms, and called to the clergyman in the pulpit, "Sir, you must come down, we do not allow such kind of preaching."[a] Basing House, the strong and stately seat of the Marquis of Winchester, was an obstacle to their London communications. Waller had attempted to invest it, but drew off, unwilling to expose his men to the delay of a siege in wintry weather. Bickerings occurred between the garrisons of this place

[a] Merc. Aulic. Feb. 1643-4.

and Farnham. The Chichester wagon was captured and retaken. In this mutual harassing the season passed away.* At the end of about ten weeks the army rose: Birch was able to rejoin his company at Arundel, and renew his command, for some measure of importance was about to be taken.

1643-4.

Much of the mischief and bloodshed in general during this intestine quarrel was occasioned by petty casual encounters, surprises, and the beating up of quarters in the shorter days. But these were at an end: the spring approached, the weather was fair; they moved in the direction of Cheriton; the trees there, from which that village is said to derive its name, and whither they were going to convert its orchards into a scene of slaughter, were preparing to put forth their leaves and bloom. The army rose on March 11, about the season when, in Scripture language, "Kings go forth to battle." Waller, flushed by his success, gathered up his strength to take the initiative, and prosecute the war in earnest. Collecting his troops he drew forth from his centre of occupation, and approached Hopton's head-quarters. He pushed on towards Alresford, not far from Winchester, where Hopton, mortified by his reverses, was as eager to meet him, and had express command from the King. Other writers have described more manœuvring and fighting than is here found. From the length of time (March 25 to 29) occupied in this dispute, and the various and distant points near which it took place, it has been distinguished by different names; but Alresford or Cheriton are perhaps the most generally adopted. The struggle was protracted obstinately in strategy for several days, attended with serious conflict: Roe has described its opening as merely a "facing at cannon-shot distance;" he could have seen only a portion of it: he witnessed the early movements, and the latter fight, the most severely contested of the whole. He has forcibly described the events of that day, and Birch's strength of resolution and valour. Other eye-witnesses of the field are not wanting; if Roe differs from them, he may readily be excused.

[Opening of Waller's Campaign.—Battle of Alresford.]

1644.
March 29.

* Appendix X.

80   MILITARY MEMOIR OF

1644.
March 29.   Nothing can be more delusive than many of the descriptions of
general battles by those who were present.[a] While the combatant
is absorbed in his own excitement, he has too often no power to
attend to what is going on beyond his own immediate post. As
Denon the artist, in his superb illustration of the invasion of Egypt
by Buonaparte the Consul, has singled out and described an individual group, and called it a *battle*, so the writer and his corrector
have here attempted to show little beyond what occurred within
their view; but the biographical particulars, so to speak, of this
encounter, so far as the principal characters are concerned, are
original; and the details broken up into portions will bear some
expansion in the Notes.

[Incidents of battle of Alresford.]   There is candour and impartiality in the brief sketch of this, one
of their greatest battles. Lieut.-Col. Sir Richard Brown,[b] Sir
William Balfour, and other officers, with the gallant loyalist Appleyard,[c] have their due. The reprobate conduct of the Roundhead
blasphemer,[d] with Hesilrige's timidity [e] at the sight of the rout at
Cheriton Wood, receive their fair admission and exposure. A
council of war, held on the evening before the last day, had, in any
such circumstances, been a symptom of distress. Each leader had
called a council of his own. In that of Hopton, here unnoticed,
it was resolved that they could not draw off without difficulty and
dishonour; that of Waller was broken up in alarm. The receipt of
the order that fires should be lit to cover their retreat involved the
duty of Birch; but with the spirit of " vestigia nulla retrorsum," he
disdained and expressed to a brother officer his disdain of the
measure. That night he had the watch, the sentries across the
valley were yet so close that the sound of their voices could be

---

[a] [The various and perplexed relations of the great battle of Marston Moor are a well-known instance of this. Fairfax himself seems to have had a singularly confused recollection of his own part in it. In his "Memorials" he expressly states that he commanded the right wing; in Fuller's "Worthies" (215, n.) he as distinctly asserts that he had command of the left.]

[b] Note 14.   [c] Note 15.
[d] Note 16.   [e] Note 17.

heard from side to side; an opportunity the captain had, as is 1644. March 29. confessed (but how it was managed does not appear), of keeping the sentries to their posts; this opportunity he improved, and by so doing produced the engagement; he had been ordered to retire, but that order he slighted. The whole is represented as arising from orders disobeyed. Disobedience in his comrade Hesilrige at Roundway Down caused Waller's defeat; disobedience by Birch at Cheriton gave rise to the claim of victory on the part of that general—a victory ill-prosecuted, but impossible to be denied. The armies came to the encounter at earliest dawn, and the dispute continued throughout the greater part of the day. Though, in the beautiful language of Waller to Hopton, theirs was a war without an enemy, it was attended by much close and internecine combat, and heavy amount of slaughter. Previous to the crisis described by Roe, great dispersion and mingling of combatants took place round the focus of the contest, in Cheriton Wood, in the valley, and on the down. In the valley the chief execution took place; it was an obstinate but scattered fight. Waller was highly excited. By an accident he became exposed without his usual body-guard and attendants, was recognised, and by his own admission in imminent peril. "At Cheriton field I was in danger to have been taken or killed, the enemy having by a charge given upon some troops of mine shutt me off from my own men, I having then but three in company with me; but it pleased God they were repulsed again, and thereby a way opened for my retreat."—" I reckon itt a mercy that upon a sudden occasion that day charging without my headpiece,[a] and being known to the enemy (as I afterwards understood from some of them), I came off safe and unhurt."[b]

Very different statements are made as to the share that the horse [Conduct of took in this murderous affair. That of the King, according to Clarendon, never behaved so ill as on that day. After the first charge they wheeled off, deserting their officers, and never could be brought to a second attempt. Of the foot, it is agreed on all hands that they

[a] Note 18.   [b] Experiences, MS.

1644.
March 29.

[Birch's share in the battle.]

[Hopton's retreat.]

[Subsequent operations of Waller.]

rivalled each other in bravery. A reinforcement had lately landed at Bristol from Ireland, were there, and increased the desperation, for they neither gave nor received quarter.[a]

Considering the distinguished part assigned to Birch, his suggestions to the general, the charge with which he was entrusted at his own request, and the consequences that attended it, some mention might have been expected of his doings in other authorities; but it has been looked for in vain. Both at Alton and Alresford other officers of City regiments find their names transferred to letters and to the press: the colonels of the Blue and Yellow and other auxiliary regiments are held up to view and applause; he only is as yet fighting his way up; his soldier-like qualities are confined to a circle around him; for aught that has yet appeared, he is hitherto but a captain; he will come forth in his time among the ablest of those regimental leaders, and surpass them all.

As to the check that he received from a nameless commander in the pursuit, and the alleged disadvantage arising from it, it savours too strongly of the air of compliment to pass as the sole reason of the escape of Hopton's army. Though Roe has but hinted at it, the meaning is easily discernible; however delicately thrown out, it is sufficiently expressive of what was universally and more than whispered even at this time, that Waller and his superior in command, the Lord General, forbore to fight to the utterance with the King. Baxter describes the public opinion of Essex at this juncture, and thus sums it up, after enlarging upon the reasons: "they now began to say that at Edgehill, at Newbury, and at other times, he never prosecuted any victory, but had stood still, and seen the King's army retreat, and never pursued them when it had been easie to have ended all the wars."[b] A similar but nameless censure is here passed on Waller himself.

But this great advantage gained at Cheriton, great as it was, was robbed of the palm of perfect victory, for the pursuit of the Cavaliers was baffled. Amidst the confusion, the little town of Alresford,

[a] Vicars, Parl. Chron. 191.   [b] Life, i. 47.

remarkable for the air of its buildings and the respectability of its inhabitants, burst into flames, but was extinguished by the Parliamentary soldiers.[a] They could not, however, so effectually harass the retreat as to prevent the greater part of Hopton's men, nearly all his guns, and many of his wounded, from being safely conveyed to Reading, and afterwards to Oxford.[b] Waller pushed forward at once to Winchester; the ruined walls and their feeble defenders offered little resistance, the mayor had sent him the keys in token of submission, the prisoners in the gaol were set free, the cathedral had already been despoiled. But at this time he was too much in haste to take notice of the city. The castle, his own inheritance, and long occupied by a sufficient garrison under Sir William Ogle, held out against him. But now a wider tract of country lay in some measure at his mercy. By marching up and down he visited remoter places with his parties, came upon Andover, entered Whitchurch in Dorsetshire, went to Romsey, pushed forward to Salisbury, raised contributions, and put the clergy to flight. In the course of this expedition he took Christchurch, its governor, garrison, with several commissioners of array recruiting for Lord Hopton's army, and made himself master of Walton the house of the Bishop of Winchester (April 6), another garrison for the King. On his return he found the gates of Winchester closed against him. Then it was that Birch, deserted by his affrighted guide, discovered the lowest part of the wall in face of the adversaries' fire. It has been omitted to add how the gates were battered, how the entrance was forced, and Waller permitted the city to be plundered. But this was an act, as the general confessed, not unvisited by remorse, and subsequent destruction of his own property.[c] A wide sweep

1644.
March 29.

---

[a] [It was subsequently destroyed by fire on May Day, 1690.—Camden's Britannia, i. 138.]

[b] Note 19.

[c] "It was just with God for the punishment of my giving way to the plunder of the city of Winchester (whereof I was a freeman and sworne to maintain and pro-

1644.
May—June.

was for a time under Waller's control, till Birch and his men were in prospect of further operations recalled to their favourite Farnham. Thanksgivings were held for the success at Cheriton on April 9 and 14 ensuing, and ministers ordered to publish in all their churches that they would "draw all their forces together to pursue this victory and put it to a day and fight with the enemy to put a speedy issue (by the blessing of Almighty God) to these lingering miseries."[a] So odious had become the state of the land.

[Essex and Waller blockade Oxford.— The King escapes them.]

The next event to which our attention is directed is the order of the Parliament for Essex and Waller to block up Oxford. So little ground had been gained by what was thought the ill-improved advantage at Alresford, that a more decisive blow seemed necessary to bring the matter to a conclusion. With two armies, each of them believed to have been of sufficient strength to defeat him in battle,[b] the King was to be shut up in his head-quarters; and if not reduced by starvation, was to be engaged, and captured should he attempt to escape. This notable project originated with a committee consisting chiefly of certain members of the two Houses, and called "the Committee of Safety for both Kingdoms." Their main object was to superintend their own generals, and direct and control the operations of their forces. For men of talent and experience this seemed a singular error in judgment, and proved to their generals the source of many evils.[c] Essex and Waller, already not

cure the good thereof as far as I could) to permitt the demolition of my castle at Winchester." Fourth fatherlike chastisement. Experiences, MS.—Rushworth, 3, ii. 655.

[a] Rushworth, 3, ii. 656. Twenty thousand pounds were ordered to be raised for this purpose.—L. J. April 3, 1644.

[b] Essex's army consisted of 10,500 men, April 8: 4,200 were ordered to join him, May 9. Waller had between 9,000 and 10,000, May 15. The King assembled 9,500, June 18, of whom about 6,000 accompanied him.—L. J. April 8. Rushworth, 3, ii. 667, 670; Clarendon, viii.; Hamper's Dugdale, 69; Carte's Ormonde, iii. 316; Vaughan's Night March of Charles I. 3.

[c] The common sense of Whitelocke and others discovered this. "It was thought strange at that time that the Committee of both Kingdoms should at that distance

well agreed, were both obedient to it in the first instance; they brought up their men, and acted in concert as though they were earnest in accomplishing the blockade. Charles had concentrated all the strength within his reach and seemed to expect it: when, just as a junction was about to be effected by his adversaries, on the morning of the 3rd of June they were astonished and mortified by the discovery that he had slipped between them during the night and escaped them. When this became known, it puzzled the public: and, after the rumours that had existed, was imputed to treachery. Essex in correspondence with the committee expressed his disdain of the imputation. The latent disagreement between him and Waller broke out afresh, and their armies were divided. Waller had been originally destined to march into the West, but Essex was peremptory and determined to exercise his authority. At a council of war he overcame the reluctance of his inferior officer to follow the King, while he himself withdrew with his army from that design, and, under plea of orders, marched to the relief of Lyme. These measures, ill-understood at the time, and favourable as assisting the King in extricating himself from his difficulties, were whispered as mysteries, but considered as treason. The impression of the army in which Birch and Roe were serving, an impression that both of them retained, was a gross mistake. Subsequent revelations and inquiries have taught a far different lesson. The King had no other "pass" but that of sagacity and vigour. He did not in this instance owe his escape to any indulgence on the part of the generals. His own ability and resolution, aided by the experience of his advisers, was

1644.
June.

take upon them to give particular orders for the services and march of their armies, and not rather leave it to the chief commanders that were upon the place; who, upon every motion of the enemy, might see reason to alter their counsels. This increased the jealousies of the Lord General and Waller, both gallant men; but the General thought himself undervalued and Waller too much exalted." In like manner, during the resistance that Austria made to the First Napoleon, the efforts of her generals were too often thwarted and brought to nought by the Aulic Council at Vienna.

1644.
June.

such as to gain for him, from judges of military conduct, impartial applause. This part of the memoir relative to the King's night-march to Worcester, despatched in a single sentence, would comprise a study for a strategist; but the commentator, for reasons already given, forbears the interesting detail. The service in which Birch and Roe were both engaged was no doubt tedious to them. It lasted from the beginning to the end of June, sufficiently tedious and vexatious to the pursuers; for the ways through a heavy soil were deep and foul, and the bridges destroyed to cover the retreat.[a] Birch and Roe with the regiment of Hesilrige, Potley and his regiment with the militia of the Tower Hamlets, the auxiliaries of London and the men of Farnham, were all in this expedition, and shared in its toils and dangers. These, though mitigated to Waller by the taking of Sudeley Castle on the way, and by reinforcements from Lord Denbigh, failed of ultimate success. Waller, though he had several times attempted Worcester, was never fortunate against "the faithful city."[b] The scheme for "King catching," as it was satirically termed, proved abortive. His Majesty came back in safety to Oxford, drew forth his infantry, much of which he had left behind, and became the aggressor by marching northward to meet his tardy pursuers. Prince Rupert, whom they thought the King would have joined, was otherwise occupied in those transactions which immediately preceded his terrible defeat at Marston Moor. Three days previous to it the King and Waller met near Banbury, where on the banks of the Cherwell was fought the battle of Cropredy Bridge.[c]

[Battle of Cropredy Bridge.]

Several accounts have been given of this action, as well by those

[a] "I must tell you, he broke more bridges than 10,000*l.* will repaire."—Arthur Trevor to M. of Ormonde, June 29, 1644. Carte's Ormonde, iii. 318. Only Evesham Bridge is mentioned by Clarendon.

[b] The motto of Worcester is "Floreat semper fidelis civitas."

[c] The King's army had partly lodged at Cropredy the night before the battle of Edgehill (Vicars, God in the Mount, 191): so that this little place had been accustomed to the tumult of armed men.—J. W.

COLONEL JOHN BIRCH. 87

1644.
June 29.

who were present at it as others (Walker, Clarendon, Symonds, Whitelocke, Bulstrode); but it does not seem to have been well understood. Rapin, looking at it with the eye of a soldier, does not attempt to explain it.[a] On the third day after they had faced each other, when the King was marching northward, Waller, by a desperate dash [b] over a bridge at Cropredy, attempted to cut off the King's main body from its rear. To that end he brought up a portion only of what was previously his left wing, and pushed them over the bridge, but committed the blunder of omitting to supply the artillery with shot. Roe seems to have been the only one who has noticed this. The consequence was that pikes, musketeers, and leathern guns were thrust into a false position, of which the King, bringing back his main body, seized the advantage, and a great part of those that had passed over, including Lieutenant-Colonel Baines, were taken prisoners. Birch, who witnessed the error, remonstrated at the time, and blamed it ever after. He was the means of stopping the Tower Hamlets militia from running into the same snare, and secured the remainder of Waller's army. Colonel Sir Thomas Middleton commanded the advance over the bridge; Wemyss the shotless artillery. When the latter, who had revolted from the service of the King, was brought into his presence, he made some awkward excuses, professing his fidelity and allegiance to his Majesty in spite of his conduct. The King, who was in good humour with his success, told him he had not yet disposed of his place.[c] Such is the account given by Essex himself, who bears

[a] [See Appendix XI.]
[b] A similar advantage was taken by Frederic the Great at Leuthen and Rosbach, by Napoleon I. at Austerlitz, and Wellington at Salamanca; all of which succeeded. Waller after all did not miss his intent so widely as might be supposed. Lord Digby, writing to Prince Rupert, says, " it was ten thousand to one but our van and maine body had been cutt off from our reare, and all hazarded, had not my Lord of Cleveland charged them without order."—Rupert's MS. Correspondence. [The Earl of Cleveland's word on this occasion was " Hand and Sword."]
[c] Devereux, ii. 418. Wemyss had been made Master Gunner of England, and for many years had received 300*l*. per annum. The guns were recently made at Lambeth,

1644.
June 29.

[Escapes of Middleton and Waller.]

[Result of battle of Cropredy Bridge.]

testimony to his abilities, and speaks hopefully of his exchange.[a] He was sent prisoner to Ludlow Castle, Nov. 15.[b] He is commonly reported to have been the inventor of the portable leather gun. It was made of the toughest leather, and girt with metallic hoops: a strong horse could carry two of them through miry roads. They could only be discharged seven or eight times.[c] But the original inventor was Gustavus Adolphus, who employed them at the battle of Leipzig, Sept. 7, 1631. However, they seem to have been experimental rather than practical.

Middleton narrowly escaped, being unhorsed and remounted in ignorance by the Cavaliers, who told him to make haste and kill a Roundhead. Few battles are without an occasional joke: and the slender partition between the grave and the ludicrous is often visible when it was least expected. "At Cropredy in Oxfordshire," says Waller, " I escaped a great danger; where being with my officers att a councell of warre, the floor of the room where we were sunke, and we all fell into a seller that was underneath itt. I lay overwhelmed with a great deal of lumber that fell upon me, and yet I bless God I had no hurt att all."[d]

The account of the fight consists chiefly in the admission and criticism of a blunder. Both parties claim to have been the last to retreat: like the battle at Alresford, the description is only attempted of what was witnessed by the writer: no notice is taken of the brilliant charges of the Earl of Cleveland and Lord Bernard Stuart on the one hand, or the advance of Sir Thomas Middleton on the other. The Parliamentary general candidly admits it was "a dis-

and he had been paid 2,000l. for them, as appeared by writings found in his pocket.— Merc. Aulicus, June 29, 1644. [Lieut.-Col. Sir Thomas Hooper was knighted in the field for his capture.—Symonds's Diary, 2.]

[a] Devereux, i. 418. Essex's letter, July 15, 1644.
[b] Carte's Ormonde, i. 71. He survived and tried to make amends for his fault by serving under Charles II. in the battle of Worcester.
[c] Harte's Gustavus Adolphus, i. 196; ii. 42, notes. [Massey was said to be constructing them in Scotland, June, 1651. Whitelocke, 467.]
[d] Experiences, MS.

honourable loss of part of his train of artillery:"[a] still he cannot be denied to have bravely stood his ground. The parting of the two hosts was by mutual consent; and the army of Waller was, shortly after, no more. The London auxiliaries, who composed a great part of it, are said to have mutinied at Northampton. Like some of the American regiments in the beginning of their late civil war, these had been only engaged for a season, and they insisted upon their return home. Frequent difficulties arose among the soldiery on both sides,—regular, if any such could be truly so called, or volunteers. There were instances in which the Cornish would not advance eastward; the Yorkshire regiments objected to move southward; the London trained-bands thought their engagement had expired when they had relieved Gloucester, and they earnestly contended homewards.[b] That which Tacitus terms "gloria obsequii," so becoming an army, they were as Englishmen unacquainted with; only some of them might have caught the spirit of it while in foreign service. Birch by some means was not included among these seceders, as will be explained hereafter.

1644. July-Sept.

We are here brought to a stand for awhile as to Birch's military actions. Though surmises may not be legitimate history, a gap in the time may be allowed to be filled in by probability when dates and admitted facts from other sources conspire. It is generally understood that the mutiny of the troops after the battle of Cropredy Bridge reduced Waller to the necessity of repairing to London for recruits; and here too a portion of his army was subsequently led off to another quarter.[c] "We," says Roe, "marched to Abingdon." This is the first time Abingdon is heard of. It had only of late fallen into the hands of the Parliamentarians, to the annoyance of the King. When his troops were concentrated in Oxford, before his expedition to Worcester, they were withdrawn both from Reading and that place. At Reading the works were slighted;

[Waller marches to Abingdon.— Birch resigns his command.]

[a] MS. *ut supra*.   [b] Clarendon, vii. Corbet, Bibl. Glouc. 57.
[c] Rushworth, *ut supra*, 687.

1644.
July–Sept.

the evacuation of Abingdon has been attributed to mistake as to orders on the part of his Majesty. It was a great detriment and a palpable error as to the Royalists, but their attempts to recover it were in vain. The command was given to Major-General Browne, called in derision " the wood-monger." He was then a zealous adherent to his cause,[a] and tenaciously kept possession of that town. Here was a place of temporary retirement and vexation for Birch. Indeed, there is no doubt that a portion of Waller's late army was ultimately diverted hither, and he with them; and, if a notion may be formed from what we find to have happened at this place, an alteration occurred in his regiment, manifestly, from what he did and suffered here, contrary to his inclination. For a twelvemonth he had retained the command of them, nominally as captain, but with an authority as lieutenant-colonel under Sir Arthur Hesilrige; and now they are converted into dragoons. Was he ready, it may be asked, to part with them? The separation was the act, as it would appear, of the proprietor; the reason given is, that he never affected the foot-service.[b] Whatever was the cause, Sir Arthur Hesilrige is henceforth withdrawn from the narrative, and never appears in it again. Whether at the time their leave-taking was amicable or otherwise, whether the lieutenant-colonel was hurt, and took disgust at this circumstance, whatever might be his compulsion or inducement, Birch during his stay at Abingdon became dissatisfied, and for very vexation impaired his health. Want of occupation renders the soldier at ease "like a chimney in summer." He even threw up his commission.[c] All this took place before September,

[a] His sentiments underwent a total change; but, like the self-condemning Fairfax, it was too late. Browne was afterwards envoy at the Court of Versailles for Charles II.
[b] Note 20.
[c] [Probably very soon after his arrival at Abingdon: for we find him nominated, July 7, one of the committee for the city of Bristol, for putting into execution the ordinances of the Parliament.—L. J. Roe seems to have forgotten this: it may perhaps be the cause of a slight alteration by Birch in the MS.: see p. 14. The battle of Cropredy had been fought June 29 or 30: see p. 13, note [b].]

1644. But thère was a powerful reason that urged his return to the service. His demand upon the State, allowed and promised, had not yet been repaid: it will be proved that he still bore it in mind. Like the adventurer in Horace, "qui zonam perdidit ibit."[a] The loss of his property urged him on, and he fortunately procured the colonelcy of a Kentish regiment but a little before the retirement of his general, who altered the sphere of his employment, and transferred it to the West.

1644. July–Sept.

We left the armies of Essex and Waller divided in consequence of the disagreement of their chiefs; and, as we have seen, Essex, who consigned his rival to his fate, hastened to relieve Lyme. When this had been accomplished, the King, from being pursued, had turned pursuer, and followed him into Cornwall. There, after a variety of evolutions, he drove his army into a trap near Liskeard, where it seemed impossible for Essex to extricate them but by surrender. The classical reader will recognise a situation of this kind in the *Furculæ Caudinæ* of Livy,[b] where the Samnites put the Romans to a similar military disgrace. Roe has a happy art of passing lightly over reverses. He might well congratulate himself that he, with others, only heard, but saw nothing, of this catastrophe. A sad sight it must have been for a Parliamentarian to behold the entire army of their generalissimo reduced to this deplorable condition. Deserted by Essex and other chiefs, who fled in a small boat to Plymouth, they were left to submit to conditions which to some of them seemed harder than death. Favoured by the darkness of the night, and the shameless debauchery of Goring, Sir W. Balfour made his escape with the horse. Brave Skippon commanding the foot seems to have alone proved firm to the thorough unyielding principle of a soldier, and at a council of war proposed to the infantry that they should take the offensive and cut their way through. But the proposal was rejected, and the

[Essex's surrender in the West.]

[a] Epist. ii. 2.   [b] Dec. 1. l. ix.

1644.
September 2.

whole of that body, with their *materiel*, laid down their arms,ᵃ and filed off before his Majesty, too happy to be set free. The conditions were humiliating enough,ᵇ but they were left at liberty to dispose of their future services; and it is an error to say, as some writers have alleged, that they broke an oath when the same men soon after appeared in arms against the King. They were bound by no such contract. The repeated violation of such a tie during the war would have rendered it of no avail. But though Roe and others of his friends were spared the melancholy sight, there were enough of those on the other side who beheld it and exulted in it.

ᵃ These were the whole of the pikes and muskets, with 42 cannon, 1 mortar, 100 barrels of powder, and nearly all the carriages. Among them was a wagon-load of musket-arrows. These were employed for the purpose of shooting letters into towns, as at Gloucester during the siege. (Bibl. Glouc. 224.) Laugharne also shot an arrow into Cardigan Castle with a letter to give notice of his coming to its relief, about Feb. 6, 1644. (Whitelocke, 125.) Sir Jacob Astley had nearly been killed by one of them at Devizes: "A bearded arrow stuck into the ground betwixt his legs. He pluckt it out with both hands, and said, You rogues, you mist your aim." (Gwynne, Military Memoirs, 39.) The editor of Gwynne, supposed to have been Sir Walter Scott, seems to have considered this arrow as shot from a bow, and remarks that the employment of the bow might have ceased from this time, though it was used by some of the remote Highlanders in the battles of Montrose. It may have been almost forgotten that the revival of archery was a favourite with Essex. It is always mentioned in the ancient Commissions of Array. He had probably had his eye upon this, when, early in the armament, he issued a precept (Rushworth, 3, ii. 370) for raising a company of archers, in which he calls the bow "honourable and ancient, heretofore found to be of good use in this kingdom;" but the attempt seems not to have been seconded. It did not, however, escape a notice and recommendation from the pulpit by John Green, M.A., a puritan, some time minister of Pencombe in the county of Hereford, preached on Nehemiah, i. 3, 4, before the House of Commons at St. Margaret's, Westminster, on the monthly fast, April 24, 1644. [A "company of pikes with bows and arrows" were found by a Parliamentarian reconnaisance in the town of Hertford, Aug. 15, 1642. Perfect Diurnall of Proceedings in Hertfordshire, 3.—The suburbs of Chester were set on fire by arrows shot from the city. MS. Letter Book of Sir W. Brereton, ii. 74.— Arrows were used with considerable effect by the Cossacks after the battle of Friedland in 1807.]

ᵇ Rushworth, 3, ii. 705.

Symonds, standing on the spot near his Majesty, and a spectator of all that occurred, has given loose to his aristocratic feelings at a view of what passed under his eye, and has preserved distinct and numerical particulars of it.[a] In general he is cool and impartial, but here he is excited.

[margin: 1644. September 2.]

"Munday, 2° Septembris, 1644.

His Majesties army of foot stood on the same ground or thereabouts as before, the several regiments by themselves, and the colours stuck in the ground flying. His Majestie in the feild accompanied with all his gallant cavaliers dispersed in severall places.

"While about 10 of the clock, Major Skippon, first or in the front, marched with all that rowt of rebels, after the colours of their several regiments. (Then follows a special enumeration of some of them.)

"It rayned extremely as the varlets marched away, a great part of the time. * * *

"They all, except here and there an officer, (and seriously I saw not above three or four that looked like a gentleman,) were strucken with such a dismal feare, that as soone as their colour of the regiment was passt, (for every ensigne had a horse and rid on him and was so suffered,) the rout of soldjers of that regiment presst all of a heape like sheep, though not so innocent. So durty and so dejected as was rare to see. None of them, except some few of their officers, that did looke any of us in the face."

As to their personal appearance, Symonds might easily have made allowance. They were starving. They had been lying drenched with the storms, and were forced through the mire. The Royalist privates reproached, and the common country people plundered, them. Essex, who at all times showed a kind feeling for his army, soon obtained relief for them. The Parliament, that had been wrangling with him, generously condoled with him. He

[margin: [Condition of Essex's army.]]

[a] Diary, 66, 67.

1644.
September.

[Birch proceeds to Plymouth.]

proceeded by sea to Plymouth, and collected his forces: "my poor naked foot," he says, Sept. 14, "came last night to Southampton." They were speedily supplied with necessaries, and by the 17th of October were able to take the field. Those very men who had just been pardoned by their Sovereign and set at liberty, pertinacious in their resistance, were eager to wipe out what they thought their ignominy, and to do battle against him.

To return to Birch. On receiving the colonelcy he immediately set about repairing his loss of time,[a] and with great alacrity advancing by land and sea entered the town of Plymouth, through which Essex had just escaped after the loss of his foot in Cornwall. The resistance of that town had been obstinate, and it had refused (Sept. 12)[b] a summons from the King with peculiar indignity and scorn. When Birch arrived there, part of the garrison had been drawn out to the assistance of Essex, and had been given up in his surrender, so that his regiment would have proved an important reinforcement, and have been there when summoned by his Majesty. From this time forth, with some little intermission at the latter end of September and beginning of October, and during the winter of 1644-5, throughout six months, the colonel is to be considered as stationed in garrison there. The siege was tedious. Prince Maurice, to whose charge the West had been committed, with his lieutenants, was altogether unsuccessful in his attempts to take it. Lord Roberts had been left governor there by Essex at his departure; but Birch was eminent in assisting at the defence. While his stay lasted, the comparative dulness of its routine to an officer accustomed, as he had been, to open action in the field, was relieved by many assaults from the leaguer before it. Among these is recounted another deliverance and success, and it is selected as worthy of remembrance.

[a] Col. Burch hath mustered his regiment of new levied forces at Knowles near Synnock (Sevenoaks) in Kent on Friday last, and gave them their armes, who are to march to Sir William Waller.—Perfect Occurrences, Sept. 2.

[b] Symonds, 81.

It was in dead of night and winter (January 1644-5) that he was 1644-5.
called by his men from his quarters to an onslaught of the enemy.
The hour was unexpected, but he was prepared. The lines were
extensive; two forts manned by his soldiers were assaulted; the one
well defended, the other for a short space taken. In recovering the
latter, when they were close upon it under a shower of bullets, they
heard the challenge from the Royalists, "Who are you for?" the
well known challenge by night or day.[a] Birch rushing forward
with the usual answer on his side, and telling his men it were better
to go on than retreat, they carried all before them, and expelled or
slew the intruders.[b] Among those who were captured was Colonel
Arundel,[c] of the life-guard to Prince Maurice. He surrendered his
sword to Birch, who wore it in token of his victory to the day when
he appeared in the senate of his country.

This part of the narrative closes with the relief of Plymouth,[d] [Birch goes to
but has not exactly told us the whole of what occurred to the London.]

[a] Note 21.

[b] [This was probably the assault of Jan. 16, 1644-5, when, according to Vicars, Greenvile got four outworks but was driven off. One of them was called Little Penny-come-quick (Merc. Brit.). In Perfect Occurrences, Jan. 15, 1644, it is stated that Col. Birch made a sally from Plymouth, and took many prisoners.]

[c] Several of the Arundel family, Royalists, were employed in this Western contest. As to the sword which Birch thought worthy of being borne about him, it appears to have continued a favourite companion in subsequent time: for when the attempt under Penruddock and Grove took place at Salisbury in behalf of Charles II., 1654, the county of Hereford with many others threatened a general rising to restore him; horses and arms were seized, and suspected persons arrested. Among them was Colonel Birch, then resident at Whitbourne. Wroth Rogers was governor of Hereford, and reported to the Protector that possession had been taken of his person, and that he had been cast into prison. (Thurloe, State Papers, III. 264, March 17, 1654.) While his sword, which he refused to deliver up, was being taken from him, he said, with some indignation, "My sword is short, but it may be long enough within a while." Berry, one of Cromwell's major-generals, paid him a visit in the following November, and released him from confinement. (Idem, iv. 237.) It is no violation of truth to believe in the wearing of this sword ten years after it had been surrendered to him.

[d] The siege was finally raised January 12, 1645-6.—Sprigge, 165.

1644 5. Colonel there. Plymouth was a distracted town. It may be fair to hint that he had been entangled in some disputes during his stay. He was sent, with other officers, as a prisoner to answer before the House of Commons respecting this;[a] but as no particular account, beyond certain shadowy allusions, was left upon the minute-books, it may be concluded that he was as successful in his explanation upon this, as upon a former occasion. Anticipation, however, as well as omission, has somewhat mystified this part of the story, when compared with other authentic sources; and it can only be hoped that the memory of the relator had suffered much in the interval to escape. But something also has been untold with regard to the early part of his employment at Plymouth; for he had hardly set his foot in the place when he obtained a necessary leave of absence. His private as well as public affairs seemed to require it. But monetary matters are kept out of sight in the narrative. He took a journey to London to petition the Parliament in person. His men were in want of supplies, and, while soliciting in their behalf, he embraced an opportunity of reminding that assembly of his own due.[b] The fact stands thus confirmed on the records of the House:[c] "Colonel Birch having lent 1,500*l*. for the service of the State, petitions to have, towards satisfaction for it, the estate of Henry Hudson, a delinquent, upon account towards the payment." But the committee, to whom it is referred, are recommended " to give him all expedition, he being speedily to repair to his charge in the public service."[d] The positive order on the part of the committee shows the immediate acquiescence with his application, but it is accompanied by an admonition that he should remain in London

[a] C. J. May 12, 1645. See also March 10, 1644-5, and May 9, 1645.

[b] "So modestly," says one version of the Parliamentary note, "that his desire was granted." (Perfect Diurnall, Oct. 16.) He was not unversed in the *mollia tempora fandi* as well as the rougher passages of debate.

[c] C. J. Oct. 16, 1644.

[d] The whole of the composition of Henry Hudson, esquire, of London, as it stands in Dring's Catalogue, amounted to 3,700*l*.

no longer. Towards Plymouth he returns, but on his road falls in with a whole group of commanders near Basingstoke—Essex, Waller, and the Earl of Manchester unmentioned before. The occasion was tempting, for it was expected that a battle would be fought, and some apprehensions were entertained that Charles would endeavour to repossess Reading,[a] or even force his way to the metropolis. He paid his respects to the Earl of Essex, and, stating that he was returning to his charge, tendered his services under the circumstances, and was accepted. The Earl's expression towards him is flatteringly given, " not as commanding, but desiring." The King however altered his line of march, and inclined towards Newbury. Essex being really ill at Basingstoke, and unable to appear personally in the field, the command devolved chiefly on Manchester, though Waller was also there. Manchester accepted Birch's services, and the action was struck upon the following day (October 27, 1644). The (lieutenant) colonel's part in it is not spoken of by Roe. He had no regiment there to command; neither does Roe intimate that he himself was there. Birch would only be an attendant on Manchester; but if as an amateur[b] attendant upon the general he had no part in the fight; yet he had in the pursuit.

1644.
October 25.

Here we arrive at one of the most interesting features of the manuscript. But more unrelated matter remains to be supplied in this place. Events crowd upon us in this part, for while Waller's

[Second battle of Newbury.]

---

[a] The officer who then commanded there was Colonel John Barkstead, originally a goldsmith in London, distinguished by the zeal and ability with which he passed through his military promotion in the Parliamentary service. After signing the King's death-warrant he fled to the Continent, where he continued for a while in a sort of sanctuary at Hanau in Germany. Venturing from that free city into Holland, he was seized, and, with others of the regicides, executed at the Restoration, April 19, 1662.—Noble's Regicides, i. 87.

[b] See in Appendix XII. an original letter containing an account of this battle. It is from the pen of Colonel Richard Norton, Cromwell's favourite "Dick Norton," who was governor of Basingstoke, and witnessed the fight only as an amateur, but got engaged too far in assisting Ludlow, who was in danger. Norton in so doing was wounded. It is the more interesting, as Ludlow himself, who confesses his horse was shot, has taken no notice of his personal escape.—Memoirs, i. 131.

CAMD. SOC.   O

1644.
October 27.

men had been dispersing at Northampton and proceeding to Abingdon, and Charles had turned off to follow Essex, the fatal battle had been fought at Marston Moor.[a] The forces of Manchester and his lieutenant Cromwell being disposable after that victory, were directed southward to outnumber those of the King, but the commanders brought heart-burnings with them: a conciliatory letter from the committee of both Houses[b] failed to unite them; so that the wranglings of Essex and Waller, added to the disagreement of Manchester and Cromwell, left their army really without an efficient head; and the orders of Essex or Manchester were neglected or disputed rather than obeyed. In this state of things Birch found the leaders when he came to Basingstoke, and it sufficiently accounts for the request already pointed out, rather than the command, of the generalissimo, that he would go to Reading; and in part for the inability that he met with in getting an answer from the sleepy Manchester on the second night after the action,[c] when all the army had been wearied, and when he and Cromwell had been disputing as to the military measures of that day. The affair however had then taken place. Newbury, wretched Newbury, unfortunate in having been a second time within hearing of the roar of a battle, to the terror of the inhabitants, was occupied by Parliamentary troops, and Birch, as it should appear, returning with some company, among whom was Roe, from the pursuit of stragglers, met accidentally with a convoy that threw a booty into his hands. He was obliged to get up a party in the pursuit, and went from house to house to form them. If the reader has already attentively cast his eye over this episode in the original, it will require but a few touches in the illustration. The triumph that it includes over a disabled old officer and his helpless lady is indeed poor; not so in a substantial sense is the booty obtained. The

[a] Baillie, the Presbyterian commissioner to the Parliament, wrote triumphantly to his Scotch friend on this striking reverse to the King. (Letters and Journals, ii. 35 et seq. ed. 1775). Baillie was not aware that at this very time those dissensions were brooding that ruined the Presbyterian cause. [b] Rushworth, 3, ii. 719.

[c] [Roe's date, Oct. 30, seems wrong, as the battle was on the 27th.]

talents and bravery of Birch come out in full partizan lustre; and the whole is consequently given in so joyous a manner as though it had sometime formed a capital story for the two comrades over a winter evening's fire. But for a proper understanding of it the way must be cleared. [1644. October 30?]

There was in his Majesty's service a general officer of considerable note. Patrick Earl of Forth, Lord Brentford, Lord Ruthven, for by this aggregate of names he is variously known in the history of these wars, was by birth a Scot, brought up in the troubles of the Low Countries from his youth. The enumeration of the parts in which he had served, and the wounds that he had received, seems well nigh fabulous. He had seen service in Sweden under Gustavus Adolphus, in Denmark, Russia, Livonia, Lithuania, Poland, and Prussia. In England alone the number of his wounds had equalled that of the battles in which he had exposed himself. At Edgehill, says Lloyd, he modelled the fight; was at Brentford and Gloucester, was shot in both the fights at Newbury, at Cheriton, and near Banbury. He had been shot in the head, in both arms, the mouth, leg, and shoulder;[a] and, as if all this had not been enough for his scars and his story, the catalogue was finished by a fall from his horse that broke his shoulder.[b] Could such an one have died a natural death after all these escapes? He survived to wait upon Charles II. in exile, and returning to his native country was buried in 1651 at Dundee.[c] [The Earl of Forth.]

From the account of him in Clarendon,[d] where he fairly balances his merits and his failings, he appears to have passed the prime of his powers, though zealously attached to his profession and the King. As Lord General he had been with his Majesty in Oxford, where he was at the head of his military committees; and, chiefly for the [His night-journey.]

[a] Dugdale, Baronage, ii. 472; Lloyd, Memoirs, 467.
[b] This was a little after the time of his laying down his command, and before his appointment as Lord Chamberlain to Prince Charles on Nov. 5, 1644.
[c] Warwick says that his lady was a Swede, and that both of them were afterwards ill-used by his countrymen.—Memoirs, 229.
[d] History, viii.

1644.
October.

[Birch's coarseness.]

sake of friendship for Lord Hopton and disinclination to be idle, had gone to assist him with his advice at Winchester, and had thus been hurt at Cheriton, as well as on this day at Newbury. Like the King, when the battle was raging, he had sought temporary shelter at Donnington Castle,[a] that overlooked part of the field: he had a considerable escort and many followers; it certainly was his wound that first induced him to repair thither. But he would be naturally desirous of placing his lady and other women under better security; and, having brought his official carriages and attendants, such as Shakspeare's Welshman calls "the poys and luggage" with him, he determined to make his way in part by a cross-country road[b] to Bath. It was then moonlight: on the evening of the battle they had fought a whole hour by it, and his Majesty had drawn off by it, and reached Bath in safety.[c] The journey was hazardous to Forth by reason of the ways; and the moon, useful to him in many respects, has its illusions, when on a track like this it would, in Milton's language, be "shadowy" in setting forth the face of things. Attempt it, however, he would; and the reader of the MS. has been told with what success.[d]

It may be deemed over-scrupulous to point out that the tone of the text, cheerful and spirited throughout, yet bespeaks an absence of the feeling that had graced some other commanders. Lady Forth and her husband appear not to have met with the best of treatment at the hands of the Parliamentarians. In another respect, while the omission of such impious expressions as some of Roe's friends might not have scrupled at, is happily consistent with his usage in other places (see p. 10), it is counterbalanced, on the other hand, by the hard and coarse manner in which he treats the putting to death of an enemy. It is true that the moment was critical, and it was in

[a] Note 22.   [b] Note 23.
[c] When the last flash, the last hurrah, and, would it might be added, the last groan had ceased upon the field, a large cavalcade consisting of a party that had taken refuge in Donnington Castle issued forth to travel by cross road to Bath, whither his Majesty also was on his way.—J. W. [But see note [c], p. 98.]
[d] Note 24.

self-defence; but the expression of making a hole in his adversary's skin is as cool as if it had been used respecting his own buff coat. It savours of the language[a] of those whose society he and his colonel might have kept in the guard-room. This touch of coarseness in expression appears, according to Burnet, to have been always retained by Birch, though the bishop refers it to another source (see Preface).

1645. October 30 ?

Treating chiefly of transactions in the field, Roe has passed over those of politics by wholesale; otherwise in this place would have intervened those important measures comprised between October 1644 and the early part of July 1645. Within these months agitations had taken place which, through the Self-denying Ordinance, destroyed the influence of Birch's party, and, in subjecting the Presbyterians to the Independents, created Fairfax ostensibly the general of a new-modelled army, and rendered Cromwell really the lord of the ascendant. This large omission may therefore, after the bare mention of it, be consigned to the general historian, with a single, though obviously pertinent, remark, that Birch, having accepted his place as a colonel in that army, had but changed his faction while he retained his cause.

[The New Model.]

We are now entering upon a new series of incidents in the military life of this adventurer: new, because from a nominal colonelcy he had been raised to a full command; new, because he is acting under new superiors, and is transferred to new scenes; new, because he is under new counsels in a new army. Essex and Waller and others are gradually to disappear, and the old system of half-measures is to be no more. Colonel Birch, ordered out of garrison at Plymouth, and obedient to the new military authority, marched to meet Fairfax and Cromwell at Bridgwater.[b] He joined the army near that place, and was present at the capture, where its reduction by a terrific fire is, for the first time, attributed

[Birch at Bridgwater.—Governor of Bath.—His bravery at the storming of Bristol.]

---

[a] It may be invidious to point out another trait, at p. 11, in the affair at Winchester.

[b] July, 1645.

1645.
July.

by Roe to his colonel's interference.[a] At this post is his earliest promotion to act as governor;[b] but though admitted with his men to co-operate with the "new model," he is not acknowledged here, or elsewhere, as a component part of the force. He is useful, however, for a short time. Removed ere long by Fairfax, he is entrusted with the care of Bath, an imperfectly fortified city, and exposed to danger. In the meanwhile the army proceeds to the siege of Bristol. While preparation is making for it under his advice,[c] a dispute or cabal is represented somewhat mysteriously as arising, in which that advice had been questioned; for during this second siege, and where he is now an experienced assailant, instead of, as before, defendant, a dangerous epidemic was prevailing. Probably ever since its last siege, the city was in so deplorable a condition from pestilential fever, that the army at first had hesitated to approach it,[d] yet Birch had earnestly urged them on. It was not till the last council of war, after many had been held, that the determination was settled to storm. In the debate on which this resolution was formed, Birch displayed, and it might be with some reference to that fever, a total absence of fear from pestilence or war. The storm ensued in a blaze from the guns of the defenders at the very hour, "the darkest hour that precedes the

[a] [Sprigge, who does mention Birch here, states that the firing of granados and slugs of hot iron was commenced by the garrison themselves, on the part of the town already taken by Fairfax. Great damage appears to have been done. This barbarous procedure seems to have been not unusual. The Earl of Newcastle adopted it at Hull; the town of Bridgenorth was burnt by granados fired by the garrison after they had been forced into the castle.]

[b] After a letter from Sir Thomas Fairfax to the House of Commons concerning the taking of Bridgwater, "The House then tooke into consideration the safety of the said towne, by appointing an honest, able, and faithfull gentleman to command the same; and, after some debate concerning it, the House ordered that Colonell Birtch shall be nominated, appointed, and constituted governour of the towne of Bridgwater." Perfect Diurnall, Saturday, July 26, 1645.—J. W.

[c] Fairfax took Col. Birch with him and a few others to view the works two days after sending in the summons.—Mercurius Britannicus, Sept. 8 to 15.

[d] [Only one soldier, however, died of it.]

dawn."[a] His knowledge of the ground and his experienced sword, urged by a zeal that would be peculiarly his own, gave material aid towards the ascent to Prior's Hill Fort, and the attack of Rainsborough's brigade, of which he forms a part, proves successful. The city which he dispiritedly left as lost to the Roundheads is once more won by them. His conduct is specially noted in the despatch of Lieutenant-General Cromwell to the Speaker of the House of Commons,[b]—a compliment totally overlooked or despised by Roe, as much as if it were nothing worth, though it could hardly have been unknown to him: let this be presented as a confirmation of what has already been observed, that the name of Cromwell throughout the manuscript is utterly ignored.

1645.
Sept. 10.

This heavy blow to the King's affairs gives rise to another correspondent remark, in the little mention that is here made of Rupert or his disgrace in the surrender. In a former passage (see p. 3) he is boldly reproved for his conduct before the walls; if that be true which has been said of him by others he might now have been as severely reproached for his behaviour within them. But Roe has on this head exercised a forbearance superior to the vulgar custom of the time when the account was written; though indeed the crisis of the civil calenture, when this was composed, was overpast. In this there is consistency; there is more; it may not be too much to attribute it to a just and generous feeling. Bold in condemning the master-vices of the Cavaliers, he scorns to employ the language common to those days in insulting over a fallen adversary. It would have been an opportunity of abuse that all might not have neglected. The Prince at Bristol, dispirited by evils arising from his own misconduct, was well known to have increased them since he had been governor; he had grown reckless, and had lost much

[Rupert's misconduct.]

[a] September 10, 1645.
[b] The words of Cromwell in his despatch are these: "Col. Birch with his men, and the major-general's (Skippon's) regiment, entered with very good resolution where their post was, possessing the enemy's guns, and turning them upon them." Rainsborough, after all, had the hardest task of all, at Prior's Hill Fort. Sprigge, 115.

[margin: 1645. Sept.—Nov.]

of his moral as well as military reputation, in the eyes of his friends as well as enemies.[a]

[margin: [Birch sent against Hereford.]]

To return once more to Birch. He had assisted in this affair with a considerable command of horse and foot; yet appears nowhere after the storm but as at the head of a volunteer regiment, governor of Bath, with Bristol in his charge. Here he was left, while Fairfax and Cromwell passed away to other successes. The position was little suited to his taste. Alternately elevated and depressed, he considered the supervision of two places already humbled to submission as no better than want of employment, where there was neither prospect of advancement nor of future gain. We are led, however, to infer that he had higher aims. In a fit of weariness he contemplated once more laying aside the profession of arms. His prospect of advancement seemed at an end. But a new opening unexpectedly presented itself. Going to London in the middle of November 1645, and communicating his intention to his friends and the Committee of Safety, he obtained a fresh appointment, coinciding more acceptably with his inclinations. From them he received a force of horse and foot, composed partly of his own men, with other provisional assistance, and a sort of roving commission. In this, with the consent and aid of the governor of Gloucester,[b] to whose superintendance Herefordshire had been committed, he was directed to march towards a part of the kingdom before unknown to him; his precise orders were to " distress the city of Hereford."

[margin: [State of Herefordshire.]]

Hitherto has the commentator accompanied the writer and his

---

[a] " Prince Rupert is so much given to his case and pleasure, that every man is disheartened that sees it. This city of Bristol is but a great house of baudry, and will ruine the King; and, by all I see, Prince Rupert is resolved to lye by it." (Trevor to M. of Ormonde; Carte's Ormonde, iii. 354.) He was so unpopular at his marching away, that the country people called out " Give him no quarter." The general himself attended him with the ladies two miles out from the city. (Sprigge, 111, 112.) Baker says that the people of the town would stand by him no longer. Chronicle, 499.

[b] Note 25.

comrade throughout their military wanderings and hair-breadth adventures in the West. The scene must now be changed to a very different quarter, where the struggle had been hardly less intense, and where it had been going on with singular activity. The story of Herefordshire in its civil miseries is one which the commentator had once thought to have opened more fully, had time and opportunities served. But though reduced here as to its dimensions it is too interesting that it should go untold, even in the part that verges towards its close. Wherefore turning his back altogether on the distractions of the West, and throwing aside the staff with which the MS. of Roe has hitherto supplied him, he must attempt for a while as a mere harbinger to prepare the way for the exertions of Birch in this hitherto untried sphere of occupation, by a short transfer to that western remoter border of Britain, where from their earliest days the Welsh had ever shown their blind attachment to their princes, and where from the beginning this civil strife had been entered into with romantic loyalty; for all classes, from the inhabitant of the hall to the peasant in his hovel, for the greater part, or with very little exception, had treasured in their hearts that sentiment which Hopton had inscribed upon his alliterative banner—

> I will strive to serve my sovereign King.

This is that western border-land which Birch is about to invade. Here is the city, into which he is about to enter, to establish himself as a governor; the country in which he is finally to settle, in which he is to end his days.

The city and county that he was approaching had done and suffered much in the cause of Charles I. By drains of men and money, through incursions by night and by day, their original quiet had been succeeded by a long-continued state of alarm and intrusion. Hereford itself had sustained several hostile visits: one from the Earl of Stamford in 1642, whom Essex had sent from Worcester on an errand of occupation before the battle of Edgehill; others from Waller in the following year. But these had been

[City of Hereford.]

1645. rather annoyances in the way of forced contribution and limited plunder. In another more recent attempt it had resisted the Scots, who had been compelled, after six weeks beleaguering, to break up from their trenches and retire in disgrace before the advance of his Majesty to its relief. The spirits of that whole county, that the Scottish army had ransacked for subsistence during its irksome continuance before the capital, had been raised to their highest pitch, and they were enjoying a temporary triumph. The cause of the King was low, but they were proud of their recent defence. In spite of all former intrusions the place had never yet been entered by fine force. The natives, both then and for many after generations, traditionally boasted of it as a " maiden city." The Parliament saw this. Their committee employed leaders upon whom they could depend. The contingency from several causes seemed favourable, and Birch was sent " to distress the city of Hereford."

[Loyal feeling of Herefordshire.] The tone in the politics of this county, when Birch directed his steps towards it, seems, at the hazard of repetition, to call for a more expanded retrospect of what had originally happened here. The Parliament's influence had not much at first affected it, when England's troubles began. On the contrary, as has been already related, its almost universal feeling had been in favour of the King. This was not altogether without some counterpoise; but for a considerable season the opposition on behalf of the Houses could scarcely rear its head. Shut out from the rest of England by wretched roads and an all-but-unnavigable river, Herefordshire was in general too content to remain as it had been for centuries before. Many of the owners of the land enjoyed ample estates, but with a single exception not one of the nobility, whose presence influenced other parts, had been in residence here. Its wealthy proprietors were chiefly baronets or knights; its clergy upholders of the established ritual; and, though there might be much ignorance in their flocks, according to the notion of the Puritans, they had been taught adherence to their Church and its temporal head the King. They ignored for the most part the new teaching of the Houses and their divines, and, when the torch was kindling, the county endeavoured to extinguish it by expressing their abhorrence of making war for the King against himself. At the season when petitions loaded the tables of the senate, theirs was of the most severe and caustic character. It was an attempt to read a lesson to the Houses: the Commons voted it "an insult," and resented it by a threat. All this was owing, in Herefordshire, to a knot of Royalists whom their opponents in derision called "the Nine Worthies;" Lord Scudamore, Fitzwilliam Coningsby, Sir Walter Pye, Sir Henry Lingen, and others; but they were feebly resisted by Sir Robert Harley, Sir Richard Hopton, old Sir John Kyrle, and some of inferior note. When the Royalists petitioned, an attempt had been made for procuring a counter-petition, but it failed, because sufficient respectable signatures could not be found. The Parliament, however, adopted means for interfering with this unanimity and fancied security, and introduced the wedge by way of arms. When the Earl of Essex went down to Worcester before the battle of Edgehill, he sent forward a force under Lord Stamford, as already mentioned, to occupy the city, and disturb the Royalists around it. This was seconded by the usual dash of Sir William Waller in one of his military rovings, when, without difficulty, he twice entered and raised contributions. At this time Lord Scudamore was captured; and some of " the Nine Worthies," previously taken at Highnam near Gloucester,[a] were carried off to Bristol. The whole of this had occurred before the latter place had in the time of Birch been wrested from the Parliament, and while, as we have already told, he was a volunteer there.

1645.

As to Hereford itself, from the time that Waller had forced his way and carried off his captives, it had been placed under authorised military government: not always at first well administered, for it had been undertaken by those who were not equal to the task; but, in process of time, when the appointment fell from the Marquis of Hertford to Prince Rupert, it had its governor to command, and

[Hereford a military post.]

[a] Corbet, Bibl. Glouc. 29.

1645.

its Committee to collect assessments, by misnomer called contributions, and its regular garrison, if necessary, to enforce them. Much of the moral influence of the landed proprietors, and the feeling of the public throughout the county, was disturbed by the military occupation of the provincial capital; yet after all it was a source from which royal levies were drawn upon emergency: a place whither the King himself, after the fatal battle of Naseby, had retreated, and where he was received, though in distress, with joy and acclamations, as if he had indeed been a fortunate King. And in truth, though this had not, like many other counties, seen its fields strewed with the slain of many battles, it had tasted some of the bitterness of this draught of sorrow.

[Governors of Hereford.]

The selection of governors for the city and county had not always been fortunate. The six that had ruled there, reckoning downwards from Herbert Price, and including the present officer, had held it for the King. Myn, who immediately preceded the existing governor, was indeed a soldier of the highest ability, maturest experience, and most encouraging hopes. But his course had been cut short. Massey, the indefatigable commander at Gloucester, surprised him and his Anglo-Irish regiment in the field at Redmarley in the county of Worcester, slew or dispersed them all, and, amidst the universal regret of soldier and citizen, bore the corpse of the colonel to an honourable funeral at Gloucester. After the brief interposition of Colonel Barnard, a temporary commander, equally

[Sir Barnabas Scudamore.]

unfortunate, Sir Barnabas Scudamore was chosen by Prince Rupert to be governor of Hereford. The post of governor, nominally under the Royal Commission, was actually under the Prince. It had been in some instances elsewhere the object of cabal and contention: it does not appear to have been so here. In some cases it had been much coveted: the present occupier had found it no easy task from the hour he had taken it in hand. The qualities for which Rupert had appointed him could not have been of a mean order, as his acquaintance and connexion with the country, of which he was a native, seemed to have rendered the appointment appro-

priate. He was a younger brother of the noble house of Hom 1645.
Lacy near the city; and, as a soldier of fortune, with the slender
and dependent means of such an one, had adopted that profession
which frequently fell to the lot of younger brothers in noble families.
He had throughout exposed his person for the King in various
places:[a] at the siege of Lichfield under Rupert;[b] at Ashby-de-la-
Zouch with Hastings;[c] in Monmouthshire with the forces at
Raglan;[d] and ever acquitted himself with a soldier's honour. If
his post were at all an enviable one it was now by no means an easy
one. His command extended over a wide district, and his commission is more stringent and ample than any earlier governor
received; and it shows the necessity of the time, and of arbitrary
and extensive power. The state of the Royalists had retrograded in
these as in other parts. The necessity and the increased arbitrary
nature of that power, exercised in whatever way it might have been,
was liable to unpopularity, and to provoke jealousy. The only plea
that could have been tendered by an officer thus circumstanced
must have been that put into the mouth of Dido :

> Res duræ et regni novitas me talia cogunt
> Moliri.

From the first hour that he had accepted it, he had difficulties [The gover-
and embarrassments of no small moment to contend with, both nor's dif-
within as well as without the walls. When he entered upon his ficulties.]
command at the departure of Colonel Barnard, the provisional successor to Myn, he found himself at the head of 457 foot-soldiers
and inferior officers in the garrison, besides townsmen in arms.
What horse he might have would be lying out in convenient
quarters within call; but their numbers, so far as this evidence goes,

---

[a] Serjeant-Major Scudamore is mentioned in a letter from Thomas Bushell to Sir
Francis Ottley as being at Shrewsbury after the battle of Edgehill at Christmas.—
Collectanea Topographica, vi. Ottleiana, 22.

[b] Ottleiana.

[c] Harl. MSS. 986.

[d] Merc. Aulicus, May 22, 1644.

1645. do not appear.[a] The weekly pay of the military amounted, when the account was taken, to 53*l*. 4*s*. 0*d*. and when the treasurer handed over his reckonings, having accounted for sundry payments of moneys lent, repairs of fortifications, and disbursements for necessaries under different items, there remained on the last day of September, 1644, a slender balance of something less than 2*l*. 10*s*. 0*d*. To meet future wants would be of course his immediate care: the issue of warrants for supply, or enlistments, would rest with the magistrates composing the committee: these would be issued to the constables of the different parishes within certain districts, and their returns were strictly enforced. The process was regular; not always easy of execution; but the officials could call in the military to its aid, in the last extremity; for these were the days of sword-law. Demands might more frequently be accompanied by mere threats on the Royalists' side, who were cautious of disgusting their own neighbourhood; they were inflicted more remorselessly by the agents of a Parliamentary committee. But the process was bad enough in any case, when ill-humour or exasperation prevailed among those who were compelled to demand and obey. The office of chief constable and his subordinates was peculiarly odious, as they were frequently forced by turns to act in making assessments for both parties, when parishes were alternately pressed upon by inroads to find subsistence for hungry soldiers, or recruits to supply their loss. But the multiplication of petty garrisons on either side, particularly in bordering

[Garrisons.]

[a] [A party of considerable strength, containing a number of "*padees*" (horseboys attending the cavalry? see Devereux's Life of Essex, ii. 353),—and including "some horse and foot from Hereford," the whole commanded by Sir William Vaughan, marched in the direction of Montgomery to the relief of Chester, about two months before the surprise of Hereford. It was reported that Scudamore sent a hasty message to recall them; but, if true, it was to no purpose. On the news of the capture of Hereford these forces, then at Whitchurch, "retreated to theire holds, all saue the Hereford men, who haue now noe garrison to retreat vnto, but curse their fortunes for leaueing Hereford to goe with Vaughan to releoue Chester, and loosing their owne, and are gone with him into Bridgnorth."—MS. Letter-book of Sir W. Brereton, ii. 49; iii. 107.]

counties, had become the scourge of the country. They consisted chiefly of the defensible houses of the nobility and gentry, and seemed to have been a favourite engine in Prince Rupert's system of hostilities. One of the uses to which they were applied was the ease with which parties might be collected out of them: their abuses were grievously oppressive. In Shropshire and the counties of Stafford and Worcester they existed to an alarming extent.[a] Established on principal lines of communication, they were set up or withdrawn as circumstances required. Sometimes they were admitted by the proprietor as his only means of defence: at other times a military occupation was forced upon him against his will. According to the dispositions of the governor they proved too often the misery rather than the protection of the neighbourhood, and were liable to be commanded by strangers or foreigners who had no sympathy with the surrounding country. A large amount of private and public suffering was occasioned by these intruders, whose exactions and insolencies became odious, and whose fortified abodes were often converted into scenes of contention and rapine. A mansion of this class existed at Canon Frome in the rich and fertile valley of the Frome. It kept open the passage between the cities of Hereford and Worcester, and was so far fortunate as to have had at this time for its governor Colonel Barnard, who made way for Scudamore when he was promoted to be governor of the city. But if Barnard had been acceptable to the natives, his garrison, consisting of a mixture of Anglo-Irish, appears to have been far otherwise to them. Canon Frome, an ancient residence of the knightly family of the Hoptons of Herefordshire, was strongly fortified. It had a moat and a drawbridge. The owner, Sir Richard Hopton, one of the few who adhered to the Parliament, had been driven out from his home: his eldest son, Sir Edward, was in Oxford with a regiment he had raised.[b] When the Roundheads marched to Hereford under Stamford in 1642, Sir Richard

[Canon Frome.]

1645.

---

[a] See Mrs. Stackhouse Acton's interesting Illustration of the Shropshire Garrisons.
[b] Hopton MSS.

1645.

[Club-men.]

committed himself to their cause by showing encouragement to them; and, when they withdrew, had to undergo the consequence. His mansion was sacked, and the furniture sold or pillaged by the neighbourhood. In this state was Canon Frome, compelled subsequently to admit a Royalist governor. In the year 1645 the peasantry were exasperated by the occupiers of this strong-hold; being subordinate to Hereford, it took part in their exactions. Between them the country became intolerably oppressed: clubmen were rising in various quarters; and here they abounded: a part of their complaint was the treatment they endured from both the garrisons of Hereford and Canon Frome. Symptoms of popular risings had appeared in the month of March in Shropshire and Worcestershire; all at once the malcontents were said to be gathering in great multitudes; by degrees the cloud had rolled on towards Herefordshire, and burst on a sudden with violence and disorder. Oppression was their plea: neutrality was their cry.[a] From some insults received at the hands of Royalist, most probably Anglo-Irish, soldiers, a large body of the peasantry had recourse to arms; a fray occurred in the hundred of Broxash between them and the soldiers of Scudamore; some blood was shed, and much threatening language employed; an armed crowd came up and faced the walls of Hereford, calling out for redress or vengeance. The governor at first had affected to despise this movement, till at length it assumed a serious form. With arms in their hands, they delivered a set of demands in writing; among others was the withdrawal of this garrison of Canon Frome. From intelligence of this movement Massey hastened from Gloucester to Ledbury in hopes of establishing a communication with them; but he found that they were neither wholly for the Parliament nor for the King, but as neutrals determined to associate for the preservation of the country from plunder. Scudamore acted with great energy: in his proclamation he firmly opposed them, denounced their unruly conduct, challenged the assistance of all loyal

[a] Note 26.

persons to come to his aid, and pointed out the ringleaders by name. 1645. After much wrangling a reconciliation was effected: some who had shown themselves most forward in the tumult were arrested and punished. Massey soon saw his hopes extinguished, and retired, unable to come to an understanding with them. Rupert overtook and slew some of them, and the remainder withdrew to their homes. This agrarian insurrection, as to Herefordshire, has been little noticed by historians, though many articles respecting it are to be found in the newsbooks: yet to the governor of Hereford it was the cause of much uneasiness. But all this disquietude was surpassed by the invasion of the Scots, who, at the instigation of the Par- [Scotch Invasion.—Siege liament, marched down under the Earl of Leven, attempting to of Hereford.] take possession of Hereford. As they passed by they took Canon Frome by assault, slew Barnard the governor, and put most of the garrison to the sword. Scudamore on this occasion showed himself worthy of what had been trusted to his care. During a regular siege of six weeks he treated their summons with a refusal, resisted their attacks, and turned a deaf ear to the persuasion of Parliamentary friends ; opposed assaults with sallies, and mines with countermines, till at length the Scots, baffled and disappointed of Parliamentary help, on intelligence that his Majesty was marching to the relief of the besieged, and that the successes of Montrose required their return to the North, broke up from their leaguer on the [The siege 5th of September, and retired amidst the derision and joy of the de- raised.] fenders. Hereford and the whole county were transported with exultation and triumph. By their presence before the outworks, as well as their intrusion and spoil throughout even the remotest corners of the agricultural borders, the enemy had irritated the whole of the country. A committee had been appointed by Parliament to supply them with provisions, but in that engagement they signally failed ; this forced the invaders to seek their subsistence where they could find it, and it was recollected that it had not been the first occasion on which the Scottish nation had done so in other parts of England. Here it was held in lasting remembrance. Tradition of their presence has from that time to this hour been handed down through successive generations: they employed their horse in collecting provisions, and sometimes money, through all the parishes: their voracity was almost proverbial: the common people on many occasions turned upon them—even the females, individually, helped to join in the resistance, and evil-entreated famished stragglers who entered their doors, though, as the writer has traditionally learned from the descendants of the sufferers in those days, where no resistance was made, the conduct of the intruders was not in general marked with wanton insult and cruelty.

[Rupert beats Massey at Ledbury.] Such had been the trials undergone in this region and its chief city during the autumn of the year 1645: so far the Royal cause seemed sustained for a while by Rupert's authority that bore down all opposition. Massey was beaten out of Ledbury with disgrace, and commanded away to strengthen the forces of Fairfax and Cromwell, on which Birch had turned his back. The departure of Massey from Gloucester had made room for a new governor there, Colonel Morgan. Herefordshire was tranquil, and for a season joyous. All except the Parliamentary occupation of Canon Frome[a] appeared to favour the Royal cause, but such information had reached the Committee of Safety in London that it led them to a resolution of making an attempt upon Hereford. In the small

[Wilton Castle burned.] village of Wilton-upon-Wye the traveller is still attracted by the remains of a once considerable dwelling, whose fragmentary windows and blackened walls owe their dilapidation to this time. Without exactly determining the date of its destruction by fire, the origin of its ruin may thus be traced. It was the residence of the family of Brydges, and had been inherited by a long descent of ancestry that

[a] Canon Frome was left by the Scots as a parting gift to the Parliament. It annoyed Scudamore, who made an unsuccessful attempt to recover it by means of a machine called a Sow—a revival of one of the contrivances of the middle ages. It was captured at Malvern. One of them had been employed by the Parliamentarians at the siege of Beeston Castle. (Brereton Correspondence, i. 308.) Two engines, a Boar and a Sow, had been used at the siege of Corfe Castle, May, 1643.—Merc. Rustic. 104.

placed them among the high-born of the country. Sir Giles
Brydges, baronet, the father, was still living, and had an heir, who
had embraced the soldier's life. Sir John Brydges, knight, had
held the command of an Irish regiment that had served among
those who were sent to that island to avenge the massacre of the
Protestants there, and had returned to recruit the losses in his ranks.
By the time he had reached his house at Wilton Castle he found all
things distracted by the war. The governor of Hereford, and Sir
Henry Lingen (the sheriff) at Goodrich Castle, had endeavoured to
persuade him to join them: his refusal was the cause of a quarrel
with them, and though the state of his house was not such as could
admit of a garrison like that of Canon Frome, so as to be occasion
of jealousy to them, their dispute came to open rupture. They sent
him notice that it should be burned down, and they were as good
as their word. One Sunday morning, according to tradition, they
joined their forces, came upon it while all the family were at church,
and reduced it to the blackened and wasted pile that now presents
itself. This is the fact, almost forgotten by those who see it in
decay, and are not generally aware that the flames of Wilton Castle
proved in a great measure the loss of Hereford, and by consequence
in no small degree the ruin of the Royal cause. After this misfortune Sir John sought refuge in Gloucester, and cherished in his
heart a hope of revenge.

This, as was afterwards evident, had not been so soon compassed, [Insecure condition of Hereford.]
but that it was aided by several concurrent causes. Hereford itself, in
spite of outward appearances, exposed as it was to spies and informers, was inwardly far from secure. The state of its society
was unfavourable to it: it had become a city of refuge: the sick
and the disabled and the destitute, those that had been elsewhere
expelled and proscribed, without a home to shelter them, helpless
females and unsuccessful soldiers, had encumbered the place. Some
were of note. There was Sir Henry Spiller, exempt from pardon
by the Houses, whose oaks had been profusely levelled by the sequestrator; Lord Brudenell, long afflicted with the dropsy, whose

1645.

painful wanderings had commenced with the beginning of the civil disturbances; Judge Jenkins, who had in his office condemned Parliamentarians as rebels and traitors to the execution of the law; and, lastly, Sir Thomas Lunsford, one of the bravoes concerned in the arrest of the five members—detested by his opponents, and not highly esteemed by his political friends, he had endured a long confinement at Windsor, and, since his escape or liberation, had commanded and lost the town of Monmouth. These were desperate, and so might the greater portion of the Royalists have been deemed on near inquiry. The character of a "cage of unclean birds" applied by the Puritans to those in Newark might have been employed to express every officer and private, for a simple staff, wielded in the name of the King, had been enough to constitute the hand that bore it delinquent to the Parliament. But all were not faithful to the Royal cause.

[Treachery of Royalist Officers.] It is rare that one in supreme authority can act without giving offence. Some officers of the garrison, not named by Roe, had contracted such mortal displeasure against the governor that they had withdrawn themselves from the defence into the country, while they still contrived to keep up intercourse with the disaffected within the garrison. The communication was set on foot by Sir John Brydges.[a] The opening of their inquiry on the part of Birch and Morgan was, however, unfavourable.. It dashed the hopes of the former; but his resolution and talent here once more came to

[a] ["Sir John Brydges being discontented for the burning of his house, and for some reproachful language given him by one of his Majestie's generals, upon the businesse of the Clubmen, and angry with me for not having something that he desired, which yet I could not give him, quits the King's quarters and goes to Gloucester, where and in the parts adjacent residing some two or three months, and coming sometimes into Herefordshire in disguise, the better to lay his designe, at length goes up to London, and presents to the Committees of both Kingdoms propositions for the taking of Hereford by the way of stratagem, as he calls it. Hereupon order is given to Col. Birch, then Governour of Bath, to joyne his forces with Col. Morgan, Governour of Glocester, for the purposes aforesaid."—Sir B. Scudamore's Defence.]

his aid. Except in the instance of Waller, Roe, to all but his hero, is chary of approbation; but it is an admission of the ability of Scudamore amounting to praise, that Birch should have thought the undertaking impracticable. Daunted in the face of danger he could not be; disappointed for a short time he might be. As at Plymouth and Abingdon, he might feel depression, for that is shown to have been part of his temperament. Upon further investigation he "screwed his courage to the sticking place;" as he had done at Crondall, so he did at Hereford. In the language of mythology, he resolved that the arts of Mercury should precede the sword of Mars, and, as is fabled of old at Troy, secured the way to conquest by a bribe.[a]

1645. December.

The means by which he compassed his end, with the concurrent aid of Colonel Morgan, are so explicitly and vividly told in detail by Roe, that the original narrative needs only a few explanations to elucidate what an eye-witness has himself supplied.

[Capture of Hereford.]

The account of this extraordinary success reached the Houses on the 22nd of December.[b] Each of the messengers by whom it was brought was rewarded: thanks were voted to the two Colonels: Lieutenant Barrow, "the Constable of Hereford," received a handsome proof of their gratitude; and a thanksgiving was appointed on the ensuing Sunday in the churches of London. The news was speedily current everywhere; the press vied in spreading the intelligence, and it was given with a variety of particulars as delightful to the Parliament as they were mortifying to their opponents. In an authorised publication of letters, and particularly in a pamphlet called "A New Tricke to take Townes,"[c] the names of the two

[Parliamentary rejoicing.]

---

[a] Note 27.

[b] [It should have been noted on the MS. that some confusion exists as to the date of the capture of Hereford, and that neither the recollection of Roe or Birch could be trusted in what might naturally have been thought so memorable an event. From Birch's interlineation on p. 27 the surprise is fixed on Dec. 17th; according to Roe's statement on p. 31 it took place on the 24th (obviously a week too late). The "New Tricke" and Vicars concur in specifying the 18th, which is no doubt correct.]

[c] Appendix XVI.

1645.
December.

other conspirators, Captains Alderne and Howarth, are added, though suppressed by Roe. These once formed part of the garrison, and had quarrelled with the governor and left him, who, it seems, had also a " difference " with the city. Sir John Brydges of Wilton was after all the prime mover, assisted by Hodges, a committee-man, and member for the city of Gloucester. Colonel Morgan too was from the beginning, as much as any one, in the secret, and held consultations with them. He, in fact, as already observed, had previously been entrusted with the superior command of the Parliamentary interest in Herefordshire, before Birch was sent thither. But affairs in the city itself had passed into such confusion, that, on the whole, had private dissensions and animosities progressed in their natural course, it was on the way to be lost to the Cavaliers.[a] The feeling of a dispassionate observer might here have exactly accorded with the proverb of George Herbert, " one sound blow will serve to undo us all."

[Easy capture.]

The forcible acquisition of a large town is a serious operation in any, especially a civil, war, and those who could have looked upon the case in an impartial light might have seen cause of congratulation that it was attended with comparatively mitigated circumstances. It were taking too wide a range here to allude to the woes that on this score have at times been endured in foreign lands and intestine wars. Here the killing of a sentry or two at the gate, a few shots upon scattered soldiers, or from inhabitants at windows, by which not many lives were lost, made up the sum of execution. There was no continuance of raging tumult amidst blood and spoil and fire: within a short time all resistance was found to be useless, and the Colonels Morgan and Birch were established in the palace of the Bishop as their head-quarters. By a side-wind,[b] and through the

[a] Note 28.

[b] Birch and Morgan's letter to the House of Lords. L.J. Dec. 22, 1645. [The townesmen have suffered by the souldier, by reason we entred it by force and that the enemy shot out of the windowes and in the streets the souldier was so inraged that we could not prevent them from plundering, which we indeavoured much to

pamphlet, "A New Tricke to take Townes," as well as the list to be subjoined (Appendix XVII.), it transpires that unrestrained plunder went on for several hours. The captors considered it as an onslaught, and the inhabitants were compelled to submit; but there is no collateral complaint of violence and disorder. Composition is admitted to a certain extent for property and personal safety. The more immediate work of ransom for person and property being over, a Parliamentary Committee appointed for the county came into operation. It supplied the place of that which had acted under the name and in the authority of his Majesty. All this must be exhibited, though Roe has not helped us to it, but so it was ordered in the first instance that each responsible citizen, as appears by the Appendix,[a] was called upon to supply his assessment, and the governor gave account some time after to his employers of his proportion of the spoil.

1645.
Dec. 18.

As to Scudamore, his escape to Ludlow, fortunate as it was, proved so humiliating to himself, and disappointing to those who had been used to look up to him, that he lost his credit in consequence, with his command. Many were the reasons resorted to for explanation, and the blame was divided among various parties. By some persons it was attributed to the drunkenness and dissipated habits of the place; by others to subordinate officials who were specially in charge—in particular to the neglect of the town-major: few who duly considered this subject could lay it altogether to the fault of Scudamore himself,[b] who had taken the usual precautions incumbent upon him, and whose conduct in the Scottish siege had called forth the utmost admiration. Wherever the sole or divisible blame might rest, his courage had been tested, and could not be called in question. Be this as it may, it was too well known to be ever afterwards forgotten that he had been reduced to the necessity

[Escape of Scudamore and others.]

have done.—From a letter of Lord Byron's to Prince Rupert (Warburton, ii. 262) it appears that his men were very discontented, "in that they think they are sent away at this time to lose their shares in the pillage of Bristol."]

[a] See No. XVII.   [b] Note 29.

of shuffling off with a crowd of others over the river on the ice. He fled an outcast to the nearest, or the most convenient and securest, garrison of Ludlow, where to hide his head,[a] as others had previously fled to him for shelter in the hour of distress. Those whom he had protected and left behind, whose names are triumphantly exposed on the list of captives, were at once pounced upon and marched off in the severity of weather as prisoners to London. Some of the chief of them, who had given signal offence to the ruling powers there, were committed without delay to the Tower. But even here a desperate plan was formed for a rescue upon the road. A body of Royalists from Wallingford made the attempt. This to a certain extent succeeded. Some Parliamentary Committee-men who were on the move were caught in the snare intended for the other escort; but the Hereford prisoners were brought in security to London, and delivered over to confinement. Yet this showed undeniably the resolute spirit with which, in spite of their overwhelming disaster, the Cavaliers were still animated.

[Birch Governor of Hereford—His difficulties.]

There was something so exceptional and startling in the case of a stronghold with all its inmates thus taken by surprise, as to give rise to an immediate burst of approbation of him who had been entrusted with the chief management of the affair. Birch was at once appointed governor, and a sum of 6,000*l.* voted for the payment of his men by universal acclamation.[b] The tide of his successes was now at the flood; yet unforeseen difficulties presented themselves by the way. As an utter stranger he could hardly be aware of, though he soon found out, the temper of the public that he had to control. If, as often happened (and actually occurred in this case), any of the military then in garrison passed over to his own side, for it was frequently done by common soldiers who thought the best cause was the best pay, still he had to look to many hundred reluctant

[a] [Thence to Worcester, intending to proceed to the King at Oxford to excuse his conduct; but at Worcester he was imprisoned seven months, and, having fruitlessly endeavoured to obtain his trial by a court of war, he published a Defence, some extracts from which will be found appended to Note 29.]

[b] [His regiment was also to be recruited, at his desire, to 1,200 men.]

citizens who had taken up arms for the King, and were not so readily prepared to desert his standard and their own homes. Besides, it must be borne in mind, what has been already hinted, that in the population of a place where the very children, to use the Parliamentary word, had been educated as malignants, as well as throughout the whole country, there had been originally a natural as well as political disposition for the greater part if not altogether adverse to the present as well all former intruders. Hereford, we are told, was " almost as difficult to keep as take." [a]

1645—6.

Their state of public feeling must be dwelt upon in forming any estimate of Scudamore's situation. The sagacity of Birch saw that in the city the old and never-to-be-forgotten remedy for curbing an unruly population would be required; and that that which was originally destined for its protection should be employed, if necessary, against it: so he repaired and strengthened their fortress,[b] the castle, and introduced a garrison of his own. He as quickly cast his eye on any probable danger that might arise from a remainder of Royalist force in other parts more or less remote.

[He repairs the Castle.]

In the "Anglia Rediviva" of Sprigge, written expressly for the purpose of establishing the triumph and superiority of the new-modelled army, under the head of the "State of the Kingdom," is the following passage referring to Herefordshire, descriptive of its condition before the Independents of Fairfax and Cromwell took the field:

[Former state of Herefordshire.]

In the County of Hereford.	*The* KING *had* That County entirely to himself, with the Garrisons of *Hereford, Gotheridge,* and *Cannon Froom.*	*In the County of* Hereford.	*The* Parliament *had* No Garrison, Place of Strength, nor Field-force.

---

[a] ["Thus we may see that even after almost a conquest, yet they apprehended no safety; such are the issues and miseries of a civil war, that the victors are full of fears from those whom they have subdued; no quiet, no security. O let our prayers be to God, never to have such calamitous times again!"—Whitelocke, 219.]

[b] Sequestr. Papers, *sub voce* Awbry, Series II. 2882, 593, as to the employment of the materials of his ruined house for this purpose.

[1645—6.
[Hereford-
shire lost to
the King.]

[Sir Henry
Lingen.]

[Castle of
Goodrich.]

The triumphant contrast is now obvious. The King has lost the whole of his military power in that ill-fated county, the strong castle of Goodrich alone remaining; and of that defensible castle the governor is Sir Henry Lingen.

This gentleman, who was of the ancient stock of this border land, and had been knighted by his Majesty when he resorted hither after the battle of Naseby, had been most resolute in his exertions for the cause he had embraced. Could his actions be rescued from oblivion they are believed to have bordered almost upon romance. "Harry Lingen" is still a household word with the natives. Wherefore it should so have been may now be searched among them in vain. A period has arrived when the remembrance of him has been nearly lost. It tells but little for the gratitude of a country that, in two centuries and a half, so much of him should have been forgotten, while he is known to have been one of the most remarkable persons of his place and time. But the march of improvement disturbs or arrests the current of tradition. The story that could once have enlivened the peasant's hearth is now no more; even his descendants can hardly point to the place of his sepulture;[a] and he has left little to posterity but the shadow of a brave and generous name.

The subject of Goodrich Castle in its present state and remote origin has so amply employed the pencil of the artist and the researches of the antiquary as to leave little room for pictorial taste or laborious investigation. It belongs not, doubtless, to the province of the commentator to indulge too far in the sentimental part of this subject; but it is impossible in the view of that ruined baronial structure, which is believed, when perfect, on a small scale to have represented the manners of the middle ages, not to regret its sad condition, as it frowns darkly on the rippling waters below. To be acquainted too with the cause of its reduction to such a condition adds not a little to that regret. The voice of time, in the language of the poet, "disparting towers," has not alone revealed the secret

[a] He and his lady are buried at Stoke Edith.

of these demolished walls; the most interesting of our structures bear traces throughout this island of the evil passions, of either the avarice or the anger of man.

[1646.]

Should any passage of warmth or floridness of description escape as in this instance from a considerate pen, its excuse may be entrusted to the feelings of the well-instructed voyager, when first he moors his bark on the margin of the charming Wye, in his ascent to the height on which this shattered fortress stands, or when he treads its court, and beholds the desolation that surrounds him.

[Present state of Goodrich Castle.]

The civil and religious heat of the new governor of Hereford brooked no unnecessary delay; with an increased force and a supply of money he applied himself in due time to remove the evils that remained to obstruct his rule. Lingen held the stronghold of Goodrich. He determined that this should not be permitted; and there were other reasons why he would not rest till the "castle should topple on its warder's head."

[Activity of Birch.]

To any one who still beholds and considers its situation it cannot but appear well chosen for such a purpose as the Royalists required. It stood between two districts that from of old, even up to that time, bore the vestiges of independent power, and by their natural privileges and aspect laid claim to it. They were lands of fastnesses. Eastward the Forest of Dean, though of late it had been harassed almost to distraction by Prince Rupert, was not as yet totally exhausted. It had furnished a Parliamentary garrison and "the constable" for Canon Frome; neither was it, on the other hand, without resources for the Cavalier. North-westward, and in the direction of Hereford itself, lay the district of Irchinfield, whence, though far away beyond, towards the Hatterel Hills, stretched out a land whose customs neither the Roman nor the Saxon had eradicated,—whose forests and marshes had formed the retreat of the patriot and refuge of the outlaw. The whole region abounded in strongholds that had been constructed by the Normans; and Goodrich Castle was one of these.

[Situation of Goodrich Castle.]

1646.
[Character of Lingen.]

To return to its present occupant and his efforts. It may be seen from the preceding observations that time and an ungrateful country have left too little of the authentic respecting Sir Henry Lingen to gratify altogether the wish of the inquirer or the reader. It is not very possible to discern how far he may have attained to the true ideal of a real Cavalier, or whether he was rather a coarse or vulgar aspirant to public applause; yet, as regards his sincere and honest resistance, sufficient is known of him from the national archives still existing as to his sufferings by pecuniary losses, and the valour and constancy with which he had incurred and endured them, till he had been deprived of the greater part of his property: in short that he did not give way till the whole of the religious and political system for which he had contended had crumbled over him, even as at Goodrich he had scorned to yield till every tile had tumbled over his head, and the breach was ready for the assault that would have ended in his own death and that of his followers.

[Goodrich Castle a garrison.]

Anthony Earl of Kent, who had not long since taken his seat in the House of Lords on the death of his father, was the owner, but resident elsewhere. It was the fate of void even as of well inhabited houses to be seized upon by either of the disputants. Thus the Earl of Stamford made Goodrich a convenient harbour for his men when he plundered the neighbourhood and reduced the celebrated Royalist Swift, the vicar, to the condition of an outcast, and his wife and children to absolute poverty.[a] The Marquis of Hertford had afterwards secured it; and, not to dwell upon any intermediate attempt at occupation while hostilities had been agitating in the parts between Hereford and Monmouth, and when the Scots were roving throughout the country, it was now a garrison, and the only one near Hereford that assisted in upholding the fallen power of the King.

[a] This, one of the earliest achievements of merciless plundering, was put in practice by Captain Kyrle, a neighbour to the vicar and his family. He was an officer under the Earl of Stamford, but afterwards, as will appear, a Parliamentary colonel, and comrade of Birch. He had the unenviable distinction of being the first to disturb his defenceless neighbours in the adjoining parish of Goodrich.— Merc. Rustic. 71 *et seqq.*

Lingen had escaped the fate of the captives and of Scudamore, though he, too, along with the latter, had scrambled over the ice. It had been among the reports of the time that his house at Sutton Frene was destroyed by fire. Wherever his family had fled for safety, the walls of Goodrich were now his military home, and hence he at once derives importance. He had stocked them as far as he could with what was necessary for defence, and with him was a company of gentry as officers and privates attached to the same cause; though after all but " a faithful few, a little band of brothers,"

Exigui numero, sed bello vivida virtus,^a

determined to resist to the last. None there were traitors. All things wore the air of loyalty about them; even the pile of coal that in the time of the writer was dug from the rubbish of 1646, was a symptom of the provision that had been made; and the very brazen saucepan of the cook, then also discovered, contained his daily admonition, for the inscription in pierced letters on the metallic handle was

C · V · B · LOYAL · TO · HIS · MAGISTEIE

—and bade him to be ready for any attempt against them. At least a hundred horses stood in the stable upon the counterscarp; the riders were bold and experienced; they knew all the intricate and hidden roads of the country, those of the hundred of Wormelow with all its loyal attachments, and especially of the district of Irchinfield, where dwelt their purveyor—and, what is still perhaps of equal importance, all the fords, of which 20 existed between Hereford and Monmouth.[b] This display may in some sense be thought insignificant or as resembling too much the struggle of a sinking cause in the late Italian troubles; but it will bear as little comparison in the mind of the dispassionate as those of the endeavours of a disinterested party who had everything but honour to lose, can bear to the feats of the torturing assassin or the professed thief.

[a] Æneid, v. 754. [b] Scudamore MSS.

1646.
[Isolation of Goodrich Castle.]

When they looked around them they could apparently reckon upon no marching force to come to their rescue, and their communications were gradually cut off; for though the garrisons of Ludlow, Worcester, Madresfield, and Raglan, as it seems by the text, were the objects of apprehension to Birch himself, they were for the present paralysed, and, strictly speaking, after the loss of Hereford, not one remained in the county. Raglan, already invested, was at too great a distance to have afforded relief to Goodrich; and as to Monmouth, Morgan had taken measures to secure that town and the part of Wales behind it.

[Courage of the Garrison.]

The whole of this attitude, rightly estimated, might therefore be thought bold and gallant enough in the eye, if not altogether to the hope, of the Royalists; and, by the way, even now may appear too much so to have been almost consigned to oblivion. But, from the point at which the Parliamentarian looked at it, it presented no more than the desperate strivings of an obstinate malignant enemy, severely crippled, but not as yet to be despised.

[Difficult task of Birch.]

The task of the governor of Hereford in overcoming his obstacles was in the meantime accompanied by no little difficulty and danger. The process of converting to obedience those who were harassed by the demands of ransom or sequestration in city and country was not an easy one, and, while the remainder of the winter was occupied in repairing the castle of Hereford, it was also vigilantly employed in an endeavour to cope with that spirit of aversion which rendered those repairs necessary. The safety of himself and of his new-modelled garrison, as well as the tranquillity of the place, were constantly at the hazard of a popular outbreak. The public continued to cast their eyes towards Lingen as their champion. While his garrison were in the saddle, for therein consisted his chief strength, he was able under all disadvantages to compete in some sort with Birch and thwart him. He could go within a certain range and enforce requirements upon Royal authority, and claimed to be the representative of his master, undisturbed by the Parliamentary committee, or their agent the newly-appointed governor.

While those whom he held to be usurping intruders were vexing his suffering friends, he ventured even to exact support from and extend protection to his adversaries, to execute warrants and require contribution in the name of his Majesty.[*] In the country throughout the southern hundreds the British trackways furnished him with great facilities; even long after, the talk of the common people would be in his favour; the Cavaliers doubted not that "they should have a day, or time, for it, again."

So disturbed a condition of government as Roe allows us to understand, of which this is but a feeble representation, could not long be endured, and accordingly the turn of events made way for a change upon the approach of spring. Three months had elapsed since the surprise of Hereford, and Lingen and his men had continued unsubdued. He could still find means of existence in the core of the country, could draw his resources from considerable distances, and obtain supplies of victual for man and horse. Corn and cattle, oats, hay, and straw were at his command. The roads towards Gloucester and Hereford were far from being entirely closed to him. Birch was at length urged by the necessity of time, and the provocation constantly offered at Goodrich, to make some attempt against it. [Birch resolves to attempt Goodrich.]

As soon as it was announced at Oxford that Hereford had been irrevocably lost, Sir Jacob, now Lord, Astley, was sent upon an important mission to collect all the force that could be spared from the remaining Royalist garrisons of Salop, Stafford, and Worcester. His immediate object was the relief of Chester, besieged by Colonel Sir William Brereton, and now almost at the last gasp. These garrisons he found in the utmost disorder, caused by supernumerary officers whose regiments were broken up, and privates who were desperate for want of pay. All things were in confusion; and, as he travelled from one to the other, his own finances were so reduced [Movements of Lord Astley—Birch's successes against Lingen.]

[*] [He made a daring attempt in Jan. 1646, to intercept the return of the guard of a convoy that had been sent from Newnham through the Forest of Dean to Hereford, but failed in consequence of the non-appearance of the expected party.]

1646.

that he was compelled to solicit money for his expenses on this journey. He found that Sir Lewis Kirke had abandoned his command at Bridgenorth, and left everything in disorder. In the course of the months of January and February he had, however, exercised such diligence and management as to have appointed a general rendezvous at Bridgenorth towards the beginning of March, to put himself at the head of a body of men desperate and valiant, wrought up to the resolution of venturing their last stake in the field. They consisted of about 3,000, and were ready to have been met by others drawn from Oxford, and making an aggregate that was hoped to be sufficiently able to cope with any that the Parliamentarians had to bring against them. It was the knowledge of this fact that hastened the preparations of Birch, Morgan, and Brereton, for the Parliament were always well informed of the measures of their opponents; it therefore behoved Birch to be ready against the time appointed, though he could not venture to leave Lingen behind him. "Wherefore," says Roe in his simplicity, "you tooke vp such a resolution as seldome hath been heard of." Under favour of a dark night, by information of the exact height of the outer wall, and a combination of stratagem, force, and fire, he contrived to enter and demolish the large stable that rested against the counterscarp of the castle. By this single master-stroke he carried off or destroyed nearly the whole of their horses.[a] An equal success attended him, arising from a dangerous endeavour to waylay his person a few nights after, as he was travelling upon what might have been considered the safest road to Gloucester. To avoid suspicion he took a bye-track, and few attendants. The road where the ambush was laid was through Fownhope, by the Old Gore, and on by Eccleswall Castle to Castle End, where it opened upon the more usual way through Ross to Gloucester: and between Old Gore and the termination are several undulations, any one of

[a] [From a letter dated at Hereford, and published in the Perfect Diurnall, March 16, 1645, it appears that Colonel Kyrle at Monmouth sent a party to join in this expedition.]

which would be well adapted for the lying in wait and encounter. It is evident that the failure of this attempt of Birch to reach and confer with Morgan upon Astley's project might wholly have thwarted the victory that, by the combination of Birch and Morgan and Brereton, was obtained at Stow. That fight and its preliminaries are fairly related, except with the usual prominence allotted to Birch's interference therein,[a] and the sole credit of his having claimed the surrender of the brave and hoary veteran, wearied by the toil of the night and the encounter of the morning.[b] Thus certain, looking through the train of events, does it appear that on the entrance of the stable of Goodrich in the first instance depended the success of the campaign that, not only in this but in every part of England, materially put an end to any serious operations in the field. As to the siege of Ludlow, Worcester, and its smaller outlying garrisons of Hartlebury and Madresfield, those places, with many others assailed elsewhere by Fairfax and Cromwell, collapsed at intervals as the resistance declined.[c] Yet while this

---

[a] [In a letter published by Vicars (Burning Bush, 398) from one of Brereton's officers who was present, that commander and Morgan are alone mentioned.]

[b] No portrait can be given more to the life than that of Sir Jacob Astley by an anonymous writer, who has left the share of our colonel in the action to the original description of Roe, and claims the servant of Major Hawksworth as the person to whom Sir Jacob Astley surrendered. It were injustice to the memory of this admirable veteran to omit his prophetic words amid the Parliament soldiers on the field of battle: "Sir Jacob Ashley being taken captive, and wearied in this fight, and being ancient (for old age's silver haires had quite covered over his head and beard), the souldiers brought him a drum to sit and rest himselfe upon; who being sate, he said (as was most credibly enformed) unto our souldiers, Gentlemen, yee may now sit downe and play, for you have done all your worke, if you fall not out among yourselves."—Vicars, Burning Bush, 399.

[c] Mercurius Civicus, Oct. 9-16, 1645, states that 20 garrisons of different sizes had been taken between April 20 and October 18. [The latter part of Roe's narrative is more hurried and less circumstantial than might have been expected. Possibly he may have been absent at that time; if so, the criticism in note [a], p. 36, may be mistaken. This seems the more likely, as a circumstance at the siege of Ludlow reflected so much honour upon Birch that Roe would hardly have omitted it had it passed under his own observation. He sat down before the town April 24, 1646:

1645-6.
March.

was going on, the flag of royalty and defiance still continued to float from Goodrich Castle. It might have been expected that such discouragement as Lingen had undergone alone in the reverses already described must have been sufficient to cast down any ordinary antagonist situated as he appears to have been. At length, as is proved by the requisition sent to the bailiff of Sir Edward Powell of Pengethly, near Ross, the hour arrived when we may see him warned and preparing for a last resistance. On the 3rd of March, 1645-6, he sent a written message to the steward of that estate, to which he had often in former raids had recourse for contribution and other help, and it was couched in these terms:—

Mr Grubb,

I shall desier you to send your three teemes loaded with boards hither presently and that they may bee of your longest size of Boardes, for I am informed that you haue very longe ones, I pray you send them away presently for I must make vse of them presentley* soe I rest

Your loueing
ffrrend
HEN. LENGEN.

Gotherig Castle this 3d of March 1645.
(Endorsed) For Mr. Grubb at Pengethley.

[Goodrich stable burnt.]

Here then is proof of the first premonitory symptom of expected hostility. Immediately after this, the nightly attack of Birch upon their stable on the counterscarp, followed up within a few days by the adventure at the Old Gore near Ross, was so successful that Birch might well have supposed that it would weaken their ability to annoy, and well-nigh deprive them of the power of future resistance. How this happened will be seen by his letter to the

on the 29th some forces from Raglan, Goodrich, and Madresfield faced him, but retired. Woodhouse, the governor, treated May 20; but Birch having left the siege, the Royalist refused to give up to any one else, and drove the Shropshire men out of the town with loss, so that Birch had to return to receive his surrender. This probably occasioned the envious feeling alluded to by Roe, p. 36.]

* The boards were burned in the siege. Sir Richard Grenville got above 1,000 deal boards from the Commissioners of Devon to make huts for the soldiers.—Clarendon, ix.

Speaker of the House of Commons[a] detailing his complete and extraordinary success.

1645-6. March.

But it was not without its drawback. To revert to what Roe has said a little previously; in recording Birch's apprehensions as to what Lingen could do, he has omitted the notice of what he actually did; for, while the governor had only gone for the sake of consulting Morgan about the expedition, his apprehensions were realised. There were intelligencers enough throughout the country to convey the news of his absence, if the attack upon Goodrich itself had not given rise to the idea that something was in hand requiring the absence of the governor from the city. There were also a great number of favourers to Lingen's cause, to help him to repair his injuries at the stable, and bring forward horse to encourage and aid him. Accordingly, while the governor and Kyrle[b] with Roe were gone to Gloucester, and the rest of the garrison were commanded to follow, he dared to do in broad daylight what his adversary had only ventured to do in the depth of night. He came down at high noon to the gate of Hereford, cut the turnpike,[c] assaulted and slew the sentries, and alarmed the garrison: but, finding that he was to be overpowered, made his retreat, and eluded all pursuit.[d] The fact is unquestionable, and the date sufficiently determinable by the interval for the consultation at Gloucester.

[Lingen alarms Hereford.]

To turn from these brief illustrations to the stream of the story. These blows, though heavy, fell upon no ordinary adversary. With the last crush of the King's forces[e] was actually annihilated all chance of revival. His Majesty had himself become a fugitive from his head-quarters,[f] and whither he was gone was at first unknown; but the flag of Lingen's master continued to float in defiance from Goodrich tower. It must have been plain to all who witnessed these proceedings, friend or enemy, that the contest now

[His resolution.]

---

[a] Appendix XVIII.   [b] Note 30.
[c] [A kind of cheval-de-frise used in fortification.]
[d] See the evidence of Nathaniel Collins upon oath.—Sequestration Papers.
[e] March 21, 1645-6.   [f] April 27, 1646.

1646.
July.

could be no other than a question of time; that the days of resistance were numbered, and ere long to come to an end. His Majesty gave himself up into the hands of the Scots: not a battalion remained to him in the field: he had ordered the surrender of every fortress from which his banner had waved: still the Castle of Goodrich continued in the hands of those who had supported his cause to the brink of despair, and not till all, but honour, and the last chance of life was at stake were these Royalists prepared to yield. The account of this transaction is dismissed by Roe in a few sentences, and reference is therefore made to the letters of the Colonel himself for his own version.[a] The call to surrender was followed by a refusal.[b] The chief attack was directed on what is still known as " the Ladies' Tower," at the north-western corner, apparently the weakest part of the building. Their supply of water, through pipes from the opposite side of a ravine, was cut off; batteries were raised, and a mortar-piece, cast expressly for the purpose, was planted at the very head of the spring; the solid rock on which the foundation had been laid was mined with great difficulty, and countermined by those within, nor could a breach of sufficient size be made till a portion of the tower was beaten into the mouth of the mine, and the foot and horse were drawn up ready to storm. The white flag was then hoisted, and they surrendered at mercy for their lives.[c] Though they had placed themselves in the hands of the victor, it was neither a time nor an occasion for further bloodshed or ignominious death, nor are many of the garrison reported to have fallen, but the roof was in a state of ruin, and the vestiges and inequalities of the court seem to exhibit it at this hour. They marched out, allowing for uncertainty of numbers, about 50 officers, reformados or country gentlemen, and privates about thrice as many. Among them were refugees, such as the Parliamentarians, on account of their religious creed, had looked upon with feelings of peculiar bitterness: nothing is at the same time said of their detention as

[Siege of Goodrich Castle.]

[Surrender of Goodrich Castle.]

[a] Appendix XX.   [b] Appendix XIX.
[c] Note 31.

captives, and Sir Henry himself will be shown to have appeared within a short time in public with his sword upon his thigh. Combination for any outward resistance might be supposed from this time forth to have been entirely disarmed of its power; but it was not so: the unconquerable feeling that had been so long cherished continued to smoulder between Parliamentarian and Royalist till the heavy sequestrations of the latter expired. In the meantime the well-known prophecy of Lord Astley was verified to the letter, as to the condition that the Parliamentarians in these parts and elsewhere, Birch among them, themselves had to encounter during the confusion and usurpation that ensued. This passage of English history belongs not to the section with which we have had to interfere; it remains only to point out that the circumstance of the election of Colonel Birch was one to which he was already aspiring while Goodrich Castle was being destroyed;[a] and it proves that he was, even in the midst of his difficulties, endeavouring to acquire sufficient influence among those with whom he was about to establish his home to secure him a seat in the House of Commons—a bloodless victory, with which the memorialist has thought proper to close.

Having carried out the theme upon which he had based his exhortations, and having applied it to the leading circumstances of his unvarnished tale, this writer ends with a fervent expression of his own grateful acknowledgments to the kindness of his patron and commander, and, after a soldiership at least of three campaigns, the comrades part. Roe, who has hitherto attended the Colonel personally throughout the whole of his military exploits, briefly waits upon him over the line that sets a limit to them, to the door of the senate-house. He congratulates him as a member of that body, and argues from the past to his future successful exertions for the good of his country: he tenders respectfully these memorials of the former, and adds a prayer for his subsequent welfare. Hardly a line escapes from him who composed, or him in whose hands these

[Roe's conclusion.]

[a] Appendix XX.

1646.

memorials are placed, as to the writer, his name, or office: they are nowhere directly to be found, nor can it be determined whether the MS. was a parting gift, or, if so, whether these two persons ever met again. All that has been ascertained has already been said of the writer,[a] and, admitting the conjecture of the preface to be correct, beyond it he is lost in the cloud of war that discharged itself on the combatants in Ireland.

[Close of commentary.]

As this imperfect attempt at exposition professes to be no more than an illustration of the military proceedings of Colonel Birch till his entrance into Parliament, and as little is admitted into the memoir with respect to the latter part of his conduct leading to that event, the commentator, having no text for amplification, may be permitted on this score to bring his observations towards a close; but a few remarks at this stage may not be inadmissible.

[Nature of Roe's Memoir.]

It is hardly possible to rise from the perusal of this singular performance without an impression that while its primary and professed object is to give glory to God, its secondary intention is to bestow praise upon man; and that, while it exhorts to gratitude, there is mingled with it a provocative and an indulgence to self-gratulation. After every allowance has been made for the admission of this its lower tendency, and for an excusable omitting on the part of Roe of anything that might operate to the disadvantage of his friend, it needs in candour to be once more impressed upon the reader that this sketch is in some parts couched in language that exalts the importance of Birch in a way of which no trace has been elsewhere found, and that expressions are used that the Governor of Hereford did not refuse to accept as his own, though they are to be discovered in no other writer. How far, to pursue the metaphor, the artist who has given us this portrait of Birch may have been induced to adopt undue proportions for the principal figure in his canvas, must be left to others to determine. The same may be noted of expressions as of events. If, from what has been brought forward in illustra-

---

[a] Preface.

tion, some of these may appear to have been presented in a one-sided view, it is believed that nothing will be discovered to contradict the leading facts of the time. Roe's statements are in the main confirmed by other authorities, and where they have been found to differ, they have not been passed by unnoticed. That his memory at all times served him perfectly on minor unimportant matters—this cannot be contended, while it may not be permitted to interfere with the honesty and heartiness of the design. On such points the most pretentious historians are often grossly defective, and occasionally all at variance. Such as the memoir is, it was offered as an only gift of gratitude to his master: it was such as he thought he would be pleased with, and such indeed it proved; for Birch revised it, and left it to his descendants corrected in many places with his own hand.

1646.

It is difficult to assign a legitimate position to this vicarious autobiography, for which it would not be easy under all circumstances, at any rate in the commentator's experience, to find a parallel in the English language. The text proves that, in the estimate of the writer, a plain soldier, sheer courage holds the place that is assigned to it by the tragedian in the old Roman sense: valour is

[Its style and spirit.]

> "the chiefest virtue, and most dignifies
> The haver;"

and, with the addition of Christian motive, that this gift is best maintained by its being derived from a sense of Divine protection, and gratitude for providential deliverance in dangers. If this be the leading impression intended to be conveyed in the text, the commentary may not be without its instruction—at least so far as it shows the advantage of discretion allied to force; and, in the instance of this individual, proves that he was endowed with the happy art of seizing on the advantages that this combination gave him, and knew the moment for sheathing as well as drawing the sword. In tracing the image of his master, Roe was firmly convinced from religious prepossession that the Supreme Protector and Disposer of events was in favour of the conquering side. Birch, it

1646.

[Close of Roe's MS.]

[The Memoir only military.]

[Subsequent events.]

[The Governor's difficulties.]

is well known, lived in this respect to alter his opinion; but this, being on the outside of the present subject, can find no entertainment here.

This view of the varied scenic changes of our eventful drama has been confined to certain limits. Such as they are, it is now closed: the curtain that had been raised upon Birch as a merchant volunteer captain on the bridge at Bristol descends upon him as a colonel, Governor of Hereford, seated in the senate of his country.

It will be borne in mind that the representation of him has extended only, as is professed in the title, to his "martiall actions." A wider sphere of inquiry and an abler judgment might have amassed and combined sufficient materials to have furnished a more ample filling-in of the outline. In lieu of this, which has not been the object professed from the commencement, certain scattered and chiefly original materials may be subjoined, to help in forming some opinion of the salient points in the progress of Colonel Birch's subsequent career.[a]

Roe has now left us, and from his revelations we are to expect no more. The commentator might have therefore exchanged his office for that of biographer; but the subject is too intricate to attempt other than brief detail, and would prove too ample for the compass of a small volume. It is too curiously entangled with the politics of the time not to excite interest, and too complicated easily to unfold.

Some men, like Belliard under Napoleon I., are of a fit talent for the government of conquered places. The Parliament could not have chosen a better man than Birch. He had been gifted with no ordinary abilities to carry him through the task to which he was appointed. He was good-humoured and cautious, strict and prompt where there was necessity for immediate action, and master of the weapon that he bore for emergencies. But he had to steer his way

---

[a] [Thus far the labours of the original Editor were left nearly complete for the press. The remainder has been compiled chiefly from imperfect sketches and memoranda.]

through a mingled population, to coerce the refractory, to conciliate the half-disposed to serve and obey, and keep a watchful eye over all; for there were some of those who took the intruder's side for interest's sake, whose hearts were all the while prepossessed and swayed by an opposite feeling, and held their peace and followed him, though they were ready on a favourable opportunity to have turned once more against him. The conqueror held the refractory at arm's length by a threat that could not be misunderstood. But in spite of the stern menace held out by the available repairs of the fortress, holding an air of defiance and punishment over every townsman's dwelling, and commanding obedience to a new state of things, where it had seemed to guarantee security under the old, it was impossible to secure the fluctuation of a public opinion that had so long taken its hold on the feelings and shown itself in the conduct of most households. Beneath all appearance of submission the current still continued to flow; and, while it was fed by the tear and fanned by the sigh of suffering in person and property through oppression,[a] could not at once be checked in its course. Lingen was well aware of this, and waited his opportunity,

1646.
October.

[a] There was a time when it was not merely the following of the Royal banner; but a word spoken almost in jest, or the indulgent kindness of a secret hour, the involuntary exchange of a dwelling to the Royal quarter, the discharge of a natural duty (as at Harewood), was sufficient to furnish the informer with a charge and constitute a delinquent.—J. W. [The case referred to seems to be that of John Browne of Harewood, in the county of Hereford, gent., who, being a minor and left destitute of the means of maintenance, was "forced to seek out his guardian and to go into the King's quarters, whereby he became a delinquent." He bore arms as a Royalist, but subsequently was a Parliamentary soldier for three years, and petitioned on that account to be admitted to compound for his estate, and was fined at a tenth, 213*l.* 16*s.* 10*d.* (Sequestr. Papers, Series 2, v. 83.) The following is an instructive specimen of sequestration. When the Earl of Derby levied forces in Lancashire, John Rycroft of Haugh, in that county, husbandman, was summoned on pain of death to meet at a rendezvous, and for repairing thither and distributing a cheese among the soldiers he was sequestered, though he ever after lived in the Parliament's quarters, submitted to their committee, and took the Negative Oath and National Covenant. — Compos. Papers, Series 1, liii. 763.]

1646.
October.

[Hereford October Fair.]

in the absence of his adversary, to prove what chance he yet had against the dominant power.

It is a well-known maxim of despotic government that in times of civil dissension a cautious regard should be had towards larger assemblies of the people. Hence markets, wakes, and fairs of unusual size have always been looked at with a jealous eye. They have often been the cause of outbreaks when the minds of those who frequented them were heated by mutual animosity. It was so in the case of this civil strife. Lady Harley anticipated with alarm the effect of the great horse-fair at Brampton-Bryan, June 11, 1642 and 1643;[a] and liberty was not yet so extinct in England as to prevent the holding of the great cattle-fair at Hereford on the 19th of October of the year 1646. A time then was approaching when, if ever, some favourable circumstance might be expected to arise. Lingen was abroad,[b] his sword by his side, respected by the common people for his family, for his gallant upholdings, his bearing up under adversity. Aware of his consequence, though stripped of power, he understood the position of his intrusive adversary, and resolved a second time to show what he could dare to do. Such an one could not be overlooked, even if he was not still the object of a host of admirers: and Birch took measures to obviate the consequences of the fair. The resources of the city just then were too much exhausted to maintain the garrison. His regiment of horse,—for now he had one of his own,—was distributed in scattered though not very remote quarters. Two months had passed since he had crushed the last fortress and dispersed its defenders: but much still remained for restlessness of thought and promptitude of action. It

[a] Letters of Lady Brilliana Harley, 168, 169, 203. A Royalist party of Col. Price's regiment came from Brecknock in July, 1645, with intention to plunder the fair, but were anticipated by another party of Parliamentary soldiers who beat them back with loss, slew and took many prisoners.—Perfect Occurrences, Monday, July 28, 1645.

[b] [He had been in prison till Oct. 1, 1646, when he petitioned to compound.—Sequestration Papers, Series 2, xxviii. 418.]

was a few days before this popular assemblage, with which no modern assumed authority could yet venture to interfere, that Birch undertook to overawe a number of those who might be coming together upon that occasion. {1646. October 6.}

In the centre of Irchinfield, the district already noticed, had long been a house of reception[a] for strangers coming out of the Welsh borders. There the magistrates in times of peace transacted their business; thither came the dealers of sheep and cattle with their droves from a wild tract beneath the Black Mountains, a district that Welsh and Saxon history have both united to celebrate in more than mere legendary story.[b] The house overlooked the further heights from Garway, Orcop, and St. Weonard's on the Hill, a succession of parishes that had been the scene of border debate, in the depth of whose morasses covered with alder and inhabited by clouds of water-fowl, at Tretire, along the thickets of the wandering Gamber, Owain Glyndwr was supposed to have sought a refuge from the pursuit of Henry IV.; and where no man could want a hiding-place. Many of the larger dwellings were fortified; all bore the marks of seclusion and resistance; and the inhabitants, as already hinted, though thinly scattered over the surface, were not to be despised. Lingen knew his popularity among them: Birch was equally aware of it: therefore he ordered a meeting to take place on the 6th of October. From backwardness on the part of the invited, or some less imaginable cause, this had been a second meeting, and that day was wearing away when Birch had returned to his quarters. What then must have been his surprise to find that in his absence the quiet of the place had been disturbed by uproar, and the remaining part of his garrison thrown into a state of alarm. [The New Inn.]

Could the secret and confidential communications of country committees with that of the Two Houses have been rescued from destruction through damp or rats or fire, they would throw a flood [Proceedings of country Committees.]

---

[a] [The New Inn, or by its ancient name *Croes Owain;* Owen's Cross.]
[b] See Domesday Book.

140   MILITARY MEMOIR OF

1646.
October 6.

of light upon events and characters, that would have corrected or shamed many a judgment formed by posterity upon men and things in this involved and trackless labyrinth. But these revelations are not now to be made. One of these curious documents, however, has been drawn from the papers of Sir Edward Harley:[a] its originality and authority are indisputable: it never was intended to see the light, but it gives us additional proof of the governor's just apprehensions from pretended friends as well as open foes: that he had to fear the insincerity of the one, as well as the courage of the other: and how either were evaded or overcome. And we may see, from this fragment that follows, how much more might have remained to give us an insight into the situation and conduct of the intruding governor of Hereford, as well as the behaviour of those who were about him.

[Report of the Hereford Committee.]

Friday the 6th of October 1646. Lieutenant Colonel Lingon, a great Cavalier and very lately in Arms against the Parl. met the Town Major of the Garrison of Hereford in the street, wearing (contrary to his Parole or order from the Governor) his Sword and there after some peremptory or high language given to the Town Major, calling him Rogue &c : So that a Company of People were gotten together, he openly with abundance of insolence challenged him : But the Town Major perceiving the flocking together of the inhabitants (whose malignity to the Parliament and affection to him and his Family are very well known), feared some Plot of the said Lingon with the Townsmen against the said Garrison—and that this occasion was taken of making an Uproar, to set on foot this Design, The rather because at that time most of the Garrison having no Subsistence in the City were drawn into the Country, And remembering that the aforesaid Lingon when he was in Arms against us he attempted with thirty horse to enter the Town at high Noon, when we had at least 700 foot and 50 horse in the Town, Charged the guards at

Gate, Slew four of our men, and, had he not been repulsed by the resolution of that Guard had entered, assured that upon his appearance in the Town the Inhabitants would rise to join with him against the Garrison ; Whereupon the Town Major immediately repaired to Lieutenant Colonel Raymond then Commander in Chief (the Governor being absent having summoned in all the Cavaliers of the Hundred of Wormelow to meet him at New Inn to give him an account of their Names, Qualities, abodes and business in those parts, as he had done by the Cavaliers of the Hundred before and acquainted the aforesaid Lieutenant Colonel with those passages, Desiring that he would give speedy order for his   apprehending, to prevent any future mischief, which he readily did unto the Captain of the Watch

---

[a] [Possibly a copy of the Report of the Council of War ?]

who found him drinking Sack in a Common Inn called the Falcon, with Mr Isaac Bromwich and Mr Harbert Parrett, both of the Committee.—The Captain of the Watch sent up to speak with Mr Lingon and Mr Bromwich. The Captain of the Watch told them his business: Lingon demanded by what order he came, and what he was—The Captain then replied he was Captain of the Watch—But Mr Bromwich told him, he knew no man that had anything to do to take any man a prisoner.

1646.
October 6.
[Report of the Hereford Committee.]

Expressing to him much violent language and carriage and refused to let the Prisoner go along with him—unless he did procure an order under hands, Notwithstanding which the Captain of the Watch understanding that they were Committee men was so modest as to forbear Disputes, but left him with them, and came and acquainted the Lieutenant Colonel with these passages. He considering the nature of his offences, not knowing the intent of his coming to Town armed, nor the event of this drunken Bout, gave a second order (and that in writing) for his being secured—With which order the Captain of the Watch went again and required Lingon to go along with him; whom though seemingly willing: Mr Bromwich would not suffer: But holding him often repeated, Thou shalt not go, Thou shalt not go—And with all reproached the Captain of the Watch, with Scurrilous Language calling him: Busy, troublesome, saucy fellow, but laying violent hands upon him thrust him as if he would have fallen upon him. Whereupon the Captain of the Watch wished him to forbear, Or otherwise he had power to call up his Guards. Mr Bromwich presently replied, And I have power to raise the Sheriffs, Constables, Churchwardens, and other Officers of the County to beat you all out of the Country. Nor was this all, But he reviled the Officers of the Garrison, Saying they were Cowards, for when any occasion is to fight You know all how to run away: Mr Parrett perceiving the Captain of the Watch and the Soldiers with him much discontented, Desired him to bear with Mr Bromwich, for (said he) you may perceive that he hath drunk very hard—But that if he would let the Cavalier alone, he would see him forthcoming: The Captain of the Watch came and repeated all this to the Lieutenant Colonel who admiring these carriages and passages out of Respect to the Committee repaired to them and acquainted them with all these proceedings. —And withal gave the Captn of the Watch special commands to execute his Order —In the Interim the Governor returned (it being about four of the Clock in the Evening), unto whom the Lieutenant Colonel with divers other Officers went, Who in the relation of these things, was interrupted by the sudden and hasty return of us, A great broil and tumult that he found between Bromwich, Lingon, and others fighting in the Inn Many people running in, and running forth—This was seconded with the same relation from others, that the Soldiers and   , they were called Cowards, and threatened to be beat out of the County, were ready to betake them to their Arms—The Governor and those Officers with him, Doubting the event of this Tumult, and gathering together of People at this Season (being the Evening feared some treacherous design to be working in the Garrison by means of this Cavalier, Which, because he could not bring to pass at his first meeting the Town Major, he took his opportunity

1646.
October 6.
[Report of the Hereford Committee.]

when it was night: Immediately therefore commanded the Captain of the Watch to do his endeavours to quiet the Soldiers and appease the Tumult; Strengthen and be ready with his Guards, and bring away Lingon Desiring the Officers then present to stay, and the rest to be sent for to advise what was best to be done. When they were come together many thoughts were spent, and the circumstances of things taken into consideration: To wit the Potent number of Cavaliers, most of them very lately in Arms against the Parliament and those very popular and of great interest in City and County, Particularly of this Cavalier whose family and person are very well known to have very great influence upon both. The late threats that were heard daily from Town and Country, Their admired Jollity, and frequent drunken meetings, and that which filled them the more with Jealousy, that he was defended against Justice by those Gentlemen of the Committee; one of them making it much of his business to countenance delinquents, and to whom drunkenness was no new thing. And the other at a drinking bout asked one then present if he looked like a Roundhead, The other being amazed at his question, was silent, But Mr Parratt proceeded with this Oath (God's Wounds), I am no Roundhead, never was, neither ever will be one—And further considering the Major lately sworn in the Governor's absence was a Captain against the Parliament, and now a bitter enemy familiar with the aforesaid Lingon and his family, and one who had great power with the City, and then the late acts of Delinquents and Cavaliers of their own party and strength, distinguishing them by White Ribbands^a at the fair, and their often giving forth that they doubted not but to have a Day or time for it again, And whether this was the intended time by all these circumstances as it was somewhat feared, Which being compared with the late strange insolencies of some Townsmen and Countrymen towards the Soldiery upon the last occasion The Officers, fully knowing the danger they were in, Concluded it was their Duty to endeavour the full discovery and the bottom of these Passages, and therefore thought good to send to speak with Mr Bromwich, from whom they hoped probably to receive some satisfaction, at least concerning these words he spoke, Whereupon a Captain from that Board was sent to him but instead of coming along with him, he burst forth in swearing against him, Asking him if he would drink with any man, and if he must drink any more he would drink. At last perceiving the Council of War had sent to speak with him and that the Captain was earnest to have him go along with him, Mr Bromwich spoke as if he himself had knowledge and had a hand in some Design against the Garrison, and that though they were prevented at this opportunity, yet there would come a time, wherein (saith he) We shall cool, and order you all. The Captain brought him to the Council of War, and informed these things of him upon Oath; Then Mr Bromwich was desired to come in, and the Governor standing up told him that he was intrusted by the Parliament for the

---

^a White inkle-strings were to be the badge of the Cavaliers in Yeomans's plot at Bristol, and in Waller's plot in London (Vicars, God in the Mount, 278, 357.) White ribbons were also worn by the Wiltshire Clubmen. (Sprigge, 55.)

preservation of that City and County for their service and that he was liable to give an account with his life for the miscarriage of either, and therefore that it concerned him to take Cognizance of all words and actions that tended thereto, Of which nature this day had produced many from him, and therefore the present Board desired to know of the Meaning and Reason of such words and actions. But he immediately told them he would make them no answer, but whatsoever he had done, he would answer it before the high Court of Parliament, Which all the Officers very readily assented unto—and said (with all our heart). Thereupon being to be dismissed, he took his leave of the Gentlemen of the Council of War, and going forth of the doors he turned himself suddenly to the Governor (then President of that Court) as if he had forgot some of his business, and came up close with a louder voice than before: spake to him: As for you, Sir, I shall answer you in any ground of England, Which words with the manner of their delivery gave occasion to debate the business anew, But in regard of the late Tumult (not knowing what this night would produce,) it was conceived best to adjourn their business till the next day to consider further of it, And every Officer in repairing to his Quarters should see all things to be in quietness and good order in the Town and Garrison. In the mean time as it follows in course to any that appeals, Mr Bromwich should go to his Chamber, and there stay until further order. The next day the Officers met together; consulted what way they could best convey Mr Bromwich to London, according to his appeal, and to draw up his Charge, which was to be grounded upon the breach of those articles which they were bound to keep inviolate, And one of those by him broken, as they humbly considered, was the 7th article: Which saith, That whosoever shall by words or Gesture affront or menace that Court shall die for the same. Which Crime of his with the rest of his Accusation they have humbly presented with him to the high Court of Parlam^t

Ex^r: Edward Winton.

[margin: 1646. October 6. [Report of the Hereford Committee.]]

The clumsy manner in which this affair is apparently communicated from the country committee to the Committee of Safety for the Two Kingdoms leaves this impression: that it was much easier to excite the alarm of the officers of the garrison than to quell the strong feeling amounting to hope that the Royalists still cherished in their favourite champion; that it required all the diligence and forbearance as well as energy of the governor to keep the mastery that he had gained. But let impartial justice plead for Birch. Baffled and defied, under the recent provocations of Lingen and the sudden revelations effected by inebriety, disclosing the secrets of the heart before his assembled council of war, he stood a memorable exemplification of the truth of that proverb which has received and

[margin: [Birch's discretion.]]

1646.
October 6.

[Bromwich arrested.]

[Birch's difficulty about Humphreys.]

shall retain the sanction of ages, " He that is slow to anger is better than the mighty, and he that ruleth his spirit than he that taketh a city."[a] Great as were the advantages that Birch had gained by courage over his enemies, by self-mastery he had obtained a victory over himself. If Roe, as his secretary, was present at this scene at the council board, he obtained a more striking practical proof of the actual superiority of his master than all the laudatory material with which his pages are garnished.

But whatever credit may be due to the wise forbearance of the governor upon this occasion, it is evident that insubordination such as that of Bromwich could not pass unnoticed; and it was so severely dealt with by the council of war, [that while his appeal to the Houses was allowed he was sent up prisoner to London as having incurred sentence of death. Being however a man of some position, and a cousin of Lord Scudamore's, he had friends in the county who resented the proceedings of Birch, and the affair became serious. It was taken up by Sir Robert Harley with much eagerness. In opposition to the version of the transaction which had been forwarded by the governor and officers, he presented a petition from the grand jury of the county, undertaking to prove the charge contained in it against Birch: a petition was also read from some of the Hereford committee, and the whole was referred to a select committee of the House, Bromwich being discharged by the Speaker upon his parole. The result remains as yet undiscovered, and the affair was probably compromised; but it must have occasioned Birch a good deal of trouble. But this was not all. About the same time, and perhaps forming part of these very complaints against the governor, the previous misconduct of one of his officers during the siege of Goodrich was brought before the House, and must have added to his many annoyances.]

No greater truth was ever uttered by human sagacity respecting the future than that already alluded to, which the defeated veteran, seated upon his drum, uttered in the field at Stow. The repeated

[a] Proverbs xvi. 32.

allusion to this may perhaps be excused, as it was constantly verified long after Birch had laid down his governorship, taken his seat, and attempted to go into comparative retirement. His next uneasiness came from his own party and his own agents. In those days it was the custom, as the only security at hand, to seek for a written protection, as the case might be, either from the Royalist or the opposite power. Thus the Royalist officer at Goodrich, while he had the command, would extend his protection in writing to a Parliamentarian, and the Parliamentarian to a Royalist.[a] These written productions were not always available, but were the best things under the circumstances that could be procured. They were a mere attempt at security; but it is quite evident that no security could be found against brute force; and therefore they frequently proved of little avail. One of these instances occurred in the case of Birch himself. A Major Humphreys in his own regiment, hard driven as they were for supplies during the siege of Goodrich Castle, laid his hands upon the property of one who had already compounded with the Parliament and believed himself to be secure. This person was no other than William Scudamore, Esquire, in the parish of Ballingham in the hundred of Wormelow near Ross. This gentleman had been a great sufferer in the Royal cause. His eldest son had been killed in a duel at Bristol by the notorious David Hyde, who had thus revenged himself, in furious and frenzied spite, on the mere name of Scudamore, for a quarrel which he had had with Sir Barnabas. Another had been accidentally shot at the siege of Hereford. A third, on the other hand, was spared to be of service to him by residence in the Parliament's quarters. Many heads of families, by this balance, while it increased the distress of such opposition, were enabled to save the wrecks of their property: and

1646.

[Protections.]

[Scudamores of Ballingham.]

---

[a] [One of these documents granted by Lord Hopton hangs in a frame in the Council Room of the Corporation at Bath. Three others signed by Fairfax, Cromwell, and Lingen are given in Appendix No. XXI. The proviso in one case, and the alleged reason in another, deserve especial remark in forming an estimate of the condition of the country under the victorious army.]

1646.

[Exactions of Humphreys.]

thus his youngest son, a man of great integrity, as will be seen, was living securely as a lawyer in London. It does not appear from which of the Parliamentarian commanders the protection was obtained; but the fact is certain that Major Humphreys, of the regiment of Colonel Birch, violated it. This immediately occasioned an outcry; and in the course of it a variety of particulars relating to the governor transpired. The evidence of this is found in certain original letters of James Scudamore, Esquire, of the Inner Temple, to his father at Ballingham. Extracts are here given from them in chronological order, which show the effect of this annoyance to Colonel Birch, extending from the siege of the castle to his introduction into Parliament [and for several months subsequently]:—

[Letters of Jas. Scudamore.]

27: Junij: 1646.

Deare ffather.

By my letter of the 22. of June sent to you by Mr Sansom, I acquainted you with my hopes to obtain a letter from Mr Pury of Gloucestr to Colonell Birch, but when I had prepared it, ready for his signing, hee putt it off, and was averse from writing at all in it. I did not much insist uppon, nor presse it to him, understanding that Colonell Birch had given an accompt of his disposing of the money, for the service of the Parliament, by his letter either to the comittee of both kingdomes, or to the Speaker of the howse of com'ons, which I am more certainly enquiring after, that a petition may thereuppon bee grounded, and the more likely to bee granted. I find by Mr Cholmeley that the contribution of the countrey is by assignement to the soldier who leavies it, and that the same comes not in to the hands of the com'ittee, soe that your money will bee more easily allowed to you out of other assessemts, wherein the com'ittee is to make the allowance, then where the soldier is to make it, and this will be more beneficiall to you then to have the same secured to you uppon publicke faith. I must now goe on in the way of petition to the howse of com'ons, in which Sr Robert Harley hath promised his assistance, and soe hath Mr Cholmeley. * * * *

18: Julij: 1646.

I have searched but cannot yet find that Colonell Birch hath given anny accompt of the disposall of the money for the service of the Parliament, either to the Committee of both Kingdoms or to the Speaker of the House of Commons; if that could bee obtained it would much expedite your businesse. If Sir R. H. hath urged this to the Committee of both Kingdoms further than the truth of the matter would beare, and mistaken the manner and circumstances of it (as I feare hee hath) it will putt many difficulties both uppon himselfe and mee, to hinder both his own desires and mine also. * * * *

[Letters of Jas. Scudamore.]

1: Aug: 1646.

* * * * The way of seeking your money was not by way of complaint, nor did the petition as it was altered, from that draught I formerly sent, complaine thereof, as anny thing rudely done by the governour. * * * I have seene a copy of the governour's letter in answer to one sent from the com'ittee of both kingdomes to him since the complaint about your businesse, and that of the Oxen; in that letter hee gives a positive accompt of the money disposed of for the parliament's service, the sum'e being about 200l, and that com'ing to his hands soe seasonably, when the contribution of the countrey did only reach to pay the soldier, hee should have thought himselfe worthy blame if hee had not disposed of it as hee did, which as his letter affirms was done with the privitie of the com'ittee of the county. Your freind expects the report from the com'ittee of both kingdomes to the howse, wherein hee gives mee hopes that you shall have your moneys; this report is to bee made by old Sr Henry Vane, and is every day hoped for. I doe wait uppon your freind once in foure or five daies abouts this, and hee hath wished I leave it to him, and hee will procure mee an order for the money. * * * * I every day expect an answer to my letter written to a freind about the protection. * * * * there is nothing in the governor's letter to the com'ittee of both kingdomes that reflects uppon you, more then the bare narrac'on of the matter, wherein hee hath dealt candidly with you. I have satisfied his secretary here in what manner the businesse was here carried, for the cleering of you, and my selfe, and you will have the opportunity to doe it to the governour your selfe, if it bee not already done.

29: Aug: 1646.

* * * There is yet noe report made touching Herefordshire, and your money, but wee have still hopes of something to bee done, and your freind Sr R: H: putts mee weekely in fresh hopes, * * *

24: Octob: 1646.

* * * Since my com'ing to London Sr R: H: told mee, hee would charge Coll: Birch in Parliamt with divers misdemeanors, & amongst others with detaining your money; yesterday hee putt in his charge into the com'ons howse, which was read and (together with the countrey's petition recommended by the justices at the last sessions to the members in parliamt for that county, to bee tenderd to the howse,) referred to a com'ittee, & coll: Birch to bee sent for to answer the same. Whether your money bee amongst the articles of his charge I know not, but shall this day enquire, and advertise you thereof by the next. I find noe way but this for you to come by your money, * * *

1646-7.

[Letters of Jas. Scudamore.]

14: Nov: 1646.

* * * I conceive uppon further consideration that you may have a trover and conversion against Major Humphreys, and the governour also, if the money came to his hands, and that you have proofe thereof, and that you make demand thereof from both of them ; I knowe by your former letters you did it to the governour, but if you declare against Major Humphreys, you must also make a demand of him. When I wrote you formerly my opinion in this case to the contrary, I had then my thoughts uppon an action of detinue, where the same thing in specie is to be recovered, which cannot bee of money, unlesse laid up in a box or purse, &c. * * * The comittee appointed to examine the charge against Collonell Birch have mett as yet but once; at this sitting the charge was read, and the orders of reference from the howse to the com'ittee, as also a letter from the Collonell and councell of war in justificac'on of the sentence against Mr Bromwich, shewing the necessitie of that severe sentence, and after debate had thereuppon, resolved, that the articles exhibited by S^r R: H: against the governour and the countrey's petition bee first taken into examinac'on, and afterward the businesse concerning Mr Bromwich. On tuesday come fortnight the governour is to appeare by himselfe, or some for him to answer the charge. At this sitting was read some deposic'ons taken at the councell of warr at Hereford against Mr Bromwich, whereby (if true) did appeare his intemperance, and rashnesse, and unadvised words, at the time when the difference happened, and when hee came before the councell of warr. * * *

19: Xber 1646.

* * * The businesse betwixt S^r R: H: Coll: B[romwich] & our governour goes on slowly, in respect of the late sitting of the howse of com'ons. * * *

Xber 26: 1646.

* * * The businesse concerning Collonell Bromwich hath preceeded the other articles against our governour, wch notwithstanding goe on but slowly, and is yet come to noe conclusion. * * *

Apr: 19: 1647.

* * * You will doe well to gett the proces I sent downe last weeke executed before the party goes into Ireland, & if hee gives an apperance then you may proceed though hee bee absent; there is noe touching the other defendant, hee is soe high above the reach of the ordinary courts of Justice, whilst hee is a judge in the most supreme. * * *

Maij: 31: 1647.

* * * I feare the ordinance of Indemnity, sent you by Mr Garston, will leave you without remedy for your money of Major Humphries, there being nothing done by anny imploied by the parliament, for wch hereafter they shall happen to bee

COLONEL JOHN BIRCH. 149

questioned, that they may not give in evidence was done for the service of parliament, 1647. and this you may remember was alleaged by the governour, to bee imploied at a time of great exigency, to further the reducing of Gotheridge castle, * * *

[Notwithstanding however the apprehensions of James Scudamore, [Triumph of we find that tardy justice was done, not as it appears through the the Committee.] representations of Harley, who had become so obnoxious to the army as to be forced, in consequence of their remonstrance, to abandon, on June 26, his seat in the House, but through the exertions of two parliamentary lawyers from Herefordshire residing in London, Walter Kyrle and Bennet Hoskyns. The close of the story comes out in a letter addressed to them by Miles Hill, an active partizan, who had, as appears from Appendix XX., in the preceding year been an intimate friend and confidential agent of Birch, but now had evidently been empowered by the country committee to transact business on the opposite side.

Gentlemen,
Yo' former kindnes done for the good of our poore Cownty I have and shall at my [Letter of returne giue Intimac'on of to our Comittee and the gent. of our Cownty. I am gon Miles Hill.] downe thyther this day from Winsor wth orders to remove the ffoote redgments and all souldiers what soever out of our Cownty into Wales, wth a Letter to Collonell * Humpfryes to make restituc'on for what money have bine receaud in Lewe of q^rter to those Inhabitance that itt was rec^d from. * * * hee [the General] have written to Collonell Humpfryes concerning the forbearinge of Collectinge of money out of our Cownty & to make the souldiers to be sivelized.

This letter bears date Dec. 3, which from internal evidence must have been in 1647 : and at that very time the unfortunate county had to pay an assessment of £60,000 per month, besides the exactions of the soldiery !]

[But while this untoward affair was in progress, Birch had other [Other transactions of and very important business in hand.] The interposition of Fairfax Birch.]

* [The reader will have observed that the former Major had at this time obtained the colonelcy of the regiment. Birch's command was not immediately annulled on his entering the House; for the self-denying ordinance had fallen into disuse; but its provisions were re-enacted on June 10, and in consequence Humphreys succeeded to the command of the regiment; as Moore had already taken that of the castle on March 26.]

1647. and Cromwell might, in the view of stamping out the war, have been thankfully received by the lovers of peace, for the hope of this was now revived. Happy had it been for them both if this had been the consummation of the nation's troubles, and the ashes of the fire had not been sprinkled with the blood of the first magistrate of the land. Such was the feeling (rightly founded or not) that occupied the joyous hearts of those who in after days brought back the throne and the Crown. But the population had passed through several stages since the dispute arose. In the alliteration of Hooker more solemnly employed, there had been folly, fury, and frenzy, the whole wrought up by man and steel—the soldier and his sword. This it was that called for immediate action, embittered the whole, and produced such alarming fruits, that, if they had not been suppressed, might have involved all the population in a double ruin. Like the legions in the days of Rome, distress among the swordsmen of Britain at this time threatened to overturn everything. [While the cases of Bromwich and Humphreys were pending, dissension between the Parliament and the army had been on the increase, and the grievances of the soldiery, though fomented by some of their leaders to serve the purposes of partizanship and ambition, had a real foundation in the financial difficulties of those to whom they looked for subsistence.] England had now become a scene of distraction. It could not be otherwise. The country had been exhausted in all its means. Not only had it suffered from the violence of those who were above the laws, but it was doomed to contribute to its tormentors, and to supply its best resources towards their maintenance. The best cause had for some time been the best pay; and this gives the true reason just now for the extinguishing of the quarrel. It was no longer a question as to the supremacy of victory. The King had given up the point, and commanded the whole of his adherents to lay down their arms. Then were those who had fought for him forced by necessity to seek a livelihood wherever it was to be had. Multitudes, inured to the habits of military life, when they found no maintenance for them in their former service, had for some time abandoned it out of necessity, to seek it among those whom they had been accustomed to treat as enemies. [But the Parliamentary forces were themselves at this time ill-supplied, and becoming insubordinate. The Houses were naturally anxious to terminate the existence of a power which they had no longer occasion to use, but which had grown into alarming importance, and began to overshadow their own supremacy, and to thwart their cherished designs.] The new model had changed the character of the Army that had been employed to gain the mastery, but had now become masters of the Houses in turn. It was attempted to be broken up and differently moulded. A portion was to be employed in a few garrisons that were to be continued, and the rest were to disband, except such as were destined for Ireland. That service was hard. They shrunk from it. Great numbers hesitated. First was the peril and misery of the enterprise, and when they had reconciled their reluctance to this, the next difficulty was in what way they were to be ultimately recompensed, or, if this could be provided for, by what means could they be supported till they were disbanded and sent to their homes?

There was a rhyming adage prevalent among these bands—

[Discontent of the Army.]

When pay-day comes, the soldier drinks, and sings;
There is no music without silver strings—

at once expressive of the absence of it, and of the mode in which the money was spent as soon as it came into their hands. This was a couplet made by some friend of their condition. But that day was so often retarded, owing to the necessities and difficulties of those to whom they were to look, that the music was frequently turned into secret discontent or open mutiny, in detachments in different parts of England, that threatened to be communicated to the whole body of armed men. They were always in arrears, either through difficulty in collecting money, or through rapacity of officers in misapplication of it: from either or both causes dissatisfaction arose; from dissatisfaction complaint; from complaint mutiny. This state

1647.
June.

of affairs was gradually increasing when Birch entered into the House of Commons [and the near prospect of service in Ireland greatly aggravated the bitterness of the feeling]. They were persuaded by Cromwell and Ireton that the Parliament intended to cheat them of their arrears, and to send them to be destroyed by the Irish. The army was enraged: disorders took place. [In the early part of June the Parliament made an effort to appease their dissatisfaction.] Birch, as the great accountant of the day, was chairman of one of the Committees [at Windsor, Goodwin presiding at the other], before whom all the reckonings of the army passed, and through whose hands the money flowed that was to appease this frenzy, while he would help to proclaim a general amnesty. Their arms would then drop from their grasp, and all, save a certain established number at home, and those that declared for Ireland, would be released from service.

[Birch's accounts passed.]

Amid the attempted satisfaction of a general settlement a trait is discoverable in the daily statements of what passed in that council where gold was tossed about by thousands, and each was zealous to claim his rightful share. On the 16th of June appear these entries in the Journals of the House of Lords:—

> Ordered, by the Lords and Commons assembled in Parliament, That Colonel *John Birch*, a Member of the House of Commons, shall have the Public Faith of the Kingdom of *England*, for the Sum of Four Thousand Nine Hundred Seven Pounds, Seven Shillings, and Four Pence; being approved of and allowed to him upon the Stating of his Accompt by the Committee of Accompts, in full of all Sums of Money and Demands now due unto him from the Parliament and Kingdom of *England*.
>
> Ordered, by the Lords and Commons assembled in Parliament, That Mr. *Francis Knight*, at the sign of *The Golden Lock*, in Cheapeside, London, Mercer, shall have the Public Faith of this Kingdom, for the sum of One Thousand and Fifty Pounds, lent by Colonel *John Birch*, now a Member of the House of Commons, and others, unto Colonel *Thomas Essex*, at *Bristoll*, the Fifteenth day of *December*, One Thousand Six Hundred and Forty Two; and likewise for the Interest due for the said Sum, from the Time of the Lending thereof, until the same shall be paid unto him.

[His great motive.]

So it is now apparent more than ever that the original views which occasionally break forth throughout the war were entertained during the whole of it,—that it was considered in the light of trade from beginning to end—of profit and loss. Birch's abilities from the first were confined to a sole object; the great leaning of his inclination in one word was "acquisitiveness." With that he set out as a merchant, and that he never lost sight of. Accordingly he permitted no opportunity to escape him. He had money embarked in trade at Bristol. His views and pursuits were changed by the troubles of his country; but, having once seen his point, he fairly made his way to it through his only resource, the dint of steel. He lent his money to the best security and some of the highest interest that could be obtained. He became a creditor at 8 per cent., the current and enormous interest offered by the State; and so he continued creditor to it while military manœuvres were necessary to support it. But this was not his only object. What had thus been gained must be if possible preserved. When once he had obtained the summit of his ambition, where we now see him, by a dexterous stroke of policy he took advantage of the moment, and availed himself of the purchase of episcopal land. The principal was thus secured upon the best ground that in the possessor's estimation the condition of the times would afford; safety, when property was changing hands, being in the opinion of Colonel Birch, a member of the House of Commons, best built upon ecclesiastical possessions. In this, according to the notions then entertained by him, he did not consider that he would be accused of injustice; though by another revolution of the wheel that notion came to be reversed. [The following extracts from the correspondence already quoted relate to the progress of this affair]:—

1646.

24: Octob: 1646.

I herewith send you the ordinances for abolishing Episcopacy, & vesting their lands in trustees to bee disposed as both houses shall appoint; there is now another ordinance drawne, and in passing that appoints a sale to bee made, assoone as 'tis published you shall have the ordinance sent to you : * * *

[Letters of Jas. Scudamore to his father.]

1649. 7: Apr: 1649

[Letters of Jas. Scudamore.]

* * * J desire your pardon for not giving you more particular satisfaction in the Coll:ª contract, then hitherto I have done, the reason was, that the Clarkes will not without order give anny copies, & all that I could carry away in memory, uppon search of the survey, I have heretofore acquainted you with, J shall search, & as much as I can certainly carry in my memory, J will, but I cannot bee suffered to carry away notes, & it will be hard to remember sum'es & multitude of other particulars, for your full satisfaction, so as to give you a good ground to make an offer thereupon to the colloncll. J find that the colloncll is engaged to another for his whole contract, & that it is not yet fully concluded, but assoone as it is, I shall have notice of it, & shall have the refusal of Shellwick mannor; the mannors for wch hee contracted are, Eaton BB:, Hampton, Tuppesley, Barton, & Shelwick, with the pallace of Heref: the scites of all these, & the demesnes hee had within his contract, except the demesnes of Shelwick, and the scite of Tuppesly, which the lessee thereof in possession, hath bought, the rents of the coppyholds in Shelwick, as hee saith, are 4.¹ p'. ann'. being copyholds of inheritance sibi et suis, paying heriotts, & the fines certified to bee uncertaine, but hee beleives the fines are certaine, & the surveiors therein mistaken.

The coll: asked mee, whether you had not some copyholds there of good value, I told him I knew not of anny; after Tuesday hee hath appointed mee to come to him, & then I shall heare Col. Birches answer touching your money, wherein Coll: Birch told him, that hee should doe anny thing with him, I find by him, that Coll: Birch is not his chapman for this contract of the bishops lands, but some one else, brought to him by a broker, to whom he com'itted the care of his businesse, & hee beleives, that Coll: Birch, having laid out much at Whitborne, & with the Earle of Monmouth, for howses here in London, hee hath noe more money yet ready for anny more purchases. * * *

[Birch purchases episcopal property.]

[By the following spring, however, the Colonel's finances were so recovered that on Feb. 22, 1649-50, he became the purchaser of the Palace ᵇ at Hereford, and the Bishop's manors of Shelwick, Barton, Tupsley, Bishop's Eaton, Bishop's Hampton, and Sugwas, for the sum of 2,475*l*. 12*s*. 5*d*.ᶜ The possessor already of Whit-

---

ª Colonel Edward Harley, as appears from another letter.

ᵇ [Birch had occupied the Palace on the capture of Hereford. According to Wood (Athen. Oxon. ii. 623) he purchased but one half, Capt. Silas Taylor having the other; and the governor subsequently divided it into two dwelling-houses. On taking up his residence there he permitted the beggars, no doubt numerous at that time, to occupy the rooms of the Vicars Choral in the adjoining "College."—Barksdale, Nympha Libethris, 60.]

ᶜ Rawlinson MSS. Bibl. Bodl.

bourne, a country residence attached to the see, which had been previously sold to other parties for 1,348*l.* 10*s.* 0*d.*, he thus established himself among the resident landowners of Herefordshire.ᵃ]

[His subsequent life.] 1649—50.

Colonel Birch has been traced to the highest summit to which he attained; but the natural curiosity of a succeeding generation may without censure be allowed to indulge a wish to be informed of the part that he took throughout in this elevation, and how he acquitted himself during the remainder of his life. That remainder was sufficiently occupied with storms of state. No common talent could have enabled him to have encountered the changes and perils of them all. Burnet insinuates that he was deficient in judgment. How far this may have obtained in higher political matters must be left to a better acquaintance with his character, and a deeper knowledge of what befel him than has occurred to the present writer. To him he appears to have been an able speculator, with a clear head, and as bold an actor in carrying out what he had decided upon ; and he seems to have succeeded in his projects, and steered his way through the obstacles that the nature of the times opposed to him, with as much worldly advantage as any of his contemporaries, and without running into the excesses and difficulties that operated to the disadvantage of many others. Some of these trammels indeed it seemed impossible for the most careful to avoid, but his skill in extricating himself from them appears to have been as eminent as the daring which at first led him into danger, and his presence of mind to have been always equal to the occasion. If he was shrewd in forming, he was honest and bold in expressing, his opinions. This will account for the risks that he ran, and the way in which he evaded them during the Protectorate, to which he was personally opposed, his passing unhurt through the crisis in which he was entangled by the defeat at Worcester,ᵇ and his bold demonstration

ᵃ Note 33.

ᵇ [His escape in this instance must have been a narrow one. From the original depositions (Composition Papers, Ser. 1, xcvii., 481 *et seqq.*) it might be thought that Birch and his brother Samuel, the Major, attended Charles II. at Worcester on in favour of King William on the progress of the latter to the abdicated throne; while his general bearing among the people in the parts in which he settled has been characterised by Berry, the major-general who watched over the district under Oliver's scrutinizing inquiries, and in the days of spies and informers. Two centuries have passed away, but the traces of these transactions, scattered among a multitude of authorities and references, have not been altogether lost. They are to a certain extent recoverable, though they resemble a chain that had been snapped at intervals, the links of which could not for a time be restored. A portion has already been given from original materials. To these may finally be added an abstract from a summary already in print.[a] It has been adverted to in the outset of this volume, but seems, so far as it goes, to be a fair and able exposition of the whole. The sketch of the late Thomas Heywood, Esquire, my literary acquaintance and fellow-labourer, has partly relieved me from some difficulties of reference, and the industry and research he has shown in the collection of a great variety of minute particulars, some of which are omitted as already noticed, are deserving of a place in the winding-up of this story.

[Heywood's summary of Birch's later life.]

"We need not follow Birch through the years 1646, 7, 8, opposed to Cromwell, acting, like Massey,[b] firmly with the Presbyterians.—Birch, after December 6, 1648, was sent into privacy. In the debate of February 10, 1672-3, he states that his firmness in supporting the King and the covenant had caused him twenty-one imprisonments. He, to a certain degree, assisted Charles the Second in 1651; they were seen riding together in Worcester the day before the battle,[c] and Birch alludes to this, when in the debate just referred to he says, 'I had never gone to the King at Worcester but with sincere intentions.' Burnet says, 'Colonel Birch was a man of

compulsion; but it was perhaps so arranged to save appearances. Unfortunately the papers are damaged by damp.]

[a] Diary of Rev. Henry Newcome, edited by Thomas Heywood, Esq., F.S.A. (Chetham Society.)

[b] [Massey, however, did not like him, as appears by a letter from him to Sir E. Hyde, March 16, 1659, in which, after speaking highly of the Harleys, he adds "only Mr. 909 is likely to prove a bad paymaster. I meane col. Birch, a vile man."—Thurloe, vii. 855.]

[c] [Thursday, Aug. 28. The battle was on Sept. 3.]

a peculiar character. He had been a carrier at first, and retained still, even to an affectation, the clownishness of his education. He got up in the progress of the war to be a colonel, and to be concerned in the Excise. And at the Restoration he was found to be so useful in managing the Excise, that he was put in a good post. He was the roughest and boldest speaker in the house, and talked in the language and phrases of a carrier, but with a beauty and eloquence that was always acceptable. I heard Coventry [a] say, he was the best speaker to carry a popular assembly before him that he had ever known. He spoke always with much life and heat. But judgment was not his talent.' Birch sat for Leominster 1646, and during the irregular duration of the Long Parliament, and in the years 1654 and 1658, he was returned for the same borough. For his proceedings as member we refer to Burton's Diary; they were sufficiently exasperating to the government. Rogers, the Governor of Hereford, writes to Cromwell, March 17, 1654 (Thurloe),[b] 'In pursuance of your last orders I have secured severall disaffected persons, and seazed many serviceable horses. Col. Birch coming hither now in the midle of the assizes (the city being very full of all sortes of people) gave out before the Judges, as they themselves told me, that the present insurrections (Salisbury & the rest) did not consist of cavaliers, but a company of silly quakers, with some other discontented persons. He also told me the same, & added further, that the greatest matter was our owne jealosies & feares. Considering this, and what we know of his carriadge when the Scots were in Worcester, & his behaviour of late, I feared such speeches were coales cast abroad to kindle divisions among the good people here, and to hinder their uniting against the comon enimy. I thought it my duty for the safety & peace of these partes, & agreeable to your former orders, to secure him; which I have done, and as his sword was taking from him (he refusing to deliver it) said, though my sword is short now, it may be long enough within a while (the sword hanging by his side being a little short sword) and very angrily asked me, whether I had orders to secure him. I answered, If I have not, you will question me. He replied, Yes, that I will. I said againe, I believe it. So we parted, and he is in custody. I have sent a party to possess his moated house (which I finde is very stronge with drawbridges, it is alsoe well provided) least at this tyme it might be surprized and manned against your highnesse, and be a great scourge to this country. I beseech your highness speedy order concerning this person & his house, whither I shall continue a guard there or make it untenable.' Birch —now was destined to remain in Hereford Gaol until November, 1655, when the Major-General, Berry, saw, and evidently liked him. 'I mett with,' writes Berry to Thurloe,[c] '(as a prisoner here) coll. Birch, who hath applied himselfe to me as to a little king,

---

[a] [Who called him, nevertheless, on one occasion, as Pepys (i. 465) tells us, "a false rogue."]

[b] [This and the subsequent letter, somewhat curtailed by Heywood, are here given as in the original.]

[c] State Papers, iv. 237.

that could redresse every grievance. I confesse upon examination of the busines, though there were some ground of jealousy, yet I cannot see any great reason he should now be kept in restraint. It is true the man is popular in these parts, and he loves to be soe. He is taken for a great wit, and guilty of some honesty, and upon that account able to doe hurt, if he have a mind to it; but he professeth desire of peace and settlement, and saith he is for the same things that we are, but could have beene glad to have them in another way; but seeing the time is not yet for it, nor we fit for it, he thinks we had better have it as it is, then make disturbance. And trully I thinke it were an easy matter to gaine him, if he be worth getting; but not to trouble you with my thoughts, I shall tell you of my actions. I have desired the governour (whose prisoner he is,) to give him liberty to be at his owne house upon his promise to appeare when he shal be called for; and because I heare my lord and the councill have been acquainted with his case, I told him I could doe noe more till I have received instructions from his highnes; which I intreate you to procure and send me.' (Hereford, Nov. 24, 1655.) To the parliament which met in 1656 Birch was returned member for Hereford and Leominster; but he never sate, and on being refused admission signed a protest with 80 others. For Birch's proceedings at the Restoration, Kennett's Register is the best authority. The convention parliament saw this colonel member for the last time, for Leominster. In the Long Parliament which followed, 1661-1678, he sate for Penrhyn, and purchasing in 1661, from Roger Vaughan of Moccas, Garnstone, and the Weobley property of the Tomkins' family, acquired by Vaughan by a marriage with Anne, daughter of Sir T. Tomkins of Monnington, Birch sate until his death for Weobley, with the exception of James II.'s Parliament, 1685, to which, owing to the part this colonel had taken in the Exclusion Bill, he did not probably seek to be returned. Birch was a brave and honest man, but he had the misfortune to speculate in church lands. In a debate, 1677-8, he observes, 'We have found that Dean and Chapter lands were sacred; they were restored. I had bought some, but now I have none.'—Birch said to Pepys, in 1667, 'Though I am in debt, yet I have a mind to one thing, and that is a Bishop's lease. I will yet choose such a lease before any other, because I know they cannot stand, and then it will fall into the King's hands, and I in possession shall have an advantage by it. I know they must fall, and they are now near it, taking all the ways they can to undo themselves, and showing us the way.'—In Kennett's Register and Baxter's Life we find both those divines, when rumour assigned to them the see of Hereford, waited on by Birch, who wished to secure the residence and estate at Whitborne, being episcopal property now about to revert to its ancient owner, and which he had for 12 years enjoyed.—The colonel was proud of his possessions, and says (Parl. Hist. iv. 756), 'I am acquainted in three or four Counties.'—His epitaph dwells on those qualities of courage and fidelity which he unquestionably possessed. We suspect they were tarnished with avarice, and he had great opportunities, being at the head of the Excise."

COLONEL JOHN BIRCH.

To sum up the whole. Bad days and good days for England had passed under his eyes. He outlived the former and closed his years in the latter. Liberty and property had been sacrificed on both sides in the interval; but royalty survived. While the walls of our churches still bear testimony to many who suffered for their loyalty in the contest, that of Weobley, where he died, exhibits the sentiments of his surviving friends:

1691.
[Birch's death.]

In Hope of Resurrection to Eternall Life
Here is Deposited the Body of
Coll' IOHN BIRCH
(Descended of a Worthy Family in Lancashire ª)
As the Dignities He arrived at in the Field, and the
Esteem Universally yeilded him in the SENAT-HOUSE
Exceeded the Attainments of most, so they were but the
Moderate and Iust Reward of his Courage, Conduct
Wisdom and Fidelity None who [k]new him denyed him yᵉ
Charatter of asserting & vindicating yᵉ Laws & Liberties of
his Country in War, and of promoting its Welfare and
Prosperity in Peace; He was borne yᵉ 7ᵗʰ of Sepʳ 1626
and died (a Member of yᵉ Honᵇˡᵉ House of Com'ons)
Being Burgess for Weobley)
May yᵉ 10ᵗʰ 1691

[His epitaph.]

Time, that in the subdued and solemn expression of Sir Walter Ralegh, on the night before his execution—

[Error as to his age.]

When we have wandered all our ways,
Shuts up the story of our days,

has so far shut up the story of this person, that, while the latter part of it has been inaccessible to the general reader, the seal of it, the inscription on his monument, as it at present offers itself to the spectator, is equally obscure. [For some unexplained reason, the date of birth is obviously wrong, as it would make him whom it commemorates far younger than is consistent with the well-

ª "The Herefordshire Visitation of 1683 describes John Birch, then living at Garnstone, near Weobley, as lord of the manors of Upper and Lower Ardwick and of Ordsall, in Lancashire, and as the son of Samuel Birch, of the family of Birch of Birch."—Heywood, 203.

1691. established events of his career. That so gross an error, in so circumstantial a form, should ever have been committed, or allowed to remain, may well be matter of surprise, but there it stands, and deprives us so far of any accurate idea of the number of his years.[a] But it is time to conclude.]

[Conclusion.] Apart from private feeling or prejudice respecting oppression or liberty, or what has on either part been assumed as the cause of these miseries, one consideration may claim a place. Among the teachings of history in this era may be seen that the efforts of Charles and Rupert, Essex and Waller, with their adherents and adjuncts, have written in letters of blood the danger of the two-handed sword. Thus, be it remembered, as good out of evil, has arisen in England the preference of civil to military power, unless in the employment of the latter by the magistrate against the rude interference of a foreign enemy. The lesson is most salutary, and never to be forgotten.

* Note 34.

[For additional illustration see Appendix, Nos. XXII. XXIII.]

NOTES.

1. "*Volunteers*," p. 38.—The origin of the volunteer system was not at Bristol. It was in the pleasant environs of the town of Shrewsbury that volunteers first came forward in favour of the King and Parliament, and they were immediately sanctioned by an ordinance of the two Houses. This seems to have been the earliest notice that was taken of them, although Messieurs Blakeway and Owen appear not to have met with it. The example was followed in several other places. In some they were suppressed by the Royalist authorities: in others they were established by Parliamentary influence: Bristol was one of these. At first there was only one company there; and, considering the population of the city, it is an intimation that a great part of them were Royalists. The captain of the first company was appointed by the celebrated Mr. Denzil Holles, who was Lieutenant of the county of Bristol; but it is uncertain whether the lot fell upon Birch. A second was afterwards appointed, as will appear.[1] The preamble of the ordinance in question, the first and basis of many others, is conceived in a mild and soothing style. "Whereas divers well-affected Persons, of the Town of *Shrewsbury*, in the county of *Salop*, have of themselves, as Volunteers, under the Leading of *Thomas Hunt*, Esquire, one of the Aldermen of the said Town, exercised themselves in the Use of their Arms, by peaceable Training and Marching in the Fields, near the said Town, the better to enable and prepare themselves for the Service and Defence of his Majesty and the Kingdom, when they shall be lawfully called thereunto;" then follows the approbation and the permissive authority of both Houses of Parliament. After this gentle exordium it might have been thought that, in the spirit of Birch's letters and the phrase of the ancient ballad, there

* * * "loyalty no harm meant."[2]

Yet these were the men that, with a multitude of others, their eager opponents, under various leaders (for the fault was not wholly on one side), like a vast cloud of locusts, arose to overspread large parts of this once peaceful land, carried terror wherever they appeared, slew, burned, and ravaged, destroyed for a time all law and order, and finally subverted the throne. Had not Europe long been inured to such scenes under such sacred names as were then assumed to sanction them, an impartial foreigner might have adopted the exclamation of the poet—

"Tantum relligio potuit suadere malorum!"

---

[1] C. J., July 18, Aug. 17, 1642, Clarendon, vi.   [2] The Vicar of Bray.

A writer of fiction, who lived at a time when he might have communed with many of those who had been carried away in this dark torrent of civil strife, and who has woven its principal events into a romantic story, has well observed, "Religion, rightly practised on both sides, would have made us better friends."[1]

2. "*Left their quarters,*" p. 48.—In the hurry and confusion of the time great eagerness was shewn by many in all ranks to return to their allegiance. Among the nobility the Earls of Holland and Bedford repaired to Oxford: among the middle class of proprietors great numbers packed up their goods and put them on board the vessels in the Thames.[2] Great was the depression through all the Parliament quarters, but especially in London, upon the defeat at Roundway Down, thus followed immediately by the loss of Bristol; and this lasted up till the period when the tide had turned by the relief of Gloucester.[3] Even at that point a violent and impassioned exhortation was produced, calling upon all, young and old, master and servant, to help in the great work of defending London. "Our pens have been too busy, and our swords too sloe. . . . . What is the matter, noble citizens, that your hearts are downe, doe you give the day for lost? doe you thinke England is lost because Bristol is lost? Alas! Bristoll is not all our strength, nor all our forts, nor all our garrisons; we have the better cause, the greater side, and the honester men; the passage to heaven is cleere for us, so that we can goe thither and fetch what we want, but 'tis shut to them. Our Parliament is standing, our forts are well managed; we have a pound for their shilling, twenty peeces of ordnance for their one. We have the seas to ourselves, and all honest Christians with us; and as for knaves and traytors going from us, lets never be sorry, for much better is their roome than their company . . . . strive to set yourselves in order, for order is the strength of an army, and of a city, but disorder is the confusion of both; take therefore away the causes of disorder; malignants are the onely cause of disorder in a city or army: strive therefore to find them out. Give them the covenant; if they refuse to enter into covenant with you, let them not live in the city with you, be they rich, be they poore, secure them and banish them: never dispute, this man is poore, and that man hath children—cast them out, spare none; unmercifull and bloody is that pitty that causeth the downfall of a city."[4]

3. "*Pious*" (*Waller*), p. 56.—Yet he had on former occasions allowed his men to revel unreproved—except by silence—in the sack of several magnificent cathedrals, the veneration of ages, and some of the best repositories and evidences of earlier

---

[1] Defoe, Military History, ii.

[2] We hear that the rebels of London are packing up their goods away for New England and other foreign parts; their own dissensions increasing daily amongst themselves.—Mr. Sec. Nicholas to M. of Ormonde; Carte's Ormonde, iii. 179.

[3] Sept. 5, 1643.

[4] "A strange and terrible sight," &c.—London, 1643.

art and story : a permission sadly expressive of compliance with party spirit, for which no defence can be offered, nor any extenuation be admitted but the extreme danger of personal resistance to the fanatical fury of an armed mob. As to resistance the probability must be admitted that he could not have attempted it if he would, and at the breaking out of hostilities it may be feared that his own disposition might not have prompted him to it if he could. His men[1] had no scruples; at Chichester they had disfigured the beautiful and spoiled the costly and valuable in the cathedral. While the sack was going on, Waller stood at least encouraging it by silence, sword in hand. In this posture he was accosted by a common trooper, with the permitted familiarity of the time, and asked why he stood there with his drawn sword. His answer is said to have been, For personal security. "If my colonel in the Low Countries were here," said the trooper, "and commanded in chief, he would hang up half a dozen of these soldiers for example's sake; it is not the custom of the Low Countries to plunder churches, for it is a mutual stipulation between the Spaniard and the Hollander, that what town soever should by conquest pass from the possession of one nation to the other, though the conqueror had the free plunder of the town, yet churches with their ornaments and whatever was conveyed into them should be inviolable, the Church being sanctuary to whatsoever was under its roof, and if they would have anything thence, it was to be purchased at a valuable price." The general listened patiently to the rebuke: the best reply for inconsistency is silence; but the work went on.[2] The followers of Essex had been guilty, at Worcester Cathedral, of the very filthiest of common indecencies, such as wants a name, before swords had been crossed in the first great battle.[3] The visitor of the noble Cathedral at Winchester will regret that, beautiful as it is, it should have been shorn of its ancient glories by the outrages of the forces under Waller and Hesilrige,[4] when the sepulchres of the early kings and honoured departed were violated and their remains trodden under foot. The truth is that the charm of the "storied windows, the pealing organ, and the choir," had not only ceased to produce the effects ascribed to them by the parliamentary poet himself, on English eyes and ears, but were deemed idol vestiges of ancient superstition, and held in actual detestation.

In the retrospect of his life not a word has escaped Waller regretting the permission of this misrule:[5] but he considers himself justly punished for allowing the

---

[1] Waller himself assisted in recruiting his fresh army (Weekly Intelligencer, July 31, 1643). He came to the Artillery Ground. His regiment of foot guards was then complete. Many listed for horsemen (Tuesday, Aug. 8). He went to Butchers' Hall near Newgate, and enlisted many butchers to serve under him (Merc. Civicus, Aug. 3 to 11). They beat up for recruits also among the watermen on the Thames. [This note properly belongs to p. 57; but was inadvertently omitted there.]

[2] Mercur. Rust. 223. [See Appendix II.]

[3] Carte's Original Letters, i. 15.   [4] Merc. Rust. 228, 12 Dec. 1642.

[5] [In his Vindication, however (p. 29), with singular inconsistency, not unmingled

plunder of Winchester by the ruin of his ancestral castle. If reverence for ecclesiastical antiquity entered not into his religious feelings, he was no stranger to such affections as may entitle him to the epithet here applied to him. His " Recollections," a small tract, will be frequently quoted from a copy of the original MS. It has been published at the end of the " Poems of Anna Matilda," 12mo. 1788, but has not met the eye of the editor in its printed form.

Those who are disposed to trace a parallel to these proceedings of iconoclasts may consult the glowing description of the defacement of the magnificent cathedral of Antwerp, and other ecclesiastical edifices, byth e Dutch Reformers in 1566. (Lothrop Motley, Rise of Dutch Republic, 2, vii.) The parallel is remarkable in its bloodless character: it had been more creditable to the English Reformers if they had proved as disinterested as their earlier examples of demolition and destruction. The armed mobs at Winchester and Chichester shewed their inferiority by the appropriation of plate and jewels, which the Dutch are said to have disdained. If what is related of the conduct of Sir Arthur Hesilrige at the latter cathedral be true, he was more than absurdly animated. It is reported to have been sullied by the abstraction of the Sacramental plate. (Mercur. Rust. 227.)

4. *Colonel Sir Andrew Potley*, p. 63.—A veteran who had served with great credit under Gustavus Adolphus, and is described by Monro as Lieutenant-Colonel of foot in 1632, and afterwards in 1637 as an " English cavalier of good worth."[1] After the battle of Lützen, where the King of Sweden was slain, he quitted the Swedish army: on taking his leave, the Chancellor Oxenstiern, by command of the Senate in council assembled, bade him formally farewell. With many handsome expressions, he put about his neck a rich gold chain with a medallion of the late King, to be worn in memory of him. He told him that, as an ancient servant of that crown, who had done them gallant service, they held him in the rank of their children; that the Senate had ordered two thousand dollars as an annual pension during his life, that he might eat of their bread; and two thousand more to bear his charges home. Such was the condition and reward of Potley; and yet he must be fighting again. He was in this year employed by the Parliament to correspond with Christina, Queen of Sweden. Whitelocke, when in 1653 he went as ambassador to that country, took him and a relation of the same name in his suite, and entertained him at his table. His name frequently occurs in the journal of that embassy; at the end of which he received another chain of gold, with a medal of the Queen. Occasionally he interpreted for the ambassador, who calls him his kinsman and old comrade; but hints at a fault in his being irregular at Divine service.[2]

perhaps with unavowed compunction, he inveighs sharply against the permitted abominations of the New Model, little more decorous than the followers of Essex already referred to.]

[1] Expedition, ii. 18.
[2] Whitelocke, Memorials, 69, and Swedish Embassy.

Monro relates an anecdote that shews him to have been as ready with a jest in the hour of battle as the Scot at Arundel, and, while in the Swedish service, as accustomed to swearing as Lieut.-Col. Layton. "Our souldiers being commanded under Major Potley to beate backe the enemy, going on service, there happened a merry accident to one of our country-men (then ensigne to my colonell's company) called James Lyle, being in sight of his Majestie; going downe a steepe hill, the enemy playing hard with cannon, the ensigne happened to fall forwards, the winde blowing off his periwigge, which tumbled downe the hill the Major sware a great oath; the poore cavalier's head was shot from him, and seeing him rise againe without his false head, sware the cannon had shot away the skinne, with the haire of his head being bald."[1]

5. "*Offered battle*," p. 66.—Waller, in the face of his late reverse, could lay no claim to uniform success, and the hand of Divine Providence therein. But Birch and Cromwell adopted a different language. They assumed too freely the interference of a Providence in crowning them and their followers with victory upon all occasions: though the latter certainly refers his success to his own training. The assertion of Roe may bring to the mind of the reader that vaunt of the Protector in one of his speeches to a Committee of Parliament upon the formation of his celebrated regiment. "Impute it to what you please, * * * from that day forward, I must say to you, they were never beaten." Some of the members whom he had been addressing might have recollected that once on a time Burgess the governor of Farringdon repulsed one of his attacks with loss.[2] Part of his men also were roughly handled by the Clubmen in August 1645.[3] This might be considered a trifle; but an unqualified assertion should have been based upon absolute truth. As to Birch, though it should be admitted that personally, and at the head of his company or column, he never suffered a defeat, he was at Cropredy Bridge, hereafter to be mentioned, at least mixed up with those who turned their backs upon the enemy.

6. *Lieutenant-Colonel Baines*, p. 67.—Lieutenant-Colonel Jeremy Baines, at this time only a captain of dragoons, was a person of some note among the citizen-warriors who took an early part in the fray: though his name is rarely found except in the Journals of Parliament. He was an earnest Presbyterian, and fought upon the principles of Essex and Waller, engaging in hostility only as the dangerous alternative of correcting the abuses of the state by the employment of the sword. The trade of a brewer seems to have been a profitable one in those days; for another wealthy individual of this class, a sufferer for the King, had been made prisoner when Farnham Castle was surprised.[4] The occupation was indeed exalted and brought into notice by him of whom the ballad affirms—

---

[1] Expedition, ii. 22.   [2] Carlyle, i. 226, 227; iii. 307.
[3] Sprigge, 80.
[4] Vicars, 223. Brecknocks—qu. Brecknock? Both of them resided on the Surrey side of the Thames. Brecknocks in Southwark; Baines in Horsleydown.

"A brewer may be a Parliament-man,
Which nobody can deny."

But both Cromwell and Baines combined it with the profession of arms. Baines kept both these objects in view at one time, and continued his military exertions, while he carried on his London business by means of one Manger Vavasour, his partner, when he was absent on service in the field. He had been with Essex at the siege of Reading, and afterwards joined the force of Waller, with whom he is shewn by letters to have been long a garrison-inmate at Farnham, and to have mixed actively with those whom the Royalists called the "disturbers of the West." Like Birch, he passed through the active campaigns of Waller, in the course of which he will be seen to have been made prisoner. At the setting up of the New Model, he laid down the sword, and refused the offer of a regiment among them. Subsequently, in 1647, he joined those who opposed the proceedings of the army on the question that the propositions of his Majesty were a sufficient ground for a treaty of peace. For this, with many others, he was expelled the House, and endured a long imprisonment, and ruin of his trade. Being a skilful surveyor, he was engaged by the trustees for the sale of the royal estates in England and Wales during the years 1649 and 1650. Once more he took up arms against Lambert, and materially lent his aid to the success of Monk in bringing about the Restoration.[1]

The intimacy and all but connection of this family with that of Cromwell are but little known. By his wife Catherine Otway he had several children: of his sons one, who appears to have been a minister, was in great favour with Henry Cromwell while he commanded in Ireland. This young man so ingratiated himself with one of the Viceroy's daughters, that Henry wrote on her behalf to Jeremy, making proposals of marriage, which the father from prudential motives declined. The letter, published in Thurloe's papers,[2] is distinguished by judgment and good sense. The other intercourse of the families of Baines and Cromwell is referable to a lower date. Rachel, the eldest daughter of Jeremy, became the wife of Mr. Thomas Pengelly, a London merchant of great respectability, by whom she had one son, Sir Thomas Pengelly, Baronet, Lord Chief Baron of the Exchequer in the reign of Queen Anne. When Richard Cromwell, the Protector, who had been about twenty years in exile, ventured to return to England, he sought a refuge under the roof of the merchant Pengelly. Here he long abode under the names of "Mr. Clark" and "the Gentleman;" for the most part in a house near the church at Cheshunt in Hertfordshire: beneath this retirement he passed the remainder of his unambitious days; and here at the good old age of 86 he died. The years of his banishment abroad, as well as those of his solitude at home, are buried in oblivion, uncared for or unknown; though the latter in particular were chequered with circumstances that might communicate an interest that as yet has not been taken in him. This is not a place to enter into a discussion of the merits or demerits of the two Protectors, of

---

[1] MSS. *penes me*. J. W.
[2] Lansdowne MSS. Cromwell Letters, i. 22, Brit. Mus.

their lives as of their deaths. While England continues as she is, there will ever be variety of opinion; but the character of Richard has been as severely dealt with as that of Oliver has been inordinately exalted. Richard, the darling of one of the fondest and so far towards him most culpable[1] of parents, was trained to frustrate the object of his own high ambition, and stamp upon the page of English story a rare example of the vanity of human wishes; for in him by neglect he laid the ground-work of his signal failure of a permanent Protectorate in his name. Here in the weakness of the father was originally founded what has by some been considered the triviality of the son. Their end was as strikingly contrasted as their course. In a private dwelling, attended by a very few individuals, among whom was Rachel Pengelly already mentioned, and in total abandonment of state, he breathed his last, whose father expired in the palace of a long line of kings, surrounded by a retinue and proportionate attendance, leaving a name and dread of him on most of the governments of the civilized world.

7. "*Spies*," p. 69.—In a review of these troubles the mention of spies and informers frequently obtrudes itself. In all, but especially in civil wars, they form no unimportant part of the system; and in this case were closely watched, and, as usual, severely punished;[2] for with the same language and habits of society, their facilities of operation were endless; and they were to be expected in every corner. Could the account of secret-service money on this score be inspected, no doubt it would be a serious one. In the court, the camp, and the senate, within and without the garrison-town, their influence was always at work, and few, as the sequel will show, were ultimately more indebted to it than Birch himself.

In the very opening of the quarrel, from the time the King left the metropolis, the eye of espionage was increasingly upon him, nearly in his most secluded hours; and when he removed to Oxford as to safer quarter, the same influence was secretly at work upon him. "A servant of my Lord Say's was taken suspiciously prying about the Court by the captain of the watch, and sent to Sir Jacob Astley, governor of the city, to be committed, if on examination he found reason for it."[3] Strict precautions were taken with regard to those who were to be admitted into familiar intercourse with his attendants; and a watch was ordered to be set upon the stairs that led to his privy and presence chambers.[4] The subtle intruder made a lodgement within the college gates, and gave notice to the enemy of the purposes and progress of the royal counsels.[5] Prince Rupert's secretary had given a remarkable instance of this species of infidelity. The Parliament allowed him at the rate of £200 per

---

[1] Men are often as culpable from the effects of misguided affection as from those of evil intentions.—J. W.

[2] [A spy, taken by the Parliament soldiers at Reading, was tortured into confession by "having lighted matches put to his fingers."—Whitelocke, 114.]

[3] Merc. Aul. Thursday, January 26, 1642.   [4] Walker, MSS. Harl. C. a. 117.

[5] Appendix IV.

month for his communications. This soon ceased with his execution. He was arrested and hanged after the battle of Edgehill.[1] The jealousy of the governors of garrisons was sensitive and alert as to the admission of strangers under any pretence. As to intelligencers, akin to spies, and alike useful and dangerous, they abounded, but were not always reliable; they often brought about mischief, and were sometimes as instrumental to success as to disaster. Through these, to go no further, Waller obtained the easy surrender of the castle of Arundel, though at a great crisis they gave rise to the King's unfortunate resolution to besiege Gloucester.[2] Two persons of this class were executed, the one at Worcester by the Earl of Essex, the other a female, by Scudamore, when the Scots were besieging Hereford.[3]

The private letters and note-books of Rupert, Luke, and Brereton supply frequent instances of the employment of spies. Their punishment on either side was certain death by hanging. Two at different periods perished thus in London; Kniveton, who was sent by the King to publish his commands,[4] and Baisley, who had betrayed many carriers to the enemy.[5] Their fate in general was looked upon with indifference and treated with levity as fair reprisal. In the caustic correspondence between Lord Digby and Major-General Brown, at Abingdon, the latter writes, " My Lord, you have hanged a spie (as you say) of mine, whom I know not, but you may be ballanced in this also; this very morning I will cause to be hanged one of yours, condemned by our councell of war six weeks since, according to an ordinance of Parliament, resolving never to be outdone by you, either in civility or justice."[6] Disguises of course were numerous. Luke arrested one dressed as a fiddler at Newport Pagnell,[7] and another was detected at Cardiff with despatches in his wooden leg.[8] The occupation of letter-carriers was attended with extreme difficulty, yet females exhibited great courage in the face of danger. Alone, over long and weary tracts, by perils of woods, bye-roads, and waters, they undertook arduous journeys, and many a despatch, now valuable as relating to an historical fact or correcting an historical error, has been thus stealthily conveyed in the hair of the head, the hollow staff, the shoe, or next the skin, and preserved to posterity. One was regularly employed in carrying them, quilted up in a truss of linen and tied next to her body,[9] between Raglan and Denbigh Castles; and another, " Scotch Nan," travelled for the same purpose between his Majesty and the Marquis of Montrose. A spy, who had been at York, reported at Newport Pagnell that " on the 31st of May (1644), order was given to all the sentinels near the Town to suffer no women or others to come out of the Town, but to examine them and send them in again. A woman that came to sell provision at the Town, being well horsed,

---

[1] Warburton, ii. 4, note 1.   [2] Rupert's Correspondence, i. 100.
[3] Sequestration Papers, Ser. 1, xcviii. 355.
[4] Nov. 27, 1643.—Rushworth. Hobbes sarcastically declines to offer his opinion as to the legality of this.—History, 133.   [5] Oct. 18, 1645. Perfect Occurrences.
[6] Merc. Brit. No. 67.   [7] June 1644. Notebook, Egerton MSS. 785, 27 b.
[8] Nov. 1645. Scottish Dove.   [9] Carte, MS. Letters, Bibl. Bodl. EE, f. 310.

rode full gallop into the City, and the guards shot at her but missed her."[1] As to letter-carriers, despatches have existed that were apparently marked by faithful resistance and had been bedabbled with blood.[2]

The success of the system, and the fidelity of the agents on the Royalist side, is remarkably depicted in the Memoirs of Dr. John Barwick, but the whole is too lengthy to be otherwise than pointed out here. [The following anecdotes are, however, too interesting to be omitted. During the siege of Latham House communication was kept up by means of a woman, who for several months risked her life in carrying despatches during the frequent sorties made by the besieged. She was at length taken and put to the torture, but she would reveal nothing, and suffered three fingers on both hands to be burnt off before her tormentors, tired out by her invincible fortitude, at length desisted. A dog was then trained to carry the despatches in his collar, and rendered eminent service for several months, till he was shot by a soldier, in mere wanton ill-temper, just as he had swum across the moat.—Lady of Latham, 109.]

Should any reader be inclined to pursue the matter further, two anecdotes may be found in print—the one of ludicrous and harmless failure, the other of extraordinary success. In both the spy escaped unhurt.[3] It was the misfortune of surgeons to be sometimes considered as spies, and they deserved it. Richard Lowther addresses Sir Thomas Fairfax from Pontefract Castle, March 9, 1644-5, "For your chirurgeon I cannot admit of him ; but if the medicaments be sent, I shall join my own surgeons with one of your party, a prisoner here, to use the best of their art in the cure of the poor wounded soldiers."[4]

8. *Death of Colonel Boles,* p. 70.—The singularity of this tragical relation consists in the entire omission of the name of the principal sufferer. It is to be regretted that in tracing the outline of such a murderous conflict it has not been once told after all what was most prominent in the group of the dead and dying. There is the bristle of arms—there are the slaughtered horses—not a single word as to the principal person, the author of that resistance, which lasted for so many hours, and ceased not the whole of the time till he was slain. Colonel Boles died, as Spencer, and Chesterfield, and other cavaliers died, refusing quarter from those whom he deemed rebels to his lawful sovereign.[5] There is however nothing in this inconsistent with the general tenour of the narrative, for it will be seen hereafter that Cromwell himself is not mentioned by name throughout the whole of the story.

The account given by Monro in his "Expedition " (i. 52) of the violation of a church by soldiers as a place of refuge exhibits a striking contrast in the treatment of a like subject by a superior mind : "Some men perhaps will blame our conduct

---

[1] Luke, MS. Notebook, 28 b.
[2] MS. Letter-book of Sir W. Brereton (Brit. Mus.) i. 306.
[3] Clarendon, vi.; Cary, Memorials, i. 351.   [4] Fairfax Correspondence, i. 185.
[5] Appendix V.

here" (at Aickilfourd in Holstein), "for pursuing men retired to a church, being a place of refuge * * * they treacherously retired themselves to a loft apart in the church, for their own safeties, and left traines of powder to blow us up at our entry, which made our compassion towards them the colder; for when the subject of our hatred is sinne, it cannot be too deepe; and, for my owne part, I refused not to shew compassion on those who did beg it of me, and what others did in their fury I did tolerate, not being powerfull to hinder them : yet truly my compassion was so much that when I saw the house ordained for God's service defiled with their bloud and ours, and the pavement of the church covered over with the dead bodies of men, truely my heart was moved unto the milde streames of pittie, and wept." This extraordinary writer, in spite of his defects, has wonderful passages of feeling and elevation.

9. "*Prisoners*," p. 71.—What increased the severity of the contest was the encumbrance of prisoners: It is evermore so in civil strife. If, in the apprehension of many, death was preferable in such a case, confinement did actually prove fatal to some.[1] Ill-usage, bad diet, and neglect in sickness were before their eyes. If all these were escaped, tedious hours must elapse before exchange could be negotiated. It is, perhaps, little considered what hardships were endured by the prisoners on either hand. The common receptacles were soon overstocked, and complaint arose on both sides; very early by the Parliamentarians of the sufferings of their friends at Oxford. The behaviour of Smith, the King's Provost Marshal, is loudly censured by Ludlow,[2] who was detained in the castle for a time. On the other hand, the confinement of the Royalists in the prisons of London in particular, and the stifling holds of the ships in the Thames, was attended with no less disastrous effects. And so it went on throughout the dispute: in the cities and garrison-towns the common prisons, besides barns and churches, were crowded to suffocation. The castle-dungeons of the ancient nobility, damp and neglected, once more called into use, were often the scenes of sufferings unknown. Bristol, York, Nottingham, Shrewsbury, Ludlow, and many strongholds in England and Wales, were employed as places of detention.[3] Smith, the provost marshal at Oxford, appears to have been eminently a coarse unfeeling gaoler, intent upon his own interests, and practising at head-quarters in a way that ought to have incurred the displeasure of his master. It may be hoped, as Baxter says liberally of Charles in other respects, that " it was kept from the knowledge of the King, and perhaps of many sober lords of his council, for few could come near them, and it is the fate of such not to believe evil of those that they think are for them, nor good of those that they think are against them."[4] The Oxford Parliament at length took up the matter, inquired into it,

---

[1] Ludlow, Memoirs, i. 57, *et alibi*.
[2] Memoirs, i. 108.
[3] Ludlow and Hutchinson, Memoirs: Drake, Eboracum: Lady B. Harley, Letters. See an article on this subject in Bibl. Glouc. cxliv.
[4] Life, 44.

and censured Smith. Sir Francis Ottley at Shrewsbury might well have demurred to the extent of Smith's authority, when, in a style of much impudence, he sent a deputy to that place to act for him, and receive his fees for such prisoners as might be committed there.[1] "As for their captives on both sides," says a writer, "they are many, and left misregarded."[2] Barwick's Royalist memoirs are replete with charges of unjust and severe detention. Against this, it must not be forgotten that the gentlemen were often upon parole, as those whom Waller took at Hereford. Instances of honourable surrender and of dishonourable escape were not infrequent. Exchanges were made as to rank: one to a considerable extent took place in the West, between Waller's Commissioners and the Royalists, during which they seem to have enjoyed a happy meeting over the general's wine: so much so that the country thought it was the precursor of peace.[3] As an instance of mercy prevailing over cruelty, the behaviour of Colonel Hutchinson and his wife towards their bleeding prisoners in the "Lion's Den" of Nottingham Castle, in spite of the revilings of their own preaching captain, Palmer, is above all vulgar praise.[4]

10. "*Pikes*," p. 73.—This picture of a body of soldiers marching to an assault shows the mixture of musketry with pikes adopted in the tactics of these wars. A stand of the latter was frequently of essential service in close encounter, and would resist a charge of cavalry. Their multiplicity of postures in the drill shews the attention that was given to this since abandoned arm: they consisted, according to Barriffe,[5] of no less than 50. The pike of the common soldier seems to have been of an unwieldy length: it is variously stated from 15 to 18 feet.[6] A military writer (1642) calls them "the onely body, strength, and bulwarke in the field." Instances of their effective employment are endless. They won the battle against Fairfax at Adderton Moor,[7] and were all but successful in the obstinate fight near Montgomery Castle, where the Royalist force was annihilated upon the mountain (Sept. 18, 1644). To these may be added the signal resistance of this arm against the cavaliers at Auldborn Chase (Sept. 18, 1643).[8] But the weapon in the hand of Birch in the lively description here given of him, is the half-pike, about 8 feet long. Monro is enthusiastic in praise of both these weapons, especially of the latter for an officer: "Thus much in briefe," he says, "for the use of the Pike, the most honourable of all

---

[1] Appendix VI.
[2] Lithgow, Somers Tracts, 502, 534.
[3] Bulstrode, 122.
[4] Memoirs, 4to. 159.
[5] Military Discipline, 3.
[6] Rainsford's Young Soldier, 8.
[7] Warwick, Memoirs, 257.
[8] [At the battle of Edge-hill, Whitelocke says, "the generals of both armies performed their parts with great courage and gallantry, leading on their forces with pikes in their hands, but were advised to change that posture, as fitter for a private soldier than for a general."]

weapons, and my choice; in day of battell, and leaping a storme or entering a breach with a light brest-plate and a good head-piece, being seconded with good fellowes, I would choose a good halfe-pike to enter with."[1] But when the employment of the pike is the subject of discussion, the singular achievement of Edward Stanley by that weapon, though at an earlier period and in a foreign land, should not be forgotten. During the brief campaign of the Earl of Leicester in the Low Countries, Stanley at the assault of a fort near Zutphen seized the head of a weapon of this class that was directed against him. A mortal struggle ensued, and while he and his antagonist were straining every effort to gain or retain it, by a happy presence of mind he suffered himself to be raised by it above the rampart. The act struck such terror into the Imperialists that they at once took to flight, and suffered him and his followers to carry all before them. The Earl knighted him and granted him a pension. The affair is circumstantially related by Strada, De bello Belgico, viii. 455. ed. 1648.

11. "*Gallant Scot*," p. 74.—The alteration of the word "Scot" to the expression "that gallant Scot" makes all the difference, and appropriates the sense to an individual of that nation, and not to an Englishman of the name. The assistance of Scotland was now the popular theme of confidence on the Parliament side. So far as the influence of the two Houses extended the English were under covenant to adopt the Presbyterian mode of Church government; in fact they were so reduced by adverse events that the taking of it became matter of security.[2] It was printed, published, and ordered to be taken Sept. 22, 1643; and the Scots were lending an army towards the support of it. Waller took it twice, while recruiting his army in London. His testimony to the nation and its soldiers may be given in his own words. The Presbyterian general thus expresses himself: "I love their constancy to their Covenant, their steadiness in their counsells, their gallantry in the field. Some of them I have had the honour to command, and braver men I am confident no man could command."[3]

A great number of individuals, old soldiers, officers, and privates, who had learned the art of war in foreign service, chiefly under Gustavus Adolphus, were mixed with the contending parties, where their presence was most acceptable, and some of them were in high commands. The approach of their regular army in aid of the Parliament[4] had been thus heralded to the public by one of their news-book writers in praise of their excellent qualities; a scornful hint to the Cavaliers of what they had to expect; as though it had never been known what their former presence had proved in England; giving them at the same time to understand more fully of what that force was composed and the improvements that they were to bring with them:—

---

[1] Expedition, ii. 192.
[2] Rapin, ii. 483.   [3] Vindication, 216.
[4] They crossed the *Bound-Rod* from Berwick, in detachments, Jan. 18, 19, 1643-4, almost knee-deep in snow.—Rushworth.

"The Scottish army hath a very able traine of artillerie, and many pretty engines for war, and devises for killing Cavaliers and Papists; the noble and able general Lisly (Lesley) hath contrived these, and many other excellent utinsells for War.

"They are setting out orders of discipline for the Army, which will be very strict and severe, for it is one of our best principles to keepe our souldiers at command; and I dare say a proud word, never was a better disciplined Army in the Christian world than ours. We have no dangerous mutinies, nor repinings, nor complaints, but an universall cheerfulnesse in our whole body. You will not believe how peacebly we marched with our Army when we came last into England, and how we kept them in order; never did Army make less spoile, commit less violence, fewer plunderings, unless he were a bad man indeede and a very enemy to the cause, and then we borrowed something of him till our returne.[1]

"Our Army is very hardy too, and can endure all heates and colds, and a small victailing will serve the turne; a little paste well kneaded in the palme of their hands is there usuall dyet, and they are not so tender as your English Cavaliers, who love ease, and eating, and carousing. They will find wee are too hard for them in our marchings; wee never scruple att winter nor bad weather, if the way will but fit for the carriage of ordnance we shall travail ourselves well enough; we can trott over the mountaines and forrests of snow when the Cavileers sett * * * over a fire."[2]

This self-produced testimonial, however coarse and vain-glorious it may appear, from causes that belong to the general history of the period, was doomed to humiliation. They gradually lost the favour of the party who had invited them, and against whom they ultimately turned their arms. Waller had very early learned the value of such men, from a proof that he had received at the siege of Portsmouth, in 1642, his first undertaking of importance.[3] They served to leaven, by discipline and experience, the materials of which his own forces were usually composed, and they were as

---

[1] [See, however, an amusing instance of pillage by a Scotch officer, in Fairfax Correspondence, ii. 14; a consciousness of some cases of this kind may have been the cause of the apologetic expressions in the vaunt. The following extract from Burnet (Own Time, i. 38) affords an interesting comment on the whole passage:—
"The Scots marched with a very sorry equipage; every soldier carried a week's provision of oatmeal, and they had a drove of cattel with them for their food. They had also an invention of guns of white iron, tinned and done about with leather, and chorded so that they could serve for two or three discharges. These were light, and were carried on horses. And when they came to Newburn the English army that defended the ford was surprised with a discharge of artillery. Some thought it magick; and all were put in such disorder that the whole army did run with so great precipitation that Sir Thomas Fairfax, who had a command in it, did not stick to own that till he passed the Tees his legs trembled under him."]

[2] The Scotch Intelligencer, Oct. 19 to 25, 1643.

[3] Vicars, God in the Mount, 158.

cheerfully brave in the danger of battle as they were resolute to meet the immediate approach of death. The Scot of our narrative may be classed as one of these. Their bearing and temper cannot be better described than by Symonds, a gentleman in the King's army, an actor and eye-witness of most that occurred. He is alluding to an event which took place several months after. "Friday, 18 October, 1644. His Majestie, &c. left Sarum and marched toward Andevor, Waller's forces being then in Andevor. Generall Goring raysed a forlorne of horse, consisting of about 200 gentlemen that were spare commanders of horse, beate them out of Andevor, took Carr a Scot colonel, and another captain, a Scott, that died, who a little before his death rose from under the table, saying he would not dye like a dog under a table, but sate downe upon a chayre, and ymediatly dyed of his wounds." [1]

12. "*Army-Surgeons,*" p. 75.—In the establishment of the Parliament's forces their allowance for attention to the sick and wounded has been thus stated. The Lord General had his own personal physician at 6*s.* 8*d.* per day; one for the army, do.; one apothecary at 10*s.* (?) per day; one surgeon at 4*s.* Each regiment of foot had its surgeon at 4*s.*, two mates each at 2*s.* 6*d.* The Horse Officers of the field had their surgeon with his two mates at the same rate. The Regiment of Cuirassiers had its surgeon and two mates on the same terms. Harquebusiers and Dragoons had their surgeon and two mates on the same. Besides these there was a surgeon to the train of Artillery at 4*s.* per day. In this list, which lays claim to accuracy, the surgeon's chest is charged at 15*l.*[2] It seems, however, upon the whole as though in the haste of enlistment the allowance of numbers could not always be filled up, as the want of surgeons was complained of after the battles of Alresford and Newbury II., that had been of a sanguinary description, when men of their profession were of course much in request. Barber-surgeons are mentioned among their forces. In those of the King each regiment had one to every company at one ration *per diem*: he was subordinate to the surgeon-major.[3] The King of Sweden, from whom most of the military arrangements of this period were adopted, appointed four regular surgeons to every regiment; but it is supposed that the Imperialists had none of this class till about the year 1718.[4] Many of the leaders in both branches of the profession improved their skill and experience in this time of

---

[1] Diary, Camden Soc. 141.—An anecdote of contempt of death, which in the mind of the reader, according as it is disposed, may be productive of admiration or awe.—J. W.

[2] Brief Instructions, &c. by J. B. London, 1661, relating chiefly to Cavalry, 17 *et seq.* They were regularly provided with instruments, medicaments, and military chests. A surgeon's chest at the beginning of hostilities was worth 25*l.*—C. J. May 17, 1642. [Many were taken in the retreat after the first battle of Newbury. Merc. Aul. Sept. 21, 1643.]

[3] MSS. Harl. 6804, 90.

[4] Harte, Hist. of Gustavus Adolphus, Essay, &c. xxxv. ed. 1807.

trouble. They shew it in their works. Wiseman treats of the cuts about the head and shoulders received by the infantry in charges of cavalry, and Sydenham of copious blood-letting adopted in fever, when he was in garrison at Dunstar Castle. They were ranged on opposite sides, but from the nature of their employment even when unattached to the swordsmen, few of them escaped persecution and confiscation. Harvey, Bates, and Wiseman for the King ; Sydenham and Mayerne for the Parliament, were all drifted into the current. The profession in general are distinguished in the public records by their exertions. They moved from place to place, wherever the calls of humanity were brought to bear upon them, through a country disturbed by armed men, with passes, but still in peril. Sir Theodore Mayerne and Sir Martin Lister were consulted by both parties, and received a pass to attend upon the Queen in her accouchement at Exeter. Two of the medical profession, the one in the field, the other in a stronghold, were instrumental in saving the lives of children committed to their charge. The artillery in the first great battle had nearly shed the blood of the celebrated discoverer of its circulation. Reclined upon the turf at Edgehill, and remote, as he thought, from its effects, while he was reading in fancied security, and two of the princes placed under his care were playing around him, he was aroused by the plunging of cannon-balls in the turf to make a timely escape from danger. Equally fortunate was Dr. Nathaniel Wright of Hereford in saving the lives of helpless wards entrusted to him. He was a practioner of some eminence, who, driven like Tombs the divine at Leominster from his home by the persecution of his Royalist adversaries, had sought refuge with his wife in the castle of Brampton Bryan. In that noble mansion, shut up without help or hope, was Lady Brilliana the wife of Sir Robert Harley, at that time (1643) one of the most active of the leaders in London, who, while amusing himself with destroying the most beautiful works of art, left the defence of his castle to his truly noble and pious lady. She shewed herself equal to the emergency, and with the help of Wright and some retainers endured a siege, at the end of which the heroic female sunk under her sorrows, and left her children to the care of Wright. A second attack ensued, which he as gallantly repulsed, obtaining honourable terms from an inveterate enemy. He is not unfit to be cited here, because he was afterwards connected for a time with Birch in the Committee of Sequestration for Herefordshire. He subsequently rose to eminence with the ruling powers, and attended the Protector, as his physician, into Scotland, by whom he was made a Baronet.[1]

In the comparison of the professions, secular and divine, it might be a question which of the two was most serviceable in the army, the surgeon or the preacher, the one who ministered to the evil passions, or he who made it his study to mitigate the fatal consequences of them. It is pleasing to see a ray of humanity breaking in from this quarter through the clouds that overcast the state of society. A reference to Appendix VII. will prove that the King's Troop of Show might console them-

---

[1] Letters of Lady Brilliana Harley (Camd. Soc.) *passim*.

selves that in the worst of their trials they were in the hands of one who with regard to humanity was no stranger to the feelings of a gentleman and a Christian. The King offered any of his surgeons to Hampden in his last extremity.[1] Justice has perhaps hardly been done by the writers on these troubles to those who were engaged in alleviating the miseries of them.

13. "*Birch got conveyed to London,*" p. 76.—Birch was certainly in the right when he preferred the practice of London to that of the country. It must ever have been a custom to do so.[2] His first surgeons had left him behind them. The Earl of Essex could not forbear indulging in a sarcasm by offering a recommendation of the same kind, as to its being the best place for Henrietta Maria. Whoever might have been Birch's favourite, Mayerne [whose real name was Turquet Mayerne] was at that time high in estimation with the public, and a consulting physician much in request. His advice was also often sought by letter. Baxter, who was always a great invalid, resorted to him more than once. He was variously employed apparently both in surgery and medicine, as appears by his "Adversaria," still existing, partly in MS. The names of Pym and Fairfax are both to be found among his patients; the latter consulted him in writing from York after the serious wound received by a shot from Helmsley Castle, and previous to his entering upon his last campaign. Tros Tyriusve, nothing came amiss to him; at different times he doctored the King's hounds at Kew, and prescribed for the Royal family.

The reader will perhaps not be displeased with a portrait of this Esculapius in his study. Sir Henry Slingsby will thus introduce him. Alluding to his wife, he says, "The physick I sent her down from London by ye Directions of Dr Myerne, of whom she had taken Physick ye year before: for his custom is to register in a book ye diseases & remedies of all his patients, if they be of difficulties, so y^t sending for his book he finds w^t he had done to her formerly, & thereupon prescribes ye same; usually I went in a morning for his advise, about 7 of ye clock, where I us'd to find him set in his study, wch was a large roome furnish'd wth books & Pictures, and as one of ye cheifest he had ye picture of ye head of Hyppocrates y^t great physitian; & upon his table he had ye proportion of a man in wax, to set forth ye ordure & composure of every part; before his table he had a frame wth shelves, wheron he set some books; & behind this he sat to receive those y^t came for his advise, for he seldom went to any, for he was corpulent, & unweildy; & y^n again he was rich, & ye King's phycitian, & a Knight, wch made him more costly to deal wth all."[3]

14. *Sir Richard Brown*, p. 80.—A citizen of London of great repute and influence, a zealous Parliamentarian in the outset, but ending as zealously on the opposite side. He has hence experienced praise and dispraise from both. It might,

[1] Warwick, Memoirs, 241.
[2] Instances of persons being conveyed from the battle of Edge-hill to a London Hospital occur in the Diary of a Surgeon. Ellis, Original Letters, Series 2, iii. 305.
[3] Diary, 69.

however, be thought fortunate for him that his services reached down to the Restoration, to which he as heartily contributed as formerly he had offered resistance to his sovereign. In the sarcastic language of the times he is called by Warwick and Symonds the Wood-, *alias* the Faggot-monger. By his soldierly exertions he proved himself to be one who, like Birch, could change from the counting-house to the field of battle.[1] He came to the aid of Waller from the troubles in Kent, and was commander of the London force. He had then the rank of Serjeant-Major-General. During that summer he occupied Abingdon with 4,200 men. There Birch must afterwards have found him, for he was governor of that place till the war was over, and distinguished himself for awhile by such severities of martial execution before trial that, like Lydford, the unjust custom of the town obtained the stigma of "Abingdon law." In this government, however, he exposed the attempt of Lord Digby to bribe him, and obtained credit with his friends for an act of honour, yet, for plain reasons hereafter to be seen, it had ceased to become a temptation. When the war was over, his real temptation arose. Appointed as one of the commissioners to attend upon the King in his temporary confinement at Holmby, Brown was so undeceived by the amiable traits of character that were then visible in Charles, the familiar intercourse with him on the greensward at bowls, the sight of his studies and devotion—a striking contrast to what he had once believed—that he became not only convinced but converted. Royalty appeared divested of the charges that he had been wont to entertain against it, and he did all that he could to wipe out what he found to be his errors, and tried not only to mitigate but to avert the dangers that were threatening his Majesty during the hour of his adversity, though all his endeavours were in vain. Brown of course has not been pardoned for this by the stern severity and illnatured hints of Ludlow, who by some may be thought to bear hard upon him. Ludlow, however, was not to be trusted on such a point. The affection with which he was spoken of in the gentler touches of Clarendon and Heath has secured his latter reputation as a Royalist. There is, however, no doubt of the sincerity of Brown, from the sufferings that he endured at the hands of the ruling party in the House of Commons. In his passing over to the other side he was as remarkable for his zeal as for the earnestness with which he had supported the Parliamentarian cause: and his conduct must be remitted to the impartial decision of posterity. He attained the degree of a Baronet at the Restoration.

16. *Sir Matthew Appleyard*, p. 80.—Sir Matthew Appleyard, of Dillingham, Cumberland; a brave Cavalier, whose name is of great repute in the annals of this war. In the army of 1640, and in the 12th regiment, he appears as Serjeant-Major under Sir Charles Vavasour. A long period then elapses[2] till the year 1644, in this battle of Alresford, though he could not but have attracted notice from

---

[1] He had been at Winchester and Chichester in 1642.
[2] [He served in Ireland with Mynne.--Carte's Ormonde.]

his courage wherever he appeared. His regiment were called "yellow-coats." Clarendon terms him a soldier of known courage and experience. He was with the King at Cropredy Bridge and at Essex's surrender. He was one of the first to enter the breach at Leicester, where he received the highest class of knighthood upon the spot (that of knight-banneret), and was made lieutenant governor. His time of occupation there was short, and Sir Matthew is to be searched for again. He is found raising levies in Radnorshire, and afterwards drilling them in Bristol, where, as in Bath, he had formerly lain disabled and in debt. Our account of him closes with the narrative that he signed in vindication of Prince Rupert after the surrender of that city. Having thus done all that he could for his general, we lose sight of him. (Lloyd: Clarendon: Rushworth: Walker: Symonds: MSS. Harl.)

16. "*Blasphemer*," p. 80.— The colloquial employment of oaths, with which the Parliament had as a body branded the Cavaliers, would lead to an inquiry as to its origin, too extensive and remote for discussion in this place. Taking some account of the case as it now stood with respect to British soldiery, previously on foot or recently called into existence, the veterans as a class, wherever they cast in their lot, would be found to be contaminated with the hereditary vice of combining the terrors of imprecation with those of the sword. Military orders on either side were against it. The punishment theoretically was most severe.[1] Their divines assisted the chiefs in denouncing it. The King in person protested against it.[2] But those who had entered the ranks of the Parliament had been sitting under popular Presbyterian teachers, who had been more successful in suppressing the habit and exciting an *esprit de corps* that cast it in the teeth of the Cavaliers. These on the other hand seem to have persevered in it obstinately out of bravado and malicious spite. Baxter charges it upon both armies.[3] The news-books and minor or ephemeral literature of the London press did all in their power to expose it. It even disturbs the gravity of higher productions, the Report of the Court Martial of Fiennes,[4] and the studied dignity of the campaign of Fairfax and Cromwell in the West.[5] Roe expresses his abhorrence of it in another instance in better taste, but coincides in the fact that in general his party gloried in abstaining from it as a distinctive mark. Some still retained it to the annoyance of their graver comrades. After all the industry that Waller had shown in the selection of officers, here has one been introduced who is looked upon by the rest as a disgrace and

---

[1] More severe than could be put in practice—boring the tongue through with a red-hot iron. [Yet it is said to have been resorted to, with other measures of the like severity, in the Parliament's army.—Perf. Occurr. Jan. 13, 1645-6.]

[2] His Majesties Declaration, &c. to all his soldiers, in the head of his army at Southam, Oct. 21, 1642. London: printed for Wm. Gay, 6.

[3] Life, 47.   [4] Hargreave, *ut supra*.

[5] Sprigge, Anglia Rediviva, 126.

prejudice to the cause, whose bad example was likely to be fatal to those with whom he acted, and who consequently failed, as is left to be concluded in the present instance. In Cromwell's "lovely company,"[1] about this time forming, he took steps to eradicate the reproach, and the offenders paid the mitigated fine of twelvepence per diem.[2] The same apprehension of its prejudicial consequences was entertained in the army of the Lord General Essex, prior to the battle of Edge-hill. Some of the subalterns in a regiment commanded by an officer obnoxious to them upon that account, were quite in an agony till they got the difficulty removed. "Wee want nothinge but a good leiftenant-colonell," says Nehemiah Wharton, writing to his master in London; "I humbly intreate you, as you desire the successe of our just and honorable cause, that you would indeavor to roote out our Leiftenant Colonell; for, if we march further under his commaund, we feare, upon suffitient grounds, wee are all but dead men. * * Touchinge Leiftenant Colonell Biddeman formentioned, I once more humbly beseech you—and not I alone, but many others, both commaunders, officers, and common souldiers—that you would endeavor to rout him."[3] In a few days after they broke out into actual mutiny, and the colonel was cashiered. The same Nehemiah Wharton represents that even the children in Hereford were familiarised to the use of oaths. The general custom had been repressed by the statute of James I. and twelve pence made the penalty of adults: but children and other offenders, of whom it could not be levied, were to be whipped or set three hours in the stocks. This statute had been revived on June 13, 1643, and was again referred to by proclamation at Oxford, April 18, 1644[4]—a singular coincidence with the period to which Roe refers. The proclamations are a testimony to the prevalence of the vice in all conditions of society. Were any other proof wanted, it is to be apprehended that the rarely expressed exception to this scandal sufficiently establishes the rule. It has been said of Sir John Digby, who was subsequently shot at Langport, and died in the flower of his age, that besides his many accomplishments in learning, his courage and conduct in military affairs, he was hardly ever heard to swear, or observed to give way to anger.[5] If this be true he must have appeared to great advantage in Goring's army, whose officers and soldiers were proverbial for their blasphemies and excesses. The behaviour of two Cavalier officers in this respect is feelingly contrasted by Corbet, the chaplain of Massey the governor of Gloucester. In an expedition in May, 1644, that Colonel defeated a party of Royalists at Little Dean, in the Forest of Dean, where Captain Wigmore and Lieutenant-Colonel Congreve took refuge in a house. They were closely pursued to the same room, and put to the sword. Wigmore retorted upon every fatal thrust with a curse. The last words of dying Congreve were a prayer.[6]

---

[1] Carlyle, i. 192.
[2] Cromwelliana, 5.
[3] Archæologia, xxxv. 313 *et seqq.*
[4] Rushworth, 3, ii. 666.
[5] Baker's Chronicle, 498.
[6] Corbet, Milit. Government, lxxxvi.

17. "*Hesilrige's timidity*," p. 80.—Sir Arthur Hesilrige is again brought forward in no very favourable light. Prince Rupert had defeated Sir John Meldrum at Newark (Nov. 21), raised the siege, and occasioned such terror in those parts that several places had surrendered. The news has produced the like effect in the camp of Waller. The text gives us to understand that, of all those in command, Birch was the only one who, seeing the manner in which others were affected, expressed his confidence and acted upon it. "Man's extremity is God's opportunity" was a favourite adage among divines and civilians as well as soldiers.[1] The Scots employed it as a truth applicable to the most serious difficulties, and Waller himself was in the habit of cherishing it, for, in mentioning his escape at Farnham, he says, "In that extremity the Lord tooke opportunity to shew himself for me" (see p. 66). Hesilrige, if only a part of what is said of him be true, was highly in need of such a consolation. By his own admission to Holles, he had little pretensions to soldier-like bearing at Edgehill; and what is here said by no means exempts him from the imputation of cowardice, when on the sight of the rout at Cheriton-wood, he calls out to Birch, "Now, Colonel, have you fighting enough?" This is clearly the language, not of a confident, but of a dispirited man. Holles tells us that he stood crying under a hedge, "Ah, woe is me, all is lost, we are all undone!" and that a great Scotch officer (Balfour?) reproved him severely for it, bade him leave the field, and not stand "gudding" (crying) there to dishearten the soldiers.[2] The sarcastic tone of Holles can no longer be set down to mere malice; nor is it too much to suppose that he could not have continued in public estimation to occupy the part of the Achates of Waller. It was a wise measure to have called in the assistance of Sir William Balfour, an excellent leader, who was lent from the army of Essex, and had the command of the cavalry on that eventful day.

The accounts of the behaviour of that body are so much at variance, that it is difficult to reconcile them. According to the noble historian, the reappearance of the Cuirassiers[3] dismayed the Royal Horse: "Sir Arthur Hesilrige's regiment of Cuirassiers, called the Lobsters, were so formidable, that the King's naked and unarmed troops, among which few were better armed than with swords, could not bear their impression:"[4] after sustaining one charge, they wheeled off, stood at a distance,

---

[1] Introduction to the late Petition to the King, Jan. 10, 1642. Parl. Hist. xii. 19.—England's Third Alarm to War, 1643.

[2] Holles, Memoirs, 27.

[3] There were horse cuirassiers in the service of the Belgic States before 1625, as well as harquebusiers on horseback. [It appears from Sir E. Walker's Papers that the King attempted to oppose the Parliament with a similar force. On May 2, 1644, a troop of 100 cuirassiers was ordered to be raised for Col. Blagge: they are not, however, subsequently mentioned. (MSS. Harl. 6,802, 126.) In 1642 William Legge had been captain of a troop of cuirassiers in Prince Rupert's regiment.—Collins's Peerage, ii. 644.]

[4] Clarendon, viii. [Hopton had complained in the previous September of the

and never could be brought up again. If they had time to recover, they were discouraged. The officers were not deficient in bravery, and Lord John Stuart lost his life there. An instructor in the art of military horsemanship shows that they did precisely what they ought not to have done: "there is no wheeling off," says the writer, "but with an utter ruin."[1]

18. "*Charging without my head-piece,*" p. 81.—There may have been a reason why the general showed himself so unnecessarily fearless. A jealousy had sprung up between the Lord General and Waller that became very injurious to both their armies. Waller thought that Essex was near enough to Oxford to have made such a diversion in his favour as might have checked the expedition against him at Roundway Down. Essex reproached him with unsoldierly neglect and want of courage there in suffering himself to be beaten by a handful of men, and to have deserted his foot and cannon without engaging his own person in one charge against the enemy.[2] He could not have chosen a better time to give a personal denial to the imputation. But they were of entirely different temperaments, and could never thoroughly agree to the last. Their connexion was broken up by the dissolution of the Presbyterian interest after the disgrace of the Lord General in Cornwall.

19. *Hopton's retreat*, p. 83.—Hopton and Forth retired that night for shelter to Basing House; the former having discharged the duty of his command by securing the retreat of his guns and ammunition and carriages, through a lane, in safety. He could not, however, protect his lady so entirely as to conceal her flight from active pursuit. Other instances occur of ladies of superior officers who attended their husbands in the hardships and perils of campaigning, and awaited the event at a safe distance, till the battle was over, following the line of victory, as the case might be, or flying from the defeat. This was strikingly proved at Naseby, in which so many of the females of the Court were captured, and many, as alleged, were slain. Either at Andover or Romsey, Sir William Balfour learned that Lady Hopton had slipped away from the confusion in the direction of Newbury; he despatched a party after her; they overtook her, capturing several coaches, and made prisoners an escort of 200 attendants. In the spirit of a courtesy akin to that of the best days of chivalry, she was treated with the respect due to her rank, released, and conveyed to Oxford. No robbery was allowed of plate or jewels belonging to herself or those that were captured with her: the residue alone was reserved as a prize.[3] The success that attended upon this incident probably stimulated Birch afterwards to attempt a similar pursuit. Monro rebukes the ambition of officers in the employ-

---

unarmed condition of his horse; and in December of their decrease.—Warburton's Rupert, ii. 291, 333.]

[1] Some Brief Instructions, &c. by J. B.: London, 1661.
[2] Clarendon, viii.
[3] Rushworth, 3, ii. 655.

ment of coaches, as matter of luxury or state. The conduct of the Earl of Newcastle by employment of his carriage after the battle of Adderton Moor in conveying Lady Fairfax, taken prisoner in the retreat, was an earlier example that might have challenged imitation. " Not many days after," are Fairfax's own words, " the Earl of Newcastle sent my wife back again in his coach, with some horse to guard her; which generous act of his gained him more reputation than he could have got by detaining a lady prisoner upon such terms." [1]

20. *" Hesilrige—never affected the foot-service,"* p. 90.—That Sir Arthur could never do anything as Colonel of the foot is evident from his delegating the command of his regiment to another; and though he " delighted all in horse," if we are to believe what Holles has told us of him [2] and is confirmed by others, it will lead to more than a suspicion that he might delight, but could do little more than delight, in horse. The predilection of Hesilrige for this arm of the service, and his preference of the horse individually, as an animal useful in war, may have been based upon the circumstance of his having been a country gentleman, fond of good stock and careful of it,[3] one who understood the value of horses, and was fond of bargaining for them in the market.[4] Here he was of great service in purchasing them for the levies. He " delighted all in horse," for he soon perceived the superiority of horse on the part of the Cavaliers, and was the author of that singular ordinance [5] by which he is seen to have persuaded the Houses to take up the subject more earnestly: ultimately, it was the cause of their establishing a superiority that helped to decide the war. Again he " delighted all in horse," for he loved the splendour and state of the complete cuirassier, which rivalled the Lord General's life-guard. He " delighted all in horse;" but it may be added, without undue severity, that he delighted not in fighting; at least to this effect was the testimony of his intimates.[6] Thus, though he was colonel of a gallant regiment, and from heat of temper always embroiled in private quarrels, he had no reason to delight in it after his rebuff at Roundway Down. Hence he was suspended at Alresford, is undistinguished at Cropredy, and though he is included among the commanders at the second battle of Newbury, was one of those who, with Manchester, gave their vote against fighting.[7]

---

[1] Memorials, 12mo. 1699, 58. [Those who are acquainted with the party-vehemence of Vicars will not wonder that he has been guilty of a gross misrepresentation here.]
[2] Memoirs, p. 11.   [3] Holles, Memoirs, 139.
[4] Ludlow, Memoirs, i. 112.
[5] Scobell, 40, April 25, 1643.
[6] Holles, Memoirs, 27, 136.
[7] Rushworth, 3, ii. 735.—His experience in that branch of service was brought into play long after, and his employment at a season of great difficulty and apprehension ensuing the death of Charles I. will be seen by the following order:—" The Councell taking into consideration the great waste and spoyle that hath been made

As to the complete cuirass, in active service it was disadvantageous for many reasons; and it may be a question whether Cromwell's soldiers, commonly called Ironsides and Lobsters, were so entirely locked up in armour as those of Hesilrige had been. Many were the inconveniences of panoply, besides the hindrances they were subject to in putting it on when a horse-quarter was beaten up in darkness: its weight in winter and heat in summer to horse and foot; to the former the danger of overthrow and difficulty of remounting. Ludlow was compelled, after he had left or lost his saddle, to walk up and down the whole of the night ensuing the battle of Edgehill to keep himself warm:[1] and Monro's own amusing confession is a feeling proof of the misery that he endured, and served him as a lesson for the time to come. Writing of military punishments he says, " I was once made to stand in my younger yeares at the *Louver gate* in *Paris*, being then in the King's Regiment of the Guards, passing my prentiship, for sleeping in the morning, when I ought to have beene at my excercise : for punishment I was made stand from eleven before noone to eight of the Clocke in the night Centry, Armed with Corslet, Head-piece, Bracelets, being Iron to the teeth, in a hot Summer's day, till I was weary of my life, which ever after made me the more strict [cautious] in punishing those under my Command."[2]

To be thus over-armed would, in some sense, be for a horseman to be disarmed. In Italy, in some of the almost bloodless encounters of the middle ages, a battle was sometimes won by cutting the girths of the cavalry and bringing the horsemen to the ground. On the return of Charles VIII. of France from his expedition to Naples, the heavy-armed Italians at the battle of Fornova suffered from this cause. They were lancers in panoply, and were unhorsed. Their situation would have been ludicrous, had it not been fatal for them. They had been encumbered with their staves, and when once upset fell into the hands of the camp-followers, who showed them no mercy. " We had a great number of straglers and seruants following vs, all the which flocked about the Italian men of armes being ouerthrowen, and slue the most of them. For the greatest part of the said straglers had their hatchets in their hands, wherewith they vsed to cut wood to make our lodgings, with the which hatchets they brake the visards of their head peeces, and then claue their heads, for otherwise they could hardly haue beene slaine, they were so surely armed ; so that there were euer three or fower about one of them."[3]

---

of horses in England during the late troubles, and the great want there is like to be of them for the future for publique service in England and Ireland, have thought fit that all care be taken for preventing the inconvenience that may come thereby, doe hereby order that it be recommended to Sir Arthur Heselreige to take speciall care to prevent the carrying of horses out of England by the northern parts."—Council of State Order Books, Feb. 24, 1648, i. 17.—J. W.

[1] Memoirs, i. 50.
[2] Expedition, i. 45.
[3] Historie of Philip de Commines, translated by Danett, 332.

21. "*Challenge by night or day,*" p. 95.—The most remarkable and earliest instance of this challenge, with the reply, that has occurred to the annotator, is given in the Letters from a Subaltern. (Archæologia, xxxv. 329.) In the skirmish at Powick, " Colonell Sands beinge in the front, the Prince asked him whom he was for; he answered, 'For Kinge and Parliament.' He replyed, 'Not for the Kinge alone ?' He answered, 'No.' Then said the Prince, 'For the King have at you.' The Colonell answered, 'For the Parliament have at you.' And so they discharged each at other." This is well known to have been the practice upon the highway. When the parties were armed it was followed by an encounter; sometimes a defenceless person was the victim. A trooper of Massey's, in an inroad into Herefordshire in April 1644, shot Pralph, the very aged Vicar of Tarrington, who replied that he was for God and the King: and a Parliamentary newsbook treats it jeeringly as a joke. (Mercurius Britannicus, May 20-27, 1644.) On the other hand, Sir Francis Doddington shot Mr. James, a minister, near Taunton, as he stood upon the way— "Who art thou for, priest?" "For God and His Gospel." (Perfect Diurnall, Aug. 19-26, 1644.) The subject of the challenge is graphically treated by Sir Walter Scott in the Legend of Montrose. [A curious instance given by Vicars may be cited. "About a mile before they came at the Town, they discovered another partie of the enemies horse. Heer, they discreetly agreed to goe soberly toward them, every man making answer to him that asked any question, nothing but *Friends, friends,* all *friends*, as if they had been of the enemies troopes, and were going upon some design, it being, yet, dark ; therefore when the enemies called to them, *Who is there*, the other all answered, *Friends, friends*, and so they passed, but as soon as they were past, and thought themselves secure, they turned faces about, and asked the enemie, *Who are you for ?* They answered, *for the King*. Then, said they, *Wee are for the King and Parliament*, and charging, the enemy fled toward *Horncastle.*"—God's Ark, 45.]

22. *Donnington Castle*, p. 100.—The following also relates to the series of occurrences that serve to fill up the outline of Roe, and complete the anecdote of Forth's attempt to escape.

The Castle of Dennington (Donnington), near Newbury, on the north-west, was a place of importance, and had been once renowned for the residence of the poet Chaucer. Like Basing House, it had been an eye-sore to the Parliament. It had been entrusted to Colonel Boys, a brave and honourable Cavalier.[1] His defence of it has been famous. More than once he resisted the assaults of his enemies, defied their summons, and beat them off. One of his spirited answers has been preserved by Heath,[2] another by Clarendon. They both refer to the day after this second

---

[1] [He was Lieutenant-Colonel to the Earl of Rivers, whose regiment, about 200 foot and 25 horse, with 4 pieces of cannon, formed the garrison. He was knighted by the King Oct. 22, 1644.—Symonds' Diary.]

[2] Chronicle, i. 100.

affair at Newbury. It should be observed that the King's cannon had during the fight been drawn up under the walls for security till they could be removed, as they afterwards were, to Oxford. "The next day they drew up their whole army before Donnington Castle, and summoned the governor 'to deliver it to them, or else they would not leave one stone upon another:' to which the governor made no other reply than that he was not bound to repair it, but, however, he would, by God's help, keep the ground afterwards.' Seeing his obstinacy, they offered him 'to march away with the arms, and all things belonging to the garrison,' and, when that moved not, 'that he should carry all the cannon and ammunition with him,' to all which he answered 'that he wondered they would not be satisfied with so many answers that he had sent,' and desired them 'to be assured that he would not go out of the castle till the King sent him order so to do.' Offended with these high answers, they resolved to assault it, but the officer who commanded the party being killed, with some few of the soldiers, they retired, and never after made any attempt upon it."[1]

This may without hazard be assigned as the very juncture when the Earl of Forth was resting here, sheltering himself after his wound, till he thought it safe to venture out on his journey and follow the King. Boys bade defiance to Cromwell, Manchester, and Waller, and the whole of the Parliamentary army. The temper of this officer may be seen in Appendix XIII. in a note written to the Governor of Farnham Castle upon the exchange of prisoners.

23. "*Cross-country road*," p. 100.—The facility of moving with a convoy over open downs was more frequent than at present. Forth was on his way to Marlborough, intending to reach Bath, and had hardly escaped from the inclosures about Newbury when first observed. The road was partly inclosed and partly open. It is difficult to point out anything more than the direction taken; for Hungerford or Marlborough are neither of them mentioned in the line of their flight, and might perhaps have been avoided. Horses might have had little difficulty in passing anywhere; but here were three coaches laden with women, and a wagon with all sorts of valuables. Owing to this, their winding course was traced by the hand of Birch, as that of the pursued has often been tracked by the North American Indian. These windings therefore must have been necessary, and have occasioned delay. Six hours were consumed by Birch in collecting the party for the chase and in overtaking them; and their fancied security encouraged the wounded general to indulge himself at length in a halt that proved almost as fatal, and from the same cause, according to the report of his enemies, as that of the unfortunate Louis XVI. at Varennes in the year 1791. Otherwise, as the license of war admits of no impediment in the demolition of hedges, the time might have sufficed, it seems, to have gained ground upon the pursuer. The coaches of the day, however, were by no means of a light kind, even for ladies. They were only closed by curtains instead

---

[1] Clarendon, viii. [It was surrendered April 1, 1646.]

of glass panels; the more modern light conveyances would not have been equal to the difficulties and dangers of the road. In the early part of this reign, an instruction given on this subject curiously contrasts with the style of an approach to a country gentleman's seat in the present day. Serjeant Hoskyns, about to bring his wife down from London to his mansion in Herefordshire, writes thus in Dec. 1627 to Miss Bourne at Morehampton "in the Gilden Vale." After the mention of conveying the coach from London, and desiring that the horses may be sent forward for that purpose, he adds, "Take care for the coach-horses to be had at this time, and go presently about it day and night : the rest we have more time to do. Study the coach-way ; where to break hedges, and how to avoid deep and dangerous ways."[1]

Towards the end of the same century (March 9, 1684-5), one of the noble ladies of the family at Troy House near Monmouth (Lady Rebecca Worcester) thus answers the inquiry of her friend Lady Hoskyns on the subject of her safe return from Harewood to Troy :

"Madam,

"I thank God I returned to Troy safe and very well on Friday night, after hauing had a happy deliuerance from two ouerturns of the coach. I giue your Ladyship many thanks for your fauour of sending to enquire after us, and for your letter."[2]

The distance from Harewood to Troy through Ross must have been considerably less than twenty miles by the highway. And towards the end of another century the state of affairs was not much improved as to sloughs and quicksands. The Duke of Norfolk of that date coming down from the metropolis to visit his estates at Hom Lacy near Hereford, thought it prudent to carry a set of country tools in the boot of his coach to assist in removing any difficulty that might occur upon the road; and the writer of this note could point to the very spot where such impediment was found. He could also show a highway in which a wagon laden with furniture was stopped till the overhanging trees could be lopped and the holes secured in the road that led to his dwelling, and that in the present century.[3]

To revert to our troublous times. With regard to the facility of travelling through byways or no ways, by tracks or over downs, it may be instanced that Colonel Birch, when he proceeded with one of the Harleys to meet King William III. on his landing, is said by his companion to have pushed through the country without keeping the highway. They met at Wycombe, "from whence we went to Wallingford out of all roads, which was the only bridge standing between Oxford

---

[1] MSS. Collections.
[2] MSS. Collections.
[3] He recollects when the Henley road to the famous University of Oxford was traversed in coaches through wintry mire, only by faggots thrown down to stop the holes.

and London: from thence we went to Salisbury keeping no road, and by a signal Providence escaped being taken by a party of King James's horse." [1]

Inclosures, the great aversion of Tusser, the writer on husbandry in the reign of Elizabeth, had reduced the mode of travelling to narrower dimensions than of old, and multiplied miry ways. So late as the earlier part of this century it was commonly understood that cattle-dealers and drovers could steal a way for their flocks and herds, avoiding turnpikes, nearly from Gloucester to London.

24. *Capture of Lady Forth*, p. 100.—Now that this adventure has been minutely recited, and Birch by revision and correction has assented to every item, and has claimed to himself the credit, such as it is, of the whole, it is curious to find a competitor starting up with an opposite claim, and appropriating to himself the origin and management of the exploit. A Lieutenant-Colonel Thorp, vindicating his character from some aspersions in the Mercurius Aulicus, brings out in the ensuing spring a very different version, and introduces us to the obscure names of some others of the party. His case is thus stated:

" At the last fight at Newbury he was commanded upon the guard betwixt Newbeury and Dennington Castle after the fight; he then, receiving intelligence from Col. Burch, drew some fourty men and horse from the guard; so he desired Col. Burch to go along with him; there were, under his command, officers as followeth: Cap. Draper, Cap. Lieutenant Evans, Cornet Mathews, Cap. Draper's Cornet; the intelligence was, that my Lord Ruthin, the King's Generall, his Lady, and divers more with him. So they pursued them some eight miles, where they tooke the General's lady, and some prisoners of quality with her, three coaches, and about fifty horse and men, a wagon with much goods in it; so Lieutenant-Col. Thorpe sent the lady and the prisoners towards Newbury with Col. Burch and some of the troopers; the said Lieutenant-Col. pursued the Generall some nine miles further, and rid in view of him the most of that way, but he having but some two men with him, and his horse being weary, he returned back to Newbury, where he and the rest of the party divided the spoile. This was done without the losse of a man. This is the true relation of this piece of service." [2]

A similarity in the name might convey the notion that the Lieutenant Calthorpe of Roe may have been the person who put in his subsequent claim, but it is more probable that the blunders of the press were really the cause of the difference, as thus, for *Lieut. Col. Thorp* read *Lieut. Calthorpe*.

25. " *Governor of Gloucester*," p. 104.—Sir Thomas Morgan was a soldier of fortune who had learned his art in the school of experience. He was a native of Monmouthshire, and of mean extraction. At the age of 16 he was sent into the

---

[1] MSS. Harl. 885, 2, 10.
[2] Kingdom's Weekly Intelligencer, April 8, 1645.

Low Countries as a recruit with a letter of introduction to an officer. The story is that, on reading it, the person to whom it was addressed, casting his eye upon the stature and mien of the youth, said, with a sneer, "What, has my cousin recommended a rattoon to me?" (a term of contempt, signifying a West Indian fox).[1] Young Morgan, indignant at the expression, left his expected patron, and went to seek his fortune in the service of the Duke of Saxe-Weimar. How he was transferred from this into that of the Parliament is not mentioned. He was sent down from the North of England, where he had been in some way subordinately employed. In the Fairfax Memorials a Major Morgan is spoken of as expert in taking garrisons.[2] [This was in March 1643-4, before, or at the beginning of the siege of Latham House. During its progress he appears as Colonel, "a hot-headed Welshman, with a sharp imperative manner," who was employed by Fairfax as one of his messengers to Lady Derby, and directed the engineering under Rigby after his departure.[3]] His name does not appear in the sanguinary roll of any great battle, but it argues no little for his ability that he was at this time chosen to succeed Massey in the government of Gloucester. Morgan was in truth a veritable and earnest soldier. The charm of his leading as an officer consisted in his identification of himself with his men. While Sir Charles Lucas and others on the Royalist side incurred the censure of keeping too much aloof, this officer, in the Parliamentary fashion of the time, was familiarly intimate with those who served under him, and won their hearts. Fairfax, who knew the merits of Morgan during the distractions of the army and the disbanding of the regiments when their number was to be reduced, strongly recommended him to the Speaker of the House of Commons as fit to be sent into Ireland.[4] He himself petitioned to go thither. He served afterwards in Scotland under the Protectorate with great credit. In the attempt of Cromwell against the children of Charles I. and the friends of the Stuarts, this leader with 6,000 of his men was sent on an expedition to Flanders about the years 1657 and 1658. There at the battle of Dunkirk they astonished Marshal Turenne and many of the nobility of France. The courage of his troops was admired. It is his own unaffected account; "See," said he to his red-coats, as the enemy stood in battalia before them, "yonder are the gentlemen you have to trade withal." They gave such a shout that the illustrious foreigners with their Marshal came up to inquire the cause. He told them coolly that it was the usual custom of the red-coats, when they saw the enemy, to rejoice. Turenne replied, "They are men of brave resolution." At the storming of Ypres they fell upon two out of the three half-moons; the French attacked the other and were beaten off. Morgan told his officers and soldiers, quietly, they had better give them a little help. With their wonted good-fellowship with their leader, they called out, whether "should they fall on in order, or happy-go-lucky?" He replied, the latter. Immediately they were on the summit

---

[1] Bailey's Dict. v. *Rattoon*. Qu. Racoon?
[2] Civil War, i. 83.
[3] Lady of Latham, 86, 93.
[4] Cary, ii. 45.

of the work, and the enemy in the moat.[1] On one of these occasions it is said that he was honoured with a visit of curiosity not only from Turenne but Cardinal Mazarin and others. Full of expectation to find something in him heroically answerable to his fame, they were surprised to see a little man not many degrees above a dwarf, seated in a hut of turf surrounded by his fellows, distinguished only by a green hat-case, smoking a short pipe, his voice stridulous and answerable to the diminutiveness of his stature. When he was angry with any of his soldiers he vented it in a squeaking tone, " Sirrah, I'll cleave your skull." This was he who, lacking the imaginary dimensions of the hero, was in common parlance "every inch of him" a warrior. His manners were as humble as originally had been his calling. He was fond of " blowing tobacco," and the present of silver cans and a beer-bowl[2] to his Excellency while he was governor of Gloucester, and occasional attacks of the gout, appear to obtain some coincidence. Under one of these he was labouring during the extremity of the march to Hereford, and it affords some clue to his state of health on that wintry night and his resolution of endurance under that malady. As might be expected from one who had seen many foreign services, he spoke Welsh, English, French, High and Low Dutch, but all imperfectly.[3]

Soon after the death of the Protector he and his men returned from Mardyk, and were sent into the North.[4] He was there " commander-in-chief of all the forces in Scotland," and resided with his lady at Edinburgh (July, 1660). He was most essentially instrumental in assisting Monk in the restoration of Charles II., and was afterwards appointed Governor of Jersey, where he repaired the fortifications ; in which post he continued at least till the year 1677. Cradled in this sea-girt isle, and occupied in the construction of its defences, with his small garrison (30 men), a memorial of his former exploits, he appears to have passed the greater part of his remaining days secure from the storms of those preceding them. Yet, like Birch, he had the discernment to select the beautiful land of Herefordshire as an agrarian possession for the property he had gained in war. The castle and manor of Kynarsley (writes a genealogist) that had passed through several hands descended to Lord Audeley : " in the last age," he says, " the Salmons had it. William Salmon left two daughters his heirs ; Lucy, and Ann. Lucy, to whose share this manor fell, married James Pit of Kyre, Esquire, who sold it to Sir Thomas Morgan ; and his son John married Hester, the eldest daughter and co-heir of James Price of Pillith, in Radnorshire."[5] Thus quietly passed away the traces of one upon whose decision the fate of a nation as to monarchy or anarchy once gravely depended for four short days and nights :[6] one whose actions, it is hoped thus not unduly magnified, may

---

[1] Somers Tracts, Collect. 4, x. 155.
[2] Bibl. Glouc. cxvi. cxvii.
[3] Aubrey, Letters from the Bodleian, Lives of Eminent Men, 2. ii. 465.
[4] [He was knighted by Richard Cromwell, Nov. 26, 1658.]
[5] Blount's MS. of Herefordshire.
[6] " If your petitioner had stayed four dayes longer at York without going into

on many accounts have merited rather than obtained a more distinct transmission to posterity.

26. "*Neutrality*," p. 112.—The oppression of the garrisons became so intolerable in many parts that it gave rise to the insurrections of what were termed "Clubmen"—peasants rudely armed for the emergency. The Parliament were jealous of this neutral or third party, and used immediate efforts to put it down. The various ways adopted by different commanders are interesting to trace. Cromwell treated the subject very curtly when he met them in Dorsetshire and put an end at once to their proceedings in that quarter. Massey went to Ledbury to treat with the Herefordshire and Shropshire part of them, and tampered with them in vain; a letter descriptive of his endeavour and their loyal tendency is given in Appendix XIV.: his idea of "the rebellion" will be found amusing. Sir Samuel Luke, writing from his garrison at Newport Pagnell, suggests to Essex, very naturally as he himself had property in that county, that his presence would be desirable among the Herefordshire insurgents.[1] The people had been goaded to desperation; but as the Parliament were now tending towards the ascendant, and the leaning of the Clubmen was towards the King, the movement met with discouragement. It is little suspected how early the disposition towards neutrality had taken its rise after free quarters and the oppression of garrisons had once been thoroughly felt and understood, and the patience of the public become exhausted by the interminable appearance of the quarrel. A proclamation by Sir W. Waller on the same subject will also be found in Appendix XIV.

27. "*Bribe*," p. 117.—It must be confessed that it derogates not a little from the heroic part of the scene, to recollect that the success of it was owing in so great a measure to so corrupt a motive. As Birch rode through the snow-white streets of Hereford on that bitter morning, he was kept too warm by the agitation and bustle that was going on, to call to mind that the glory of the victory had actually been sullied by a bribe. The application of such means runs through and stains the brief annals of the dispute; and was chiefly attempted, for a reason that will be obvious, by the Cavaliers. They resorted to it as the royal cause grew weak, and in them (not as in this instance,) it was the unfailing symptom of a losing game. There are honourable instances on both parts when it was rejected: as might be expected, it was refused mostly by the Parliamentarians; for they perceived, as the affair went on, that the stakes would surely enough be in their own hands. Cases are too numerous in which the Roundhead had the advantage over the Cavalier, and published and gloried in it. Backhouse, the lawyer turned soldier, whose loss Massey had to lament in the battle of Ledbury, cajoled and gave to the world his correspondence

---

Scotland to joyne with the Generall his Lordship had been in very great danger."
Petition of Sir Thomas Morgan to King Charles II.

[1] MS. Letter-book, 66ª.

with Stanford[1] at Gloucester, and Sir R. Brown exposed and flung into his teeth the letters that passed between him and Lord Digby while he was governor of Abingdon. Whitelocke dwells with evident satisfaction upon a list that he gives of these fruitless intrigues towards the end of hostilities; but the plain truth appears to have been that the Roundheads felt themselves secure of their winning without stooping to the disgrace and meanness of a bribe.

In the present instance, however, allowing all the credit that can be claimed for the exertions of Birch and Morgan, who carried off the public applause, it is but due to the vindication of Scudamore to put in the strongest light that the whole of the success was the result of the grossest bribery. The text insinuates nothing that can lead to a conclusion of this kind; their letters offer no direct revelation of it; but to have ensured success by any means was the object of Brydges and the Parliament; and again, all the agents concurring thought it no dishonour. The Governor must be acquitted. The plot was aided by circumstances and the season. Unless his own honour could be impaired by his flight, setting this aside, with them alone would rest the secret shame. It is plain that there was little reason for exultation, and the praise was best secured to the relators of the narrative by suppressing the origin of the plot in silence. [It is thoroughly brought to light, however, in the Journals of the House of Lords, as will appear by the extract given in the Appendix, No. XV. Mercurius Academicus, Jan. 1, 1645-6, says that Hereford "was sold by that perfidious Major Price, who was Major of this City when the Earl of Stamford was there."]

28. *Dissensions in Hereford*, p. 118.—In Hereford matters were not cordial among officers. Besides other sources of uneasiness with which Scudamore had to deal, there was a duel pending between two Cavaliers. About a fortnight before the surprise Sir Nicholas Throckmorton, the lieutenant-governor of Hereford, the same from whom a sconce at the time of the siege derived its name, "told Sir Thomas Lunsford that he lost Monmouth basely. Sir Thomas told him he lyed: to fight they prepared," says Symonds (Diary, 276), "but stopt by the guards. 'Twas referd to six gentlemen, but could not end it; they were both confined." Scudamore had no power like that of Gustavus Adolphus (Harte's Life, i. 154) [to repress this practice, which was not confined to the Royal army, a duel having been fought in August, 1644, in a street in Gloucester, between Major Hammond and Major Gray, with a fatal result to the latter.—Bibl. Glouc. 109.[1]] It appears by this that the usual discontent and ill-humour that is often prevalent among men engaged in upholding a sinking cause, was showing itself in Hereford. The governor himself had enough on his hands, and had given offence to many persons by the difficult course he had to pursue. The private society and conversation of the officers may be judged of from this specimen and from the company of David

---

[1] Biblioth. Gloucest. 285, *et seqq.*
[2] [An ordinance was passed for the suppresion of duels June 29, 1654.]

Hyde, one of the most infamous desperadoes, whose attendance upon the King was a disgrace to that misdirected cause, when on the 4th of January, 1641-2, he was present at the House of Commons with Lunsford to help in the arrest of the Five Members. David Hyde had quarrelled with Sir Barnabas Scudamore, as he was ready to do with anyone who opposed his will. He then threatened that he would take vengeance on the first that he met with of the name. This happened to be Sir John Scudamore, of Ballingham in Herefordshire, who was with Prince Rupert in Bristol. Hyde met with him in the street and thrust him through with his sword [on May 12th, 1645. He had been created a Baronet July 23rd, 1644. It appears from Scudamore's Defence (see Note 29), that he was about to hold a court-martial on mutineers the very morning that the city was taken.]

29. *Sir Barnabas Scudamore*, p. 119.—It is but fair to let the Governor speak for himself in this instance. It adds to the many versions of the story that were current at the time. The Committee of Salop gave immediately the following account to Sir William Brereton. "Worcester is much dejected at this suddaine loss of Hereford, and say as wee heare amongst themselues they must yeild that City or they must be vndon. Wee haue not yet receiued the particulars of the takinge of Hereford, but haue sent a speciall messinger to be fully informed of the same, whose returne wee cannot expect of three or foure daies But out of the seuerall relac'ons wee haue heard and conferrence wee haue had wth those that haue receiued it from the Governo^r of Hereford his owne mouth since he came to Ludlowe Wee conceiue the truth to be that Colonell Morgan ye Governo^r of Gloucester wth a partie of Horse and Dragooners drawn out of Gloucester, Monmouth, Cannon-froome and other of ye Parliam^{ts} Garrisons, laying hold on ye opportunity now that soe many of Hereford forces were drawne out for the reliefe of Chester and other sent to Ragland vpon an unknowne designe, and makeing use of the mist vpon Thursday morneinge, marched all night and Earely the next morning vpon the Letting downe of ye bridge a small p'tie first rushed upon the sentinell and the rest came vp presentlie and wth speed rushed vpon the maine Guard, there was noe resistance at all made as wee heare of. The Lord Brudnell, the Bi'^{pp} of Hereford his sone, 16 knights and manie other persons of quality are taken, wth aboundance of Treasure and Rich prize. The late Governo^r of Hereford saith for himselfe that he vpon advance of this partie gaue notice thereof to ye Governo^r of Ludlowe, rid the rounds all night himselfe till 5 of ye clock, and gaue order to ye Towne Maior he should not let downe the bridge before halfe an hower after eight of ye Clocke and should double the Guards, but ye Maior let downe ye bridg an hower and a halfe before the tyme appointed and left but one vpon ye Guard blowinge his fingers, soe that hee concluded there was Treacherie, in ye Maior."[1]

A person upon whom reliance could be placed was appointed to watch the bridge, but according to ancient tradition this important individual, on whom so much depended, was taken off his guard. The constable and the supposed countrymen being

---

[1] MS. Letter-book of Sir W. Brereton, iii. 119.

NOTES.   193

come to the gate, and having specified who they were, the drawbridge was let down and the gate opened for them. "Being come neare to the gate," according to the old story, "they called upon John Wilder to drop the bridge, and open it ; the said John beinge a trusty man, had superintendance of that porte, and was answerable for his right conduct in the same." This is the relation that is made in an ancient MS. quoted by Price.[1] The anecdote so far helps to complete the particulars as to shew that due attention had been paid to this point.

[The courtesy of R. W. Banks, Esq., of Ridgebourne, near Kington, has enabled me to subjoin to the previous statements some very interesting extracts from a Defence of his proceedings published by Sir Barnabas Scudamore in 1646.

" Upon Wednesday in the afternoone I was advertised that the enemy was marched out of Ledbury, and that the discourse of the common souldier in Ledbury was that they were going towards Hereford. This newes the messenger delivering privately by word of mouth, when Master Major and some halfe a score gentlemen and townesmen were in the roome with me, I did instantly communicate it in publique to them, and directed Master Major to make proclamation, that the townesmen might have notice of this intelligence, and withall be required presently to shovell off the snow from the walls, that the place might be fit for them to stand on with their armes on the first alarum."

* * * * * * *

" About 3 a clock that afternoone, I gave Major Chaplaine orders to double the guards, which he performed not, as by the list he gave me appeares. At 9 a'clock, I dismist the said Chaplaine to goe to his rest, telling him I would goe the grand round myselfe, and should expect him to be with me at 5 a'clock in the morning to receive from me the defects of the guards, and to look to the towne while I might catch an houres rest or two, being at 8 a'clock in the morning to sit at a court of warre upon the mutineers of the day before. The grand round I went about one of the clock. * * * * Going on the round at every port I charged them upon paine of death that neither officer nor souldier should stirre off from their guard ; ever adding that the enemie was advancing and the towne in danger. Coming to Byster's gate, at which port they that come from Ledbury enter, I found the corporall so drunke that he could not give me the word, whom I corrected for the present with my cane, and commanded my Capt. Livetenant Ballard, who commanded the round with me, to place an officer in commission at that port as soone as the grand round should be ended, and to lay the corporall by the heeles. Looking up I called to the sentinel that stood at the top of that gate to swingle his match, and answer being made that he had a snap-hanz, for the more surety I sent another souldier up and called him downe, and finding it to be so, and fixt and laden, I returned him up to his sentry place, and added one more to him, leaving a strict charge that the sentries should be often visited and relieved every halfe-hour. * * * * The grand round being ended about 5 of the clock, I ordered my Captaine Livetenant Ballard to continue rounds without ceasing

---

[1] Account of Hereford, 1796, 46.

until 8, and to give me an account. * * * * In place of it, 'tis very well knowne by testimony of some who entred the towne with the enemie, that he, the said Ballard, drew off the guard from Byster's gate, where when the towne was entred were but foure souldiers : and further that he had beforehand poysoned, or by some other meanes disabled, the murthering peece which lay in the mouth of Byster's gate. * * * * The keyes received, away he" (Lieut. Cooper) " hastens * * * * and passing to Byster's gate, opens not the wicket, sends out no scouts,[1] but opens the great gate, lets downe the great chaine, lets fall the drawbridge, and going over himselfe, while he saw upon the other side of the mote the Liev. and six souldiers who acted the part of the constable and labourers (whose reported pretence of being sent for by warrant Cooper could not but know to be untrue, for hee was the overseer of the works and writ all such warrants and saw the snow upon the ground which made it unfit for work and knew that the ice was every day broken by the garrison,) cryes out (and to them certainly) 'Now or never.' With this the enemy enters : Captaine Howorth being in the forelorne hope of foot that seconded the said personated constable and labourers, Sir John Bridges in the forelorne hope of horse, and Captaine Aldern in the second division. Being entred the gate, where they found but foure souldiers, the forelorne hope of horse takes the right hand and seizeth upon the maine-guards, where were but six souldiers and one ensigne ; and Captaine Aldern takes the left hand to my house and the castle. My man brings word to my bedside the enemy was entered. I leapt up, commanded him to get me a horse, and slipping on my cloathes I ran instantly downe with my sword and pistoll in my hand to the foregate towards the street, where the enemies horse already come fired upon me, and shot my secretary into the belly : at which I retreating, another of the house shuts the door, and out I got at a back way toward the river, in hopes still of my horse. Upon the left hand at the castle I was shewed the enemy gallopping towards me ; upon the right hand going to the Bishop's pallace I found a body of their foot comming into the pallace yard ; and seeing myselfe thus beset, my boy shewing mee that a couple were gotten to the other side of the river over the ice, by which I perceivd it would beare, I passed over, and got to the gate at Wyebridge, where intending to get into the towne at the wicket I saw most of the guard gone, and a body of their horse comming upon the bridge ; and then understanding the enemy to be fully possessed of the towne, and no possibility of resistance left, I resolved to cast myself at the King my master's feet. * * * From hence then I went to Ludlow, and from Ludlow in like manner to Worcester, professing there my purpose to ride to Oxford."]

30. *Lieutenant-Colonel Kyrle*, p. 131.—A word must be added with respect to Kyrle. There is something remarkable in his association with the party. The

---

[1] [Cruso, in his "Order of Military Watches," 1642, thus describes the duty of the Sergeant Major in the morning : " In places of danger he openeth the wicket onely, and sends out some men a pretty distance, to discover whether there be not some Embuscado or the like, and finding all safe, opens the great gate." 65.]

abode of this notorious character was at Walford Court, in the parish and near the church of Walford, in the hundred of Greytree, three miles to the south of Ross, beneath and in sight of the windows of Goodrich itself, but on the opposite side of the Wye. This mansion was sufficiently fortified to prevent surprise, and he kept it, according to appearance, uninjured from any attack till the war was over. It stood at a place where two or three roads meet, and exhibited in after times a circumvallation that commanded them from an interior mound, on which a gun was planted.[1] The premises were further defended by strong walls, provided with salient angles against assaults. The house itself contained a considerable number of small chambers for the accommodation of his men ; there was also one called the Armoury, whose name sufficiently indicates its use. Communication with the Forest of Dean was easy, and almost immediate ; and a hill is shewn in the neighbourhood called "the Warren," on which he is said to have exercised his garrison. To the eye of one who surveyed the dimensions of the walls early in this century, they exhibited nearly a mile in circumference, with a height of eight feet. Shorn of their dimensions, and reduced to those which invested more immediately the house itself, they appeared afterwards as above described. The whole is now transformed so as from the description to be scarcely known.

The owner, who was connected by marriage with the families of John Hampden and Sir William Waller,[2] had done more than enough to deserve hostile attack, for he had followed the example of Colonel Urry in the dishonourable German system of fighting on both sides. First on his return from Continental war he had fought for the Houses ; then he published a recantation and turned over to the King ; then to serve against him ; and once more in mere treachery had dissembled with the Royalists while he proved their foe.[3] He ended on the conquerors' side. His life is a specimen of the genuine turncoat of the day ;[4] his person was exposed in several encounters : it is unnecessary to say how far he acquired the estimation of posterity. He had been lately active against Sir Henry Lingen's comrades in Monmouthshire, and once by treachery captured Monmouth itself for the Parliament.

31. *Surrender of Goodrich Castle*, p. 132.—Goodrich had fallen, but not the spirit, nor the lives, of its defenders. They were admitted to terms of "mercy for their lives." Such was the distinction, often adverted to, in their laws of war,

---

[1] By the size of balls there found of 8 lbs. the piece of ordnance seems to have been a saker.

[2] Fosbroke's Ariconensia, 91.

[3] [Merc. Aul. says he had been on three sides in less than two years. Nov. 23, 1644.]

[4] This was not the only instance in Herefordshire, according to Symonds. (Walter) "Baskervile of Canon Peawne, small estate, (*jure ux.*) first for the Parliament, then for the King, then theirs, then taken prisoner by us, and (with) much adoe gott his pardon, and now *pro Rege*, God wott."—Diary, 196.

between mercy for life, and mercy alone; and with the former of these Colonel Birch thought fit to comply. Not as at the sad and rash defence of Hopton Castle on the border of Salop, where a few brave spirits, by "stouting it out," in the language of the private soldier, through ignorance or obstinacy incurred the fatal forfeiture, and were in cold blood put to death, those of Goodrich claimed and obtained the favourable terms by which they were required to yield their persons to the hands of the victor, but admitted to retain their lives. They marched out gaily, if tradition can be relied on, to a favourite air, which was known by Sir Harry Lingen's name. It was long kept up, and played in the dances of that time, in commemoration of the event, but is irrecoverably forgotten.[1] This anecdote was current in the last century, and told to Heath by Dr. Griffin, the then possessor of the Castle. He had in his service a gardener, who in his youth knew and remembered the air. All inquiries of a later date to recover it among the minstrels of the country have been in vain.

It may be thought that too large a space has been devoted to the actions of Lingen and the scene of his exertions; but the desultory manner in which they have been passed over in the MS. has drawn from the commentator what he considered impartially due to his memory and the loyalty of that district in particular among whose romantic scenes and wild traditions his lot has been for half a century cast.

32. *Demoralisation of Soldiery*, p. 150 (where the reference has been accidentally omitted).—In times of civil dudgeon, now long grown high, when authority and law in some sense were for awhile inverted, and misrule on all sides appeared to be gaining the ascendancy, the eye would be reasonably directed to the power by which affairs were actually swayed while matters are thus balanced. This power is only found in the sword. It is the sad sequel to the heat of continued personal provocation and strife of tongues, and after four years of unrestrained employment throughout more or less of the affected districts. This chastisement going through the land could not be otherwise attended, in principle as in practice, than by sad deteriorating effects. In a word, the injury to the inflicting as well as suffering part of the community was manifest, and in both was exhibited in gross demoralisation. Religion and manners were alike violated, and in particular by those in whose hands the weapon was grasped. The character and composition of those who constituted the mass of the forces at their height, conquering or succumbing, has been variously estimated, according to the prepossession of subsequent lookers-on, and the merits or defects of their leaders have been as variously censured or applauded; but, without descending much into particulars, it is evident that principle, where any had existed, had now degenerated into the love of gain, and the root of all evil, combined with the unlicensed extravagance of other passions, prevailed.[2] Some of the severest

---

[1] Heath, Excursion down the Wye.

[2] We may accept the confession of one of the coolest judges upon the subject, when, as to the real worth of the military towards the conclusion of these miseries, he told Sir Philip Warwick, who went to visit him (Sir T. Fairfax) after the sur-

paroxysms of the disease were past. The terrible atrocities of Sir Marmaduke Langdale's forces by land, the brutal excesses of Swanley by sea against the Irish, rewarded with applause [and even more substantially] by the Parliament, and the unexampled ordinance for hanging every one of those soldiers taken in arms, passed by the two Houses and retaliated by Rupert, but disowned after the shame of compliance and disgust by both him and Essex, may be set aside as glaring and offensive blots in the page of history ; but there are revelations of another kind which throw a shade on the winding-up of this story. It cannot be pretended that the blame rests wholly with the conquerors where all contributed their share to the effect ; but it was so remarkable to those who were in the secret as loudly to demand redress. The Parliamentary force, in spite of the claims of its leaders to religious superiority, had by this time grievously degenerated and subsided into a chaos that exhibited the utmost moral disorder and threatened to corrupt the mass of society. This it is hardly too much to conceive of it, while such hints as exist in the secret memoranda of those who had not originally intended to expose them to public gaze, remain unexpunged from the impartial hands of those who were thoroughly acquainted with their truth, and ashamed that it should ever have been divulged. Sir Samuel Luke, who was a droll, as was his clerk (Butler), tells us what were amusing were it not serious [as to the intoxicated condition of the Parliamentary recruits, as well as details of a more revolting nature concerning the state of his garrison-town]. It needed an iron hand to reduce it to order. That stringent pressure was found in the final exertions of Fairfax and Cromwell. It is thus that succeeding ages, from whom truth has long been hidden, are by such revivals warned from the breakers on which their ancestors have suffered shipwreck.[1]

33. *Purchase of Episcopal Lands,* p. 155.—[Birch's investment in episcopal property was at first a very profitable one. His hop-yards at Whitbourne (notoriously however an uncertain crop) are said to have produced in one year upwards of 700*l*. But he would have suffered materially at the Restoration had it not been for a stroke of that time-serving policy which distinguished his course. His exertions in the

---

render of Oxford, that the best common soldiers he had came out of the Royal army, and from the garrisons he had taken in : " so (sayes he) I found you had made them good soldiers, and I have made them good men."—Memoirs, 253.

[1] [The following letter from Col. Venn at Northampton to the Committee of both Kingdoms, dated April 11, 1646, gives a curious insight into the state of the Parliamentary levies at that time : " Most countries press the Scum of all their Inhabitants, the King's Soldiers, Men taken out of prison, Tinkers, Pedlars, and Vagrants that have no dwelling, and such of whom no account can be given, it is no marvel if such run away " (desert).—L. J. See Waller's Vindication, 120, for a remarkable statement as to the number of Royalist soldiers included in the newly-modelled army].

cause of royalty obtained a promise from the King that he should not be damnified "for severall sums of money by him layd out and for purchasing at second hand sixe mannors and severall other thinges part of that Bishoprick, and for mony expended in building, repairing, and improving the lands of the Bishoprick amounting in the whole to about nine thousand Pounds;" and consequently he obtained from Bishop Croft leases of the whole to the trustees of the widow of Bishop Monk, the General's brother, and Croft's predecessor, who had held the episcopate for less than a year. However, a very serious misunderstanding afterwards arose, which Clarendon, mediating for Birch, failed to terminate; and it was referred in 1671 to the arbitration of Sir Edward Harley of Brampton Bryan,[1] the very man who had lodged such strong complaints against the Governor of Hereford, and whose character for justice thus received the highest attestation. Many recriminations passed in an unfriendly spirit, and the Bishop especially was moved to great warmth of language.[2] Harley's award, though not wholly, was substantially in favour of Birch, to whom the lease for three lives was confirmed; and it was signed by both parties, April 12, 1672. The disputants had confronted one another on a previous occasion, when the one was Dean of the Cathedral, the other, Governor of the Castle. The doctor is said to have preached so vigorously against sacrilege that the soldiers were preparing to level their fire-arms against him, but were restrained by their commander. The Bishop in his correspondence shews no sense of gratitude for the interposition that protected the Dean; but perhaps he felt none, for he must have known that the Governor could hardly have ventured to sanction such an outrage. It is pleasant to be able to relate that, on one occasion at least, probably towards the end of the Bishop's life, the Colonel was a visitor at the Palace. And after all, these opponents died about the same time, Dr. Herbert Croft expiring May 18, 1691, in the 88th year of his age, eight days later than his former adversary. He was a younger son of an ancient Herefordshire family.]

34. *Birch's Epitaph*, p. 160.—[The remarkable error in the date may probably be connected with a circumstance mentioned in the life of Antony à Wood (i. 304, edit. Eccles. Hist. Soc.) under the date of May 1694. "We hear from Hereford, that the bishop of that see with his attendants went to Welby [Weobley] to deface an inscription on a monument erected in that church in memory of coll. Jo. Birch, the minister and churchwardens thinking some words thereon were not right for the church insti-

---

[1] One of the most irreproachable and impartial of neighbours.—J. W.

[2] An amusing specimen of this occurs in a letter to Harley, in which he speaks of "the claws of ye Greedy Harpye who notwithstandinge all that I have giuen him would yet scratch my eyes out could he find the least piece of Gold und^r them. God forgive him and deliver me from him. Amen." It is however due to the Bishop to state that in a subsequent letter to the arbitrator he offers an excuse for his expressions.

tution. The words were these "—The whole inscription then follows, with a few unimportant variations from that now existing; the date—no doubt the correct one—is "the 7th of Apr. 1616." Wood adds " The colonel's nephew designes to bring an action against the bishop for defacing it." This may have been a mere threat; it is more probable that the matter slept during the time of Bishop Ironside, and that the epitaph was restored as we now see it after his decease in 1701: but though we may thus account for the disappearance of the true date, the substitution of one inaccurate alike as to month and year, within so short a time after the colonel's death, is as far from explanation as ever.

In leaving in his final resting-place the old Presbyterian, whom we may suppose to have become a conformist in his later days, it is pleasing to record a fact indicative of liberal feeling. In the admirable Camden Edition which Mr. J. G. Nichols has given of Dingley's History from Marble (I. clii.) is a representation entitled "The South prospect of Weobleys Church as its steeple now stands Anno MDCLXXXII beautified repair'd and adorn'd by John Birch Esq[r] one of the Hon[ble] Burgesses for this ancient corporac'on."]

[ADDENDUM.—It should have been remarked in foot-note[b], p. 55, that, according to Heywood, Birch is set down as a Major in his kinsman Thomas Birch's accounts in 1643.—Newcome's Diary, 204n.]

APPENDIX.

APPENDIX I.

(1.)

The two following letters will perhaps be amusing, as they expose the different dispositions of persons employed on the same side. All accounts concur in the dispersion of great numbers of those who had fought at Edge-hill and suffered in the diseased camp at Reading. The writer of the first letter shews the coolness or ease with which his object was accomplished, in spite of his having subjected himself to military law and to the punishment of death. He had served for a while as a dragoon under Captain Baynes, and when he found his commanding officer was ordered into the West, he turns his back upon him and sends this excuse.

Captaine

    noble Sir my due respecs waite vpone you Sir this is to sertifie you that I being Left att reading one wedings day night Being secon of nouember did not know whether to Come to you but retired to your hous att London and Coming att hid parke Sargent Smith vnder Captaine Burns liuing in the pallis yard tooke my hors and my sword from me and thay said they shoold be safe for you and soe gaue me libertie to goe for I was not very well att this present I find my selfe not able to doe you seruis Els shoold I be ready to waite vpon you soe haing noething Els worthie to informe you with I Rest your humble seruant att Command

                                                                   WILLAM BACON

from london this fowrth of nouember 1642

(2.)

The next letter is still more strongly descriptive of the desertion of the army, but expresses an opposite feeling in the writer. Goodwin, the intimate friend and neighbour of Hampden, held like him a command under the Earl of Essex, and was quartered at Aylesbury in the first campaign. Whitham pleads in his excuse for apparent neglect of duty, among other reasons, his having given proof of his attachment to the service, by sacrificing the comforts and charities of private life.

Most Noble S^r.

I beseech you to excuse mee in that I doe not waite vppon you for orders accordinge to my duty, the grounds whereof meerely arisinge from my care to the states good, for if I should bee but a small while absent our dragooners would for the most part all bee gone wch as I conceiue would bee p'iuditiall to us in incouraginge our enimies and discouraginge us to hear y^t our forces disband, beesides the loss the state would suffer in regard of their horse and Armes, wch yet notwthstandinge for all my care of them and engagem^{ts} for them are some allready gone as my Leiftn^t: this bearer can more fully informe you: Truly S^r my most humble & honourable esteem of yo^{r}selfe and my unfayghned respect to the cause brought mee first unto you, and though I left a son'e dead ou' night and a sorrowfull woman hauinge longe had a wounded conscience and troubled spirit (and then much more increased by that temporall afflic'on) yet I most willingly in ye morninge left all to obey orders I rec^v: to waite uppon you, wch I hope together wth yor owne goodnes & charity may perswade you of ye faithfulnes of him to doe you seruice who unfaighnedly desires to bee yor humble (though unworthy seruant

NATH: WHITHAM.

To his much Honourd and Noble Com'ander Coll: Goodwin Com'ander in chiefe of the forces at Alsbury these p^{r}sent.

(Indorsed by Goodwin,)
   Serg^t Maior Witham 1642.

(Carte's MSS. Letters, Bibl. Bodl. EEEE. 57.)

Whitham (if he be the same person) appears to have risen in the army, and was afterwards Governor of Northampton, and brought a party of horse to join in besieging Banbury Castle. (Perfect Diurnall, Aug. 26 to Sept. 2, 1644.)

APPENDIX II.

Through the kindness of Lady F. V. Harcourt, the following curious and in more than one way instructive letter is now published for the first time. It appears to be in the hand-writing of Sir W. Waller.

S^r:

Our greate Care and desire was and is to p'serue the Cyttie of Chichester from vtter ruine and wee haue Cause to blesse God that there hath not bin (though the souldiers lay nine dayes and nights in the open feilds) since our entrance any plundringe to satisfie the souldiers Wee jngaged our selues to giue them one monthes pay the

Cyttie is not able to make this good wch Compels vs to moue the house that some plate raysed by the Cyttie vpon the p'posic'ons may be returned to assist as a helpe in this greate Charge w^ch: jf the house please not to grant wee knowe not what miserie may fal vpon the towne our souldiers haueinge hethertoe wth much patience expected our p'mise but jf they find our jnabiletie Wee knowe there rudenes. The valew of the plate is about one thousand pounds. Wee had in this towne about one hundred Com'anders and officers aboue three score are sent vp and the rest shalbe with the fittest Convayance wee Can. The Co'mon souldiers gathered out of the Country and keept in by force wee sett att liberty but the Dragoons sent from Oxford will Come vp by sea; wee looke vpon those (jf set att libertie) as men that Can'ot but doe mischiefe & only fitt for a pla'tac'on. Wee p'sent our seruices to your selfe, and will euer bee

                                              your seruants

Chichester this 6   WILLIAM WALLER.
   of jan 1642   ART. HESILRIGE.
                                        WILLIAM CAWLEY.

Indorsed,
    For the much Honored John Lentall Esq. speaker of the house of Com'ons——

with this note by Sir Robert Harley,

Fro' S^r: W^m: Waler et. to Mr: Speaker.

                                                             (Brampton Bryan Papers.)

APPENDIX III.

(1.)

When Count Mansfeldt arrived in England in 1624 to raise an army under his command for the recovery of the Palatinate, in the 4th regiment of foot, under Colonel Sir C. Rich, were enlisted the following officers : Lieutenant-Colonel Hopton, and Sir William Waller. They had been comrades in that expedition, and served and suffered together. (Rushworth, Hist. Coll. i. 153.) On the strength of this ancient connexion Hopton addressed a letter to Waller, desiring an interview, since they were on opposite sides. This is the answer of Waller to Hopton, before the battle of Lansdown, 1643 :

Sir,
    The experience which I have had of your worth, and the happinesse which I have enjoyed in your friendship, are wounding considerations to me when I look upon this present distance between us: certainly, Sir, my affections to you are so

unchangeable, that hostilitie itself cannot violate my friendship to your person; but I must be true to the cause wherein I serve. The old limitation of *usque ad aras* holdeth still: and where my conscience is interested all other obligations are swallowed up. I should wait on you according to your desire, but that I look on you as engaged in that partie beyond the possibilitie of retreat, and consequentlie incapable of being wrought upon by anti-persuasion, and I know the conference could never be so close betwixt us, but that it would take wind and receive a construction to my dishonour. That Great God, who is the searcher of all hearts, knows with what a sad fear I go upon this service, and with what a perfect hate I detest a war without an enemie, but I look upon it as *opus Domini*, which is anough to silence all passion in me. The God of Peace send us, in his good time, the blessing of peace, and in the mean time fit us to receive it. We are both on the stage and must act those parts that are assigned to us in this Tragedy, but let us do it in the way of honour, and without personal animositie; whatsoever the issue of it be, I shall never resign that dear title, of

Your most
Affectionate Friend
and faithful servant,
WILLIAM WALLER.
(Vindication, 13.)

(2.)

Another letter shows his courteous disposition, more akin to the Cavalier than the Roundhead. The lady to whom it was addressed had suffered from the capture of her noble husband at Hereford, and her expulsion by night from their seat at Hom Lacy near that place. She had been forced to take to flight from the visit of his troops. The other house that is mentioned in this letter was at Newark near the city of Gloucester, and now in the hands of the Parliamentarians. It is doubtful whether he could perform his promises of relief from sequestration, or if so in the first instance, whether such relief from damage and sequestration could be continued.

NOBLE LADY,

I shall ever take itt as a great honour to receive your commands, and I shall, with a ready obedience, entertaine them.

In obedience to your ladyshipp's letter, I sent for Alderman Pury, and questioned with him what wast had been committed on your ladyshipp's house or grounds. I finde some trees have been felled, and have given order there shall be no more touched; but I am assured nothing about the house hath been defaced, only a tower of an old chappel adjoyning thereunto was pulled down, in regard itt might have been some annoyance to the workes. For your ladyshipp's rents I have given order the sequestration should not bee executed; so that, Madam, they are still at your command. If there be any thing else wherein I may advance your ladyshipp's service, I humbly beg the favour to be commanded, that I may have opportunity to give some demonstration with what passion

I am, Madam,
Your devoted humble servant,
WALLER.

Gloucester, June 4, 1643.

For the Right Hon. the Lady Scudamore,
  att Homelacy, humbly present these.

(Duncumb, Hist. of Herefordshire, i. 264.)

(3.)

This address to the Royalist General proves his talent at hitting upon the temper of the King's officer, and how nearly in some respects he approached to the bearing of a Cavalier. When these two commanders were beating up each other's quarters in Wiltshire, the Parliamentarian being worsted, and desiring an exchange of prisoners, wrote thus:

Waller to Goring.

Noble Lord,

God's blessing be on your heart, you are the jolliest neighbour I have ever met with: I wish for nothing more but an opportunity to let you know, I would not be behind in this kind of courtesy. In the mean time, if your Lordship please to release such prisoners as you have of mine, for the like number and quality that I have of yours, I shall esteem it as a great civility, being your Lordship's most humble and obedient servant,

WILLIAM WALLER.
(Bulstrode, Memoirs, 120, ed. 1721.)

APPENDIX IV.

S^r.

I am now lodged at the Maidenhead over ag'st Lincoln Colledge, & hope to haue my quar^{tr}: in the great quadrangle a corner ground Chamber of my sonne, even in Ch: Ch: ye Court it selfe. I found all passages less difficult then I expected wthin theyr quarters & in Court & Citty, (They being noe less carless then yow strict for wch yow owe them thanks, & they none to yow) am taken for a high Cavallier and shall not

I hope want opportunity for effectuall service in due time. That I writt noe sooner was, that I could perceive noe danger to your Garrison upon the best inquirie I could make; the Prince Rupert wth horse & some foot drawne from ye severall Garrisons to ye number of 6000 being to have his Rendesvous at Lamborne on tuesday night, and the desseign to bee for the Devises, Gloccster, Bristow, as success should invite him. And knowing that my Lo: Digbyes Troope quartred in Whatley was drawn up, I was confident it could not bee for yow, and indeed yow, doe not soe much feare them as they the deepe wayes to yow, the strength of your Garrison &. fortifications wth the affection of the adiacent Country; Howsoever yow shal doe well to stand on yowr guard and observe well his reverse, And I shall not fayle to lett yow timly know what I may if yow will butt send a witty confident fellow to mee & place another at some reasonable distance from the Towne, wch I wonder our scout Mr Gen^ll: hath not done in all this time though promised long since & wth out wch I shalbee of noe vse. This messenger is mine owne servant, I am therfore confident. Pray giue him this inclosed seale back againe, that he may retorne by yow if need bee, or view well the man, yow may know him another time; his name is W^m: Snape. Though in hast; I am S^r

         Your verie humble and carefull servant
           (no signature)

Oxford 25° ffeb: 1642

Here is noe certayne newes what the Prince hath done as yett. The Secretarie ffalkland went to him last night I hope he hath not lighted on our Convoy of mony & Armes wch they say Neale theyr Scout M^r. gaue them notice of howrly Butt I hope they missed theyr marke, for surely it would haue been known here ere this.

(Seal a death's head.) (No address—indorsed C. S. 1642.) (This figure on the back.)
      (Carte's MS. Letters, Bibl. Bodl. EEEE. 64.)

APPENDIX V.

Six and forty years after this event his memory was recalled and perpetuated by a descendant in an inscription on a monument in Winchester Cathedral, which, as a curiosity, is given verbatim, since, proceeding from a Master of Arts, it is as remarkable in its way as the character it records:—

"At the south-east end of the pillar at the head of Bishop Morley's vault, on a square piece of brass fixed against the pillar, is this inscription:

A Memoriall

To the Renowned Martialist Richard Boles of the Right
Worshipful Family of the Bolses of Linckhorne Sheire,
Colonell of a Ridgment of Foot of 1300, who for his gracious
King Charles the First did Wounders at the Battle of Edge
hill. His last Action to omit all others, was at Alton in
the County of Southampton, was surprized by five or six
thousand of the Rebels; which caused him, there quartered,
to fly to the Church with near fourscore of his men, who
there fought them six or seaven Hours, and then the Rebells
breaking in upon him, He slew with his sword six or seaven
of them was slain himself, with sixty of his Men
about him. His gracious Sovereign hearing of his death
gave him his high Commendation in that passionate
expression.

Bring me a Mourning Scarf, I have lost
One of the best Commanders in the Kingdome.

Alton will tell you of that famous Fight
Which this Man made, and bade this World good night
His vertuous Life found not Mortality;
His Body must, his vertues cannot die.
Because his Blood was there so nobly spent;
This is his Tombe, that Church his Monument.

Richardus Boles Wiltoniensis in Art. Mag.
Composuit, Posuitq: Dolens
An. Dni. 1689."

(Gale, Hist. of Winchester, 54.)

APPENDIX VI.

Noble Sr

I once more increase my ill manners to you which is to let you know that in all his Majes^ties Garissons I am allow'd a Deputy, Yors being so I am bold to entreat you will allow of this my Deputy George Crosse, who being one born near you and as he tells me known to you wilbe the more readily well allow'd by you, my fees are 20s for a Gent. 13s 4d for a Cittizen 10s for a Farmer or Yeoman, & 5s for a Com'on Man so much severally for every day, I pray you let him have your Countenance & Assistance in his Service, wch I assure myself he will perform dilligently and Honestly so rest

Sr yor humble Servant
W SMITH.
Oxford Jan. 6. 1642.   P. Marshall Generall.

I hope this Letter with yor Com'ission & permission wilbe sufficient Authority for him, if not I will send him a deputation at large but have done no more but this in other places & am obey'd.

 For Sr Francis Oately my most honoured Friend
  This & my Service at Shrewsbury.

(Ottley Papers at Pytchford.)

APPENDIX VII.

Honored S^r

 At yor late beateing up o^r Q^rters at Kidlington among^t. other Prisoners there taken was a Boy named Beniamin Gill my Apprentice It is very well knowne how carefull I haue ever beene in dressing y^r wounded men whensoeuer they have fallen into o^r hands Therefore S^r if y^u will give him a speedy release & safe passe to Oxford, I am very confident ye favour shall not passe wthout an earnest endeavour of Recompence ffor if at any tyme any Chirurgion or wounded men of yo^{rs}. shall fall into our hands my care of getting releasem^t. or dressing those y^t have need thereof shall manifest how greate a favour y^u have done S^r to

yor obleidged seruant
HEN. JOHNSON

Kidlington 11th of March,   Chirurgion to his Ma^{tys} owne Troope.
  1644.

The boy is mentioned as having been sent back 16th May, 1645.

(Letter Book of Sir Samuel Luke.)

[When the estate of Stephen Fossett, surgeon to the Duke of York, was under sequestration, he produced two certificates setting forth that he, during his residence in Oxford, constantly and carefully dressed all such as were taken prisoners and wounded of the garrison of Abingdon, without any satisfaction for his pains, and with much care and willingness, at his own charge, dressed all such wounded soldiers of the Parliament as from time to time were brought in wounded, and relieved them with such other necessaries as were needful for them in the times of their extremity.—Sequestration Papers, 2, xxiii. 71.]

APPENDIX VIII.

The Devonshire Ditty.

The Devonshire Ditty, a ballad of the most poignant kind, in which wit and ribaldry are sufficiently intermingled to bear the impress of the Cavalier rather than the Roundhead. It had perhaps been intended for the service of the King, by its attacking neither side in particular. Its dialect determines it to a district where some of the grossest spoil and misery had been endured, and especially from the rude soldiery of Waller. It may be worth preserving, nearly entire, on another account, as a philological curiosity, since it no doubt represented accurately the existing phraseology of the county :—

—— Chill work no more,
Dost think chill labour to be poore?
No no, ith chave a doe,
If this be now the work and trade,
That Ise must break and rogue be made,
Ich chill a plundering too.

Chill zell my cart and eke my plough,
And get a zword if Ich know how,
For Ich mean to be right,
First chill learne to zwear and roare,
  * * * *
Tis no matter where Ise can fight.

But first a warrant it is vet
From Mr. Captain that is get,
And make a zore adoe.
For then chave power in any place,
To steale a horse without disgrace,
And beat the owner too.

Ich had six oxen tother day,
And them the Roundheads got away,
A mischief be their speed.
Ich had six horses in a hole,
And them the Cavalieres stole,
Ise think they be agreed.

If chave any mony left in store,
There comes a warrant straight therefore,
Or Ise must plundred be.
As soons chave shuffled out one pay,
Then comes another without delay,
Was there ever the like azee?

Her's do labour, toil and zweat,
Endure the cold, the drie and wet,
And what does think Ise get?
Fags, just my labour for my paines;
The garrisons have all the gains,
For thither all is vet.

They vet my corn, my bean and pease,
Ise dare no man to displease,
They do so swear and vaper;
And when Ise to the Governour come,
Desiring him to ease one zome,
Chave nothing but a paper.

But dost thou think a paper will
My back cloath and my belly fill?
No no, goe take thy note.
If that another year my vield,
No better profit do me yeeld,
Ise may go cut my throate.

And if all this be not griefe enow,
They have a thing call'd Quarter too,
O! tis a vengeance waster.
A plague upon't; they call it vree.
Cham zure theyve made us slaves to be,
And every rogue our master.

(Wits Interpreter, 1655, 143.)

APPENDIX IX.

TAYLOR THE WATER-POET.

John Taylor, a zealous Cavalier, so called as having been bred a waterman. He is less brilliant than the Devonshire Ditty, and even uncouth, but not less intended to be severe. A fragment, in spite of its dulness, may not prove unacceptable:

> Tell me, experienc't Fooles, did not your dayes
> Glide smoothlyer on   * * *
> When no grimme saucy Trooper did ye harme,
> Nor fiercer Dragon, when no Stranger's Arme
> Did retch your yellow Bacon, nor envy
> The richness of your Chimnye's Tapestry?
> When good Dame Ellen (your beloved Spouse)
> Bare to the Elbow in the Dairy-house,
> With fragrant Leeks did eat the Cheese she wrought,
> Not sent it to the Garrison for nought.
> But see what love of liberty affords,
> And the strange lusting after new coyned Words.
> How much the better are ye now, I pray,
> That yee with much expence have learn'd to say
> *Quarter* for *Lodging*, and can wisely well
> What *Carbine* signifies, and *Granado* tell?
> Which would have pass'd with you the other day
> For six legged Monsters out of Africa.
> Was not your Ale as browne, as fatte your Beefe,
> Er'e Plunderer was English for a Theife?
>   *   *   *   *   *
> It is the greatest Misery of Mankind
> Fortune at once makes happy and makes blind.
> How richly were yee blest in house and Field
> With all the store that a fat Land could yeild,
>   *   *   *   *   *
> Those dayes are gone   * * *

And thus he continues to sneer and reprove through several pages of alternate dulness and sarcasm, till the contrast ends in an exhortation to return to the King.

(Ad Populum, or A Lecture to the People. Printed in the Yeare 1644.)

The evils of the garrisons, to be spoken of hereafter, began to be fully experienced and cried out against in this stage of the war.

An account of Taylor is given by Anthony à Wood, ii. 393, Edit. 2, 1721, under the article "Withers."

APPENDIX X.

These two letters, the one from the pen of Cheynell, the cruel adversary of Chillingworth, written before the capture of Arundel, the other from Onslow, both of them committee-men, describe the disturbed state of the country in Sussex and Surrey.

(1.)

Noble Sir,

The Committee of Chichester present their respects and humble thankes to you for your care and vigilancy in this busy time: and in particular for your dispatching of a party towards Basing for ye redeeming of Chichester-wagon, when the greatest part of our strength was attending of the Winchester forces, and Sir Edw. Ford; It is ye desire of ye Committee that the Souldiers should have a faire reward for their magnanimous adventure, but the goods, horses, wagon, &c. being not in the enemyes hand for ye space of 24 houres, they conceive that the souldiers by ye law of Armes are not to make their owne markets, they therefore intreat you (though souldiers doe vsually sell cheap) to moderate the buisnesse, and they will acknowledge it for a favour: we shall hereafter look more towards your quarters, and if the guarrison at Godalming did every Fryday send out a party to Chidingfole or Haslemeere to wait there till Saturday in ye afternoone, I beleeve your County and ours would be more secure, and we should serve one another in love, wch is ye desire of, Sir,

Your affectionate Servant
F. CHEYNELL.

Endorsed,
  To his much Honoured friend Lieuten^t-Colonel
  Baynes at Farnham present these.

(2.)

S^r

I am credyly enformed that some scattering trop^{r}s of the king's are vp & downe this County: vpon Fryday there were some at Guildford & went from thence to Napp hill: on saturday night there went some that had beene of Mr Lee his troope towards Rygat and that night the Countesse of Nottingham of Lethered had her house broke open & some of the company were trop^{r}s. there is one fox a glouer of Lethered that as I am enformed kept close a horse that was to be conueyed to Oxford, it is fitt he should be examined: one of them that was at Guildford on Fryday was one Mr Christopher Gardyner, I beleeue there may be some newes of him about Croyden at the Lady Heyden's, but I very beleeue his Brother that liues there at Halyng knowes not of him, for he has beene from Oxford once before in those parts & robbed his owne Brother of all his horses in the night, but if you carry the enquiry hainsomly, you may bbly find him out, he is there in a dangerous corner of malignants & may with his company much preiudice the Country. S^r, I hope you will be carefull to take these p'sons if you can, and soe I rest

Your assured loueing frind

Sept: 18th 1643. RICHARD ONSLOW.

(Baynes Papers.)

APPENDIX XI.

[BATTLE OF CROPREDY BRIDGE.]

[The following sketch of the probable military operations at Cropredy has been drawn up, as appearing to the writer to afford a plausible solution of the difficulties which have been admitted to attend upon an accurate understanding of the affair.

The town of Banbury is seated upon the river Cherwell, the course of which is here from N. to S. (not from E. to W. as erroneously supposed by Roe): a few miles above it is a ford, and about a mile further a bridge, called Cropredy Bridge, from a village near it. Between Banbury and Cropredy Bridge, on the west side, is a rising ground called Crouch-hill, of great advantage as a military post. Both parties tried to reach it, but Waller was the first to seize and occupy it. The King drew up opposite to him on the east bank of the Cherwell; and thus they stood facing one another for two days. Here Waller, intending, it would seem, to attack the King's left wing, which was nearest Banbury, strengthened his own right wing at the expense of his left, drawing from his own, Potley's, and Weems's regiments, a number of musketeers, to form a forlorn hope of 1,500, who should fall on with the horse: the attack, however, was not made during the two days, and on the third the King, intending to draw Waller from his strong position, commenced his march northwards, on his own side of the river, securing Cropredy Bridge, as he passed by the end of it, with a body of dragoons, anticipating Waller's intention of employing it to fall on his left flank during his march. Waller immediately pursued on his own side of the river, preserving the formation of his troops, so that what had been his left wing became his van, and the right wing his rear, and here he committed the error blamed by Birch, of leaving the previously formed forlorn hope of musketeers for a rearguard, where they would be useless, as the King was marching a-head, instead of recalling them, so as to make up the complement of the regiments from which they had been drafted, and which now led the pursuit. The King having the start, his van and main body had got beyond his end of the bridge by the time that Waller's van had come opposite the other end of it. Here the prospect of cutting off some reinforcements that were on their way to join Waller induced Charles to push forward his van and main body, but the rear receiving no orders to close up, a gap was left in the middle of his army, somewhere opposite the bridge. Waller judging the opportunity to be favourable for cutting off the King's rear, sent Col. Middleton, with several troops of horse, to force the bridge, himself passing (according to his own letters) with another body of cavalry by the ford a little below, intending to attack the extreme rear, while Middleton cut them off in front. Finding them, however, strongly posted, he waited while Middleton pursued the dragoons whom he had driven from the bridge, and had been followed in support by the infantry forming the van of the Parliament army, who crossed the bridge with their artillery, but without their shot,[1] and without the musketeers from their ranks who had been converted into a rear-guard. Middleton, having halted before attacking, was suddenly charged, without orders, by the Earl of Cleveland, who routed one body of horse, but would have been taken in flank by two others had not Lord Bernard Stuart been sent to his support by the King, on which they gave way: in a second charge the Earl overthrew the main body, capturing their guns (which were mounted in two wooden barricades on wheels), and clearing all his side of the river as far as the bridge, which, however he did not pass, not knowing whether the main body were near enough to support him. At the same time the Earl of Northampton, who was in the extreme rear, facing about upon Waller and his cavalry, put them to a disorderly retreat across the river. The King then, having re-united his army, took post on one side of the bridge, and Waller on the other. Charles attempted in vain to force the bridge, but his men carried the ford and a mill beyond it, and held it all the next day, during which the

---

[1] Clarendon, however, states that the cannon were shotted.

armies faced each other, but afterwards drew off in opposite directions, Waller being weak, and the King unwilling, according to Clarendon, to bring on a general action until he could remove certain officers on whom he had little dependence.]

APPENDIX XII.

Col. Norton to Richard Maijor Esq.

Noble ffriend $\qquad$ y^e 19th Oct^r.

I doe beleeue you haue had an accompt of y^e late businesse at Newberry, yet I am willing to gieue you a short relation of it because I beleeue those that could be wth you soe soone did scarce stay to see all. on Saturday last y^e two armies drew out but little was done, but on y^e Saboth day, iust as I came to be a spectator, about 3 of ye clock they beganne to fire, our horse charged and routed ye first party, a second party routed an other, but there was litle doings betweens ye horse, but soone ye foot fell to it, and truly to God's glory be it spoken the enemies foot were as many in number they were held to be as good foot as any in ye world and to helpe them they had fortified themselues wth as good brest workes as they could desire soe y^t they were as confident as men could be & nothing but staruing could prejudice them My Lei Gen: & ye citty foot fell on and wth a great deale of resolution, being affected by ye great God of battell, they beate them from one work after an other till they beate them from all their ground, tooke 9 peeces and some prisoners, truly they might wth much more ease haue stormed Basing: after this it was night ye enemy stole away, left all their carriages vnder ye shelter at Doneington Castle, and are fled toward Oxford but our horse are (close?) after them and I hope will ouertake them but I heare nothing of it; yet we killed some men of note, and lost some, amongst wch was Lieu^t Col: Knight sonne to John Knight who was to me much lamented by my Ld Man[che]ster and many others and died wth ye reputac'on of as gallant a man as any in all ye army and as much beloued, truly I am sorry for himselfe and not lesse for poor John Knight's sake, but as he liued to be a good Christian soe he died like a good souldier. Many we had wounded; amongst ye number I receaud a faier admonition (by musquet shot in my legge) for medling where I had noe charge, but I thanke God my bone was to hard for ye bullett and I hope I shall be vpon both legges againe ere it be long. I could not helpe it, for I thought there was need when engaged my selfe to lead vp Col: Ludlowes Regiment, his horse haueing broken his bridle, soe y^t he was faine to
quit

(Here the remaining part of the sentence, probably with some others, is lost, from the paper having failed at the fold: on the other side, the postscript, for such it seems to be, is as follows):—

pray will you hea(?)...ther Gullett wth mony may be had and lett him...me away wth it for my men neuer wanted more. I haue an other order for 2 Monthes more wch I will send by ye next conueniency but I cannot come at it now. I desire to heare w^t forces are at any time neere those parts.

(Endorsed,) Coll. Norton. 29 Octob. 1644, Newbery battaile.

(Maijor Letters and Papers, British Museum.)

APPENDIX XIII.

S^r:

if Clarke my souldier may be returned to me, & his wife, I shall not detayne Boddeley from his, it being yor p^rtey that seperate man and wife, and not myne, beinge alwayes desirous y^t prisoners should bee Exchanged, for the other my Prisoner his tyme I gaue him is Expired, and hope yo^u will not longer detayne him; w^ch: is desired by, S^r: yor Humble Seruant Jo: Boys:

Den: Cast:
ffeb: 27th:

Endorsed,
ffor Lieu^t: Co^ll: Baynes
these.

(Baynes Papers.)

APPENDIX XIV.

(1.)

Colonel Massey to Sir Samuel Luke.

S^r.

Maior Harlyes hasty departure hence meeting wth my extraordinary occasions was such that hee overran my Intenc'ons and L're purposed by him vnto yourselfe for the paying of that tribute wch I acknowledge to owe & you may iustly clayme from mee S^r, This Post can relate the Hereford busines the whole County being now in Armes in a confused manner and before the Citty of Hereford and some of the Worcestershire side haue ioyned wth them; they keepe the soldiers in the Garrison, and are resolued to haue the Gouernor and soldiers out of it ere they leaue it, there being together since Tuesday last 15 or 16000 and amongst them as is reported at least 6 or 7000 musquitts and other fire armes. I haue sent you a Coppie of their articles and demands from the Gouernor of Hereford. S^r, vpon this noyse I advanced upon Wednesday last to Ledbury wth 500 foote and 150 horse being as many as I could spare or make at pr'sent and demaunded their resolutions and desired them to ioyne wth mee in observing the Parliam^ts commands. They would faine haue mee assist them (for they dare trust mee) but they will not as yett declare themselues for the Parliam^t but they conceiue themselues able to keepe of both the Parliam^{ts} forces and the Kings alsoe from contribution and quarter in their Contry. That is their vaine hope and vpon that ground I vnderstand they haue taken up that Resolution. S^r it's an opportunity offered to the Parliam^t if they lay hold on this occasion, and send mee speedy force to gaine them all to the Parliam^t: if not the losse will not bee small to vs. bee it how it will I haue vsed all the best Arguments I can to moouc them to declare themselues for the Parliament then they may haue protecc'on and authority for what they doe. Now their act is a perfect act of Rebellion to bee iustified by noe Law or Stat. and their confusion will be certaine. My humble request to you is to furnish this my Post wth a Horse to London that my L'res sent by him to the Committee of both Kingdomes on this behalfe and to his Excellency may find a speedy resoluc'on and returne whilst I hold faire way wth the Contry S^r I am

Gloucester March the .
22th 1644.

Your affectionate and
euer deuoted Seruant
EDW: MASSEY.

(Sir Samuel Luke's Letter-book. Egerton MSS.)

(2.)

Sir William Waller's Warrant against Neutrality.

Sussex. Being entrusted by both Houses of Parliament to do our utmost to preserve the peace of this County, and to defend it from the enemy; we hold it our duty not to omit the least meanes tending thereunto: and finding by experience that there are some men that neither regard the miserable condition of our brethren in other Counties, the present danger of their owne, nor the cause of God, but do go on in a way of Neutrality; To the intent that all may know how detestable such persons are, we are constrained to declare, that whosoever hath or shall continue in such Neutrality, and not shew themselves forward for the maintenance of the Common Cause, tending to the advancement of God's glory, the Parliament's service and the Kingdomes good; We shall take them for no other then enemies to the State, and men accordingly to be proceeded against. (Merc. Britann. April 15-22, 1644.)

The following remarkable letter on the same subject may find place here:

Right Worthy Sir

I take so much boldness on me to write my mind unto you. I have left my Father, my wife and Children, with what mind there's one above knows, and how much I desire to return you shall see by this. I never had an Intention, nor yet have, of takeing up Arms of neither side, my reasons this, my protestation already taken binds me both to King and P'liam^t. I am not so senceless (though it were almost to be wished I were) that there are two Armies the one the Kings the other the Parliam^{ts} each seeking to destroy other, and I by Oath bound to preserve both, each challenging the Protestant Religion for their Standard, yet the one take the Papists the other the Sismatikes for their Adherents, and (for my part) my conscience tells me they both intend the protestant religion, what reason have I therefore to fall out with either:—now if you'll be pleased to shelter me by your power, to live at Home is my earnest desire, beseeching you that no mock protestations be urged upon me, for I find in my own Conscience I have sufficiently enough of this, nor be compel'd to bear Armes, nor clapt up as disaffected to his Matie, which very word I abhor from my heart. Thus wishing God to deale with mee as I wish to you or either of you, I rest yours to be commanded

JONATHAN LANGLEY.

To the Right Wor^{ll} Henry Bromley Esqr high Sherriffe of Shropshire Sr Francis Oatley Knight Governour of the Towne of Shrewsbury   present   These from Birmingam
ffe: 22.

(Ottley Papers.)

APPENDIX XV.

JOURNALS OF THE HOUSE OF LORDS.
Tuesday, 27 October 1646.

The Earl of Warwicke reported a paper from the Committee of both Kingdoms; which was read, videlicet.

Die Lunæ 26° Octobris, 1646.

At the Committee of both Kingdoms, at Derby House.

Ordered, That it be reported to both Houses, That, the 11th of November last, upon a proposition made by Sir John Bridges to this Committee concerning the reducing of Hereford, power was given to him, the said Sir John Bridges, to treat with such persons as he should think fit for that purpose, and to promise a sum of money, not exceeding three thousand pounds: That, the 5th of December following, order was given to Colonel Birch, to march with some forces to attend that service, and letters also written to Colonel Morgan, and Sir John Bridges, to give them notice thereof, wherein there was again power given to them, to promise a sum of money to such as should be instrumental in that work, not exceeding, as before, three thousand pounds. The work being effected, upon report thereof made to the House of Commons, Three thousand pounds was ordered for that service, which was paid, as was appointed, under the hands of Sir John Bridges, Colonel Birch, and Colonel Morgan; That in May following, Colonel Birch signified to the Committee, that there was a promise made, by himself, Sir John Bridges, and Colonel Morgan, unto Major Howorth and Captain Daniell Alderne, two persons that they were to make use of in that service, that, if the work succeeded, they should have, each of them, (besides the money they were to receive) two of their nearest allies such as they should name, freed from delinquency and sequestration, and in June following, Colonel Birch and Colonel Morgan sent to this Committee the original papers containing that promise.

APPENDIX. 219

That the said Major Howorth and Daniell Alderne have now desired that Rowland Howorth, Charles Booth, Doctor Edward Alderne, and James Rodd, senior, should be freed from Delinquency, according to that Agreement.

That the Committee for Sequestrations in Herefordshire, notwithstanding that good service of Sir John Bridges, who was the first instrument that appeared in the county for the reducing thereof, have sequestered his estate, for something done when the county was under the power of the King, and he being now engaged in the service for Ireland, to desire the Houses that his sequestration may be taken off.

And for that it appears there was such a promise made as aforesaid to the said Major Howorth and Captain Alderne, by those who were intrusted with the managing of that business, to offer it to the House to do therein as they shall think fit.

Ex^r. Gualter Frost, Secretary.

Ordered, That this House thinks it fit that the Sequestrations be taken off the Estates of the persons mentioned in this report, according to the agreement, and that the concurrence of the House of Commons to be desired therein.

It would appear that Birch had already received a part of the money, an order having been made on June 11, 1646, for the payment to him of 1,000l. with interest, " to be employed for the disengaging of an undertaking made unto him by the Committee of both Kingdoms."

APPENDIX XVI.

A
NEW TRICKE
TO TAKE
TOWNES
or
THE just and perfect relation of the sudden surprisall
of HEREFORD
Taken *December* . 18. 1645.
WITH
A true Copy of the returne of the
Warrant, sent by a Lieutenant in the
habit of a Countreyman.
*And the names of six men his assistants
Published by special Authority.*

LONDON.
Printed by E. G. 1645.

Divine Providence (the Governour of humane actions) brings that to passe with much admiration that is least expected by mans judgement; Gods handy worke shined most cleare through the cloud of the greatest difficulties, and appeared with the fairest splendour when it passeth the most hazzard. Mans power doth execute what God decrees. By experience we finde that the meanest of his creatures becomes the instruments of his sacred pleasure. The King and Kingdomes differences unreconciled seem incureable without a conquest, and God is pleased by his victories to declare the justice of that cause he so much prospers. The particulars of Herefords affaires with some obscurity hath past the Presse, but for the generall satisfaction of the whole Kingdome (being an instrument in the designe) I have presumed to enter upon a large discovery.

Sir John Bryges in his affections most reall to his Countrey, after his continuance a while at Gloucester he came to London, where with the honourable Committee of both Kingdomes, he undertooke with his best endeavours the reducing of the City of Hereford, and the introducing of the Parliaments forces into that Garrison, being cherished by their Honours to proceed in the attempt he returned to Gloucester; from thence disguised he travel'd into some private parts of Herefordshire, and sent to Cap. Alderne, and Cap. Howorth who upon his first summons repaired to him, they being together met, Sir John Bridges delivered himselfe and desired their severall opinions, so that after an oath of performance and secresie past betwixt them, they concluded that for these reasons the designe was feazable.

First, the conveniancy and scituation of Ailstons Hill which faced the draw-bridge where an army might lie in ambush, yet undiscovered by the Sentinells.

Secondly, the usuall neglect of the Guard and the common custome in not sending out Scouts to Lug-bridge.

Thirdly, the walls of the Priory within Carbine shot of the Gate, being then standing gave an advantage there to lodge the Forlorne party of Fire-locks.

Fourthly, the constant Intelligence Captain Aldern had from the Citie, the which might have prevented any danger, if the busines had eyther been suspected or betrayed.

Fifthly, the contrivall of sending in an Officer with 6 men in the habit of a Constable and his Parishioners. Captaine Alderne drawing a Warrent and subscribing the Constables hand of his owne Parish as a returne thereunto.

Sixthly, the assurance of a Reformado Officer in the Citie who was to be neere the Guard at the time of entry, and to hinder the drawing up of the Bridge, as also to be readie to repaire to us if he found any preparation against us. After the disputeing of these reasons Sir John departed back to Gloucester, with a resolution to Post his man to London for orders from the Honourable Committee of both Kingdomes. Captaine Howorth and Captaine Alderne desired a speedy expedition, and thus determined to dispose severally of themselves. Captaine Howorth was to converse with the Officers in the Citie, and being acquainted with their designes to give upon all occasions intimation to Captaine Alderne in the Country from whom Sir John was to receive instructions, so accordingly to persevere therein. The Committee of both

APPENDIX.   221

Kingdomes, for the perfecting of this project, finding by these Gentlemens particular ingagements there was some possibility in the effect, their Honours sent for Colonel Birch, whose Regiments was commanded to draw into Gloucestershire, there in readynesse to attend the event. Colonell Birch receiving his instructions, came with Sir John to Cannon Froome, from thence he sent privately to Captaine Alderne by some Troopers belonging to that Garrison, and Captain Alderne according to their message, prepared himselfe, and, avoyding all the meanes of suspition, he came with Captain Howorth unto them, we blinding the busines that very instant, that his owne family were possessed with an opinion that the Parliaments approach was for no other end but contribution. Colonell Birch, Sir John Bridges, and the two Captaines being met, the particular reasons were repeated, and all with one assent agreed upon the execution, the day limited, which was the 16th Day of December. There was a messenger dispatched to the Officer within the City, with a Letter from Sr John, which intimated in short figures, both the time, and his duty, according to the agreement of all parties. Colonell Birch and Sir John Bridges hastned towards Gloucester, and about two of the Clock, upon Tuesday morning the Governour of Gloucester with Colonell Birch marched to Cannon Froome, from whence they drew towards Hereford, the Foot by reason of the deepnesse of the Snow, grew weake and were unable to march further, the Horse though willing were not able to accomplish the busines, therefore Colonell Birch advised with Captaine Alderne, what was best to be done, and freely offered, if Captaine Alderne conceived it fit, to march with 500 Horse, and 100 Foot to prosecute the designe. Captaine Alderne imagined that the Citie might be entred with that few number, but in regard of the strength and desperatenesse of the enemy, he was doubtfull of a repulse, thereupon he advised that the Horse and Foot should retreat to Ledbury, which was accordingly effected. After some discourse betweene Colonell Morgan and Col. Birch, and the other Gentlemen, it was concluded that upon Wednesday night, (that) the Army should march betimes to Cannon Froome, and from thence in a continuall motion draw to Hereford. In this intervale of time Captain Alderne kept correspondence with some of his friends in the City, and had the particular relation of the Governours proceedings, most part of the Horse being on a march towards the reliefe of Chester, the Governour himselfe being in some difference with the City, Captaine Alderne imagined that opportunity the best to compasse a surprize, so that Colonell Birch and the Governour of Gloucester drew from Ledbury to Cannon Froome, from thence Captaine Alderne with two troopes of Horse secured the three Bridges, vizt. Lugbridge, Lugwarden bridge, and Wordifords [Mordiford] bridge, by meanes whereof there could no alarm or notice passe unto the Garrison ; betwixt the houres of three and foure of the clocke on Thursday morninge the Governour of Gloucester marched up with his horse, the foot seconding him, all rendezvouzd together on this side Aylstons hill ; Cap. Howorth and one of Col. Birch his Captains commanded the Fire-locks to the Priory, the counterfeit Constable and his men were disposed to their station ; Cap. Alderne shewed Col. Birch the place upon the hill to draw up the forlorne hope of Horse, which was in a large dingle; the Morning-prayer-bell rung out, the Travalley was beaten in the City, and a musket of ours by accident was discharged, which possessed us with a great feare that our projects were frustrated, our hopes a while dead; at last about eight of the clock the drawbridge was let fall, the Constable observing his season killed the Sentinell, Cap. Howorth and the Fire-locks possessed the gate, Cap. Temple with the horse behaved himselfe most gallantly, Captaine Alderne according to command with others routed those at the Castle, Col. Birch and Col. Morgan being active in their commands kept the enemy from drawing in a body, so that without the effusion of much blood we became conquerours and masters of the Garrison. The souldiers strucke with apprehension of danger betook themselves to shelter, the Citizens knew no refuge, but kept themselves close in their houses, and he thought himselfe most happy that could secure himselfe till the storme was past, the two Governours preventing with their utmost power the citizens generall losse and ruine. The garrison thus by policy and force surprised without remedy was plundered, neither could the commanders rhetoricke or threat prevaile with the souldier to keepe their hands from pillage. The number and quality of the Prisoners, as also the Ordnance and Armes taken, I am as yet uncapable to expresse, but in the generality I presume it was the largest prize taken since these warres began; to attribute that to man which is proper to God argues a sinne as high as presumption. God's finger points out that line the which notwithstanding all windings man must follow; and since weak mens policy hath atchieved that great mens power from other Nations could not accomplish, we are more bound to God in the strong linkes of constant gratitude, and with an acknowledgement: we must conclude, the strongest Cities that are most and best fortified by art and nature are easily taken if assaulted by the Generall of Heaven.

A Copy of the returne which a Lieutenant in the habit of a Countreyman brought in with six men.

Whereas we have received a warrant from the Honorable Governour of Hereford, for the bringing in to the Garrison six able men to worke with such tooles as are fit for your said service, we have in obedience thereunto by our Neighbour Hugh Morris sent a returne of the names of the said parties, viz:

John Baily.   Phil. Mason.
Wil. Edwards.   Ja. Baskerville.
Rich. Deeme.   Wil. King.

These we have sent in by our aforesaid Neighbour, not daring ourselves to appeare in respect of the enemies Garrison at Cannon Froome.

Dated Decemb. 17.
1645.

The mark of (J. S.) Jo. Searle.
Roger Hill. Const.

As to any parts of this pamphlet which may appear to disagree with the contents of Roe's description, they may, if fairly sifted, assume the character of amplification rather than absolute contradiction. Compared side by side, they certainly are not such as would be justified by the strict rules of legal evidence. But the variations, so far as Roe is concerned, are such as may have proceeded from a long retrospect in the writer, and a partial desire or habit of representing Birch as the principal figure in the canvass. To some, such versions, rightly weighed, may heighten the interest of the story rather than injure the cause of truth. The editor wishes it were otherwise, but must take it as he finds it..

A similar remark may be applied to Vicars's very minute and graphic account in the "Burning Bush," where the look-out, and the signal with the hat, are referred to Birch's lieutenant-colonel, Hammond, who was in command of the firelocks, and seems to have claimed a prominent share in the capture.

APPENDIX XVII.

An Accompt of the sen'all som'es of money rec^{vd}: for the Ransome of the Persons and Estates of such As were taken prison^{rs}: Jn ye Cittie of Hereford which Cittie was taken by Surprize and Assault wthout any composic'on wth other moneys and goods of the like nature.

Which money hee conceaveth apperteyneth nott to the State.

Due to him As Gou'no^r: of Bathe & Hereford f' 1th of Augst 1645 to ye 17th of Nou^r: 1646 48 weeks att 20^l. p' weeke . .   £ 1360

ffor satisfac'on whereof hee rec^d noe money Butt what Js hereafter Exprest to defray ye Charge which hee conceiues Belongs nott to the State.

An Accompt of all the moneys as hath bene Rec^d: By Colo^l John Birch or his order for the Ransome of the Persons and estates of such as were found Jn Hereford disafected to the Parliament and theire taken without composition.

of m^r Edmunds	004 : 00 : 00
of m^r Diggars	010 : 00 : 00
of m^r David Bowen	010 : 00 : 00
of m^r Richard Philpott Senio^r	020 : 00 : 00
of Doctor Skynner	040 : 00 : 00
of m^r John Cooke	050 : 00 : 00
of m^r Edwd. Trehearne	020 : 00 : 00
of m^r Joseph Bowecott	025 : 00 : 00
of m^r West ffaylin	040 : 00 : 00
of m^r Moare of Chilston A papist	100 : 00 : 00
of m^r Tho: Cicyll	020 : 00 : 00
of m^r Alderman Evans	027 : 10 : 00
of m^r Edmund Aston	008 : 00 : 00
of m^r Robert Walker	005 : 00 : 00
of m^r Tompkins	025 : 00 : 00
of m^r Keynall	020 : 00 : 00
of m^r ffrancis Powell	020 : 00 : 00
of m^r Wingfeild	006 : 06 : 08
of m^r John Andrews	030 : 00 : 00
of m^r Thomas Bond	004 : 00 : 00
	484 : 16 : 08
of m^r William Cater	20 : 00 : 00
of m^r Tho: Barrowe	04 : 00 : 00
of m^r John Smith	10 : 00 : 00
of m^r John Trehearne	04 : 00 : 00
of m^r Thomas Davis	05 : 00 : 00
of m^r Scrivener	05 : 00 : 00
of m^r Edward Kinge	12 : 00 : 00
of m^r Thomas Church	10 : 00 : 00
of m^r Thomas Sower	05 : 00 : 00
of m^r John Pember	15 : 00 : 00
of m^r W^m. Seaborne	03 : 00 : 00
of m^r John Barnes	05 : 00 : 00
of m^r Lawrence	06 : 00 : 00
of m^r John Milward	05 : 00 : 00
of Griffith Harris	05 : 00 : 00
of m^r W^m. Butler, 2*l*: 10*s* and Mr David Bowen 5*l*.	07 : 10 : 00
of m^r Pynnock	02 : 10 : 00
of m^r Philpott Junio^r	03 : 00 : 00
of m^r Jeremie Adis	02 : 00 : 00

APPENDIX.

of mr Phillipp Symonds	10 : 00 : 00
of mr Thomas Veynall	12 : 00 : 00
of mr Rawlins	02 : 10 : 00
of mr James Barrowe	03 : 00 : 00
of Leift Colo'l Price Jn money goods & quartr	100 : 00 : 00
of mr Price of Whitston A papist	20 : 00 : 00
	276 : 10 : 00
Of Richard Lewis 2l: 10s: and mr David Bowen 5l.	07 : 10 : 00
of mr Henry Melin Butcher Jn Hereford	30 : 00 : 00
	37 : 10 : 00
The Totall of the P'ticulr: Receipts aforemenc'oned Js	798 : 16 : 08

John Birch

Recd: from two Souldirs. of my Regiment about the 20th of June 1646 The summe of 200l being P'te of a more som'e wch they found in the Earth about that tyme J say	200 : 00 : 00

John Birch

More of mrls Homes	020 : 00 : 00
of ye Widdowe Trehearne	025 : 00 : 00
of mr John Cooper	007 : 10 : 00
of Doctor Hartford	010 : 00 : 00
of mr Seaborne ye Apothecary	004 : 00 : 00
of mrls. Veynall	005 : 00 : 00
of mrs: Hill	002 : 10 : 00

(MS. *penes* Major Peploe.)

[From the style and caligraphy of this schedule it may be fairly inferred that it was part of the formal statement of Colonel Birch's account, passed by the Committee on June 15, 1647.]

APPENDIX XVIII.

COLONEL BIRCH TO THE SPEAKER OF THE HOUSE OF COMMONS.

Honourable Sir,

Since my last the 7. instant, finding the forces of Goodrich under command of Sir Henry Lingen so active that a passenger could not be safe between Gloucester and Hereford, nor could I quarter Horse abroad but they were in much danger, nor could I draw forth towards Ludlow or Worcester but they would come neer unto the City to plunder, therefore I chose rather to run the hazard of storming the House wherein they kept their out-Guard upon their Boats and Stable, being within 20 foot of their Castle Wall, than to suffer those former inconveniences, which was done thus: I marched out of Hereford Munday night last with 500 Horse and Foot undiscovered, untill I came within Pistoll shot of Goodrich, a little before day: then fell on with 100 firelocks for the Forlorn, and entred over the Wall neare the end of their stable; the wall was very high, yet got over before they had a full alarm; and found in the stable about fourescore Horse, and five men, which Horse I took all, digging thorow the walls, and turning them out; the men were slaine and taken: the stable with hay and other provision burnt; In the mean time I fell on their out-Guard, in a place called the Boat-House, which was within Pistoll shot of the Castle, which held out two houres untill it was digged thorow; then they desired quarter for their lives; wherein was Major Pateson, Commander of the Horse, and Major Benskin and 15 Gentlemen more and Troopers, whom I brought to Hereford. This success it pleased the Lord to give me with little losse, which is very advantageous, and especially enabling me to perform those commands laid upon me by the right honourable the Committee for both Kingdoms. And this day in the way as I was comming to Gloucester for that purpose, some Horse belonging to Goodrich Castle way laid me, which were out on a party when I took the rest Munday night, there being with me Collonell Kirle, and about 12 more, but not so many ready; the Enemie staid in the way, which we perceiving, gave them a charge, their number being 14, tooke and slew 12, and the other two escaping through the River to the Castle. * * *

(Vicars, Burning Bush not consumed, 396.)

APPENDIX XIX.

COLONEL BIRCH TO THE SPEAKER OF THE HOUSE OF COMMONS.

Truly Honourable,—In my last I gave you an account of all passages here, since which I sent in my summons, here inclosed, but they within resolve to stand it out, as you may perceive by their answer: they are excepted persons, and Papists very desperate: they never left sallying whilst they had one horse to sally out with, having lost in all, upon their sallies, above one hundred.[1]

I am approached within the reach of their stones, which they throw abundantly,[2] and am now almost ready to play upon them with a mortar piece, which I have cast here, carrying a shell of above two hundred weight; and have planted my battery, and am going on with my mines; for effecting of all which, a considerable quantity of powder will be speedily necessary.

I therefore humbly entreat your honour will be pleased to move the honourable house for eighty barrels, which will much forward the service, and exceedingly engage

Your honour's most faithful and thankful servant,
JOHN BIRCH.

From Goodrich, June 18, 1646.

COLONEL BIRCH TO THE GOVERNOR OF GOODRICH CASTLE.

Sir,—Before this, I question not but you expected what I have now sent unto you, which I did the rather forbear, being informed of your strong confidence of a speedy relief, and no less in your own ability to prevent such near approaches as are and may be made upon you, (being willing you should try the utmost of both;) though instead of the former, I must let you know that Oxford is to be delivered up the 19th instant.[3] In the mean time, I have been studious of your welfare, which to advance I find no visible way left, but that you submit unto the pleasure of the high court of Parliament; in whose name, and for whose use, I demand of you the possession of this castle of Goodrich; which if you shall assent unto, you may command my utmost service in any thing which may tend to the public good, your honour, and future welfare.

And for those gentlemen now under your protection, if they shall put themselves under mine, I shall not deceive them of that civility which they may expect; and shall thankfully acknowledge the goodness of Almighty God in sparing a further effusion of blood: it being my desire hereby to declare unto you my especial care to prevent; which if you shall occasion by your refusal, (that being at another time honourable which now will not appear to be the part of a soldier, whose prudence is required as well as resolution,) but that you shall persist to a further enraging of those under my command, so that you make me incapable of doing that which, it may be, you may think (and not without ground, were it not the eleventh hour) to have at

---

[1] [The loss when the stable was burnt must have been soon in part repaired, as 10 weeks afterwards 70 horses were captured at Raglan, "most of them belonging to Goodrich Castle."—Cary, i. 63.]

[2] [Wallenstein at his leaguer before Nuremberg employed "barrells or hogsheads filled with sand and stones for throwing, placed on the batteries."—Monro, ii. 134.]

[3] The treaty for the surrender of Oxford was signed June 21st; the city was surrendered to Fairfax on the 25th.

last, and that blood and utter ruin follow, I hereby desire to be excused if I prosecute my present business in such a way as will be grievous unto him, who rather desires to approve himself   Your real friend,

JOHN BIRCH.

June 13, 1646, at 2 o'clock.

P.S. That you may perceive my willingness to give you full satisfaction in any scruple that you may make hereunto; if you desire it, myself, with two gentlemen more, will give you the meeting with the like number, where you please; or if you desire no such satisfaction, I shall desire your answer in writing within twenty-four hours: which length of time I am willing to give you, because to me it looks like a business of great concernment, to yourself especially, because you bind my hands from any more lines passing in this business.

SIR HENRY LINGEN, GOVERNOR OF GOODRICH CASTLE, TO COL. BIRCH.

Sir,—I received yesterday a summons from you, wherein you demand of me this castle to be delivered into your hands for the use of the Parliament. The King placed me in it, by his commission, to keep it for him and to his use, and, until I shall receive an immediate order or command from him to the contrary, I shall do it to the uttermost of my power; otherwise I conceive I should not discharge the part of a soldier and an honest man, which I hope to carry with me to my grave. As for the information you had of my strong confidence of a speedy relief, truly it was a thing I neither desired nor expected in so short a time; yet happily may have it before my necessity will require it; as for the delivering up of Oxford, (if it be so,) the fortune of another man's command shall not be a leading case for my loyalty, and the trust reposed in me, and this I will assure you is the resolution of

Your loving friend,

HEN. LINGEN.

Cotheridge Castle, June 14, 1646.

COLONEL BIRCH TO SIR H. LINGEN.

Sir,—I have received your resolution by your drummer, which far better contents those under my command than myself, who really desired your welfare.

In honour, Sir, Your loving friend,

J. B.

At the Leaguer, June 14, 1646, 4 o'clock.

(Cary's Memorials of the Great Civil War, i. 102-108.)

[See also Perfect Diurnall, June 22, 1646, where there are a few verbal discrepancies.]

APPENDIX XX.

The Strong
CASTLE
of
GOTHRIDGE
taken by Colonell
BIRCH.
Sir Henry Lingen, and fifty Gentlemen taken
Prisoners, All the Officers and Souldiers at mercy, and
all the Armes and Ammunition, Bag and Baggage
taken by the said Colonell BIRCH, on Fryday
last. July 31. 1646.

Monday the 3ᵈ of August. 1646.
This Letter of Colonell Birches with the
two other Letters are examined and printed, and published according to order of
Parliament.

London : Printed by Jane Coe. 1646.

The taking of Gothridge Castle by Collonel Birch, with all the Armes, and Ammunition, and all Prisoners at mercy, certified by a Letter from Collonel Birch
Himselfe.

Honoured Sir,

No time hath been neglected by me in the prosecution of this service, but as the ground would admit I have carried on my Approches, Batteries, and Mynes ; And after I had very much torne the Castle with my Mortar piece, that no whole roome was left in it (that not doing the worke) I resolved to go on with the mines, and Battery (where I could not myne) both of which went on so succesfully, that in a few howres I intended to enter by Storme And to that end drew my horse and foot together, which the Enemy perceiving, rather then they would run the hazard, took down their Cullers, and put up white (without which I denyed them any Treaty) their desires were honourable tearms, which I thought not fit to grant, neither to give them any thing beyond mercy for their lives, their Persons to be wholly at my dispose ; upon which tearms, I have this day received possession of this Castle. And when the Parliament shall please to command Sir Henry Lingen to waite upon them, I shal carefully bring him up to attend their pleasure. In the mean time I desire that the Parliament will be pleased to signifie their pleasure concerning the demolishing or keeping this Castle ; The condition of which, and of all other passages here, this Bearer Major Blackmore will give a perfect accompt, who hath been very active and helpfull in this service, together with the condition of the Horse and Foot under my command, how much they have been discouraged by those who with earnestnesse seek their owne ends, notwithstanding all which, no duty hath been omitted, nor any meanes left unattempted which might forward the Publike Service.

Your most humble and reall Servant,
JOHN BIRCH.

Gotheridge the 31 of
July 1646.

The Copy of another Letter from Colonell Birches Leagure.

Sir,

I know not how enough to commend the gallantry of Col. Birch, in his deportment before Gotheridge Castle, a Nest of Papists, and rigid Malignants, that were very desperate in their resolutions, which the more encensed our Souldiers. Sir Henry Lingen would fain have had another Summons to begot a parley; but the former offers refused, made our Colonel look upon that as uncapable of so much favour. It is a place very strong, and Mining hath proved very hard work, yet Col. Birch hath used all possible means, and lost no opportunity in the speeding of the reducing thereof, to the best advantage of the Kingdome, which I believe the surrender of Worcester hath something hastned.

But the Colonell made his approches, and mined with all the speed that the cragginesse of the place would permit, and not onely plied them with his Batteries, but had done very good execution upon the Castle with the Granados shot from our Mortar peece. And all things were in so faire a way that wee were almost ready to storme; then which the Souldiers desired nothing more, so that all, both Colonel, Officers and Souldiers, should not have needed to have beene hastned, had not the worke been shortned another way. We were so neere the storme, that Colonel Birch had drawne up the Horse and Foot, and was ordering them into a posture for falling on. But the enemy in Gotheridge Castle perceiving in what posture wee were in, and seeing how they were on all sides surprized, their hearts began to faile them, so that they took a most fearfull Alarm; and (whether by Counsell of Warre, or otherwise) they speedily took their condition into consideration, and (perceiving that wee would not balk with them) being unwilling to endure a storme (which was much the more terrible to them, because of divers Gentry amongst them) they desired a Parley, but my Colonell would not grant that, though much importuned for it: insomuch that when they saw wee would not admit of any delay, they tooke in their Standerd Colours, and held out their white Flagge of Truce, and begged that they might but march out Honourably to their owne homes, and some to Garrisons. But nothing would bee granted more then quarter for their lives. And in short it was agreed to thus :

First, that Sir Henry Lingen the Governour of Gotheridge Castle, with all the Officers and Souldiers therein, shall have mercy for their lives.

Secondly, that the said Sir Henry Lingen the Governour, with all the Officers and Souldiers, shall surrender up themselves prisoners to be at Colonel Birch his disposing.

Thirdly, that all the Armes and Ammunition, provision, and whatsoever else is in Gotheridge Castle, shall be delivered up to Colonell Birch for the service of the Parliament.

Fourthly, that the same bee performed presently the same day (viz. July 31, 1646).

All which was done accordingly, this present day, and Colonell Birch is now in possession of the Castle, wherein, besides the Governour, were about 50 Gentlemen, and others of Quality, and 120 Souldiers, of whom I will give you a List of their Names with all convenient speed.

My Colonell hath this day received a letter from Hereford, dated yesterday, of which I sent you a Copy. I hope care will be taken to make all lovers and frinds, and that we that have fought together in one cause, and been ready to shed our blood one for another, shall not now spill one another's blood, but live in unity, and enjoy peace through all the Kingdome, which is the prayers of

Your most humble
Servant

Gotheridge July 31. 1646.

N. H.

The Copy of a Letter sent to Colonel Birch from Hereford, then before Gotheridge Castle.

For the honourable Colonell Birch, Governour of Hereford, at his quarters before Gotheridge Castle.

Sir,

Here is given out by some, That as soon as Gotheridge Castle is reduced, you are to march away from this City, and another Colonell to possesse your place: And truly I think the design is working: wherfore, if you may use all the meanes you can to prevent it, that your Brother, or some other friends may command the Castle and Forces which shall be left here, if you do not your self. Sir, your businesse for the County Voyces may hold if managed wisely. I have writ to Sir Richard Hopton again in the businesse, a copy of which you shall see at your return, and am now writing to Sir John Bridges, but I hear of none that stirs in it but myself. They have severall in most parts of the County. We earnestly desire you here. I pray you haste. I conclude, and subscribe myself

MILES HILL.

Hereford July 29.
1646.

I pray you set businesse in agitation in those parts where your Commands are by your Assignation Officers.

APPENDIX XXI.

These are to require you on sight hereof to forbeare to p^rjudice John Hall of South Tawton in the County of Devon either by plundering his House, or taking away his horses, sheepe, or other cattell or goods whatsoever, or by offering any violence to his p'son or the p'sons of any of his familie, as you will answer the contrarie. Provided hee bee obedient to all Orders and Ordinances of Parl^t. Given under my hand and Seale at Columb-John the 31th day of March 1646.

T. FAIRFAX.

To all Officers and Souldiers under my Com'and.

These are to require of you on sight hereof to forbeare to preiudice ye House of Thomas Soley of Worcester or to offer any violence to his person or any of his Family or to take away his Cattle houshold Stuffe or any other of his goods whatsoever he being well affected to ye Parliament and Army. Given under my hand & seale ye 4th of September 1651.

O. CROMWELL.

To all officers & soldiers und^r my Comand.

Theese are to requier and desier you not to take away any of the goods or Catles of S^r. Edward Powells nowe being or that shalbee hereafter vpon his estate at Pengethley hee haueing compounded with mee for them nor to molest or trouble any of his seruants or tenants there hee likewise haueing Compounded for his rents Giuen vnder my hand at Gotherig Castle this 16th of March 1645.

HEN. LENGEN.

To all officers and Souldiers of his Maiesties
    Armies and all others whome yt may
    concerne.   (MS. Collections.—J.W.)

APPENDIX XXII.

BIRCH'S REGIMENT DESTINED FOR IRELAND.

[It may be interesting to trace, as far as we have the means of following it, the history of this body of men, who had done such important service in the capture of Hereford.

Their former commander had, on March 25, 1647, agreed with the Committee for Ireland to send for that service a regiment of 1,000 foot, and two troops of horse of 100 each, on the terms of the payment of two months' arrears and one month to come, in all 6,740*l.* to be advanced by the County Committee and repaid with 8 *per cent.* interest, by that at Goldsmiths' Hall. But they did not set out at once, and the delay proved dangerous. They were expected at Chester in the early part of May,[1] but did not arrive. They probably heard in the mean time a bad account (and it must have been bad if it was true) of their future prospects of starvation and misery; at any rate, on July 19, 1647, we find Birch writing to the House of Commons and the General "concerning some distempers and differences that have happened among the forces at Herefford," engaged for Ireland. They had even gone so far as to "secure" their Lieut.-Colonel, probably the active but indiscreet Humphreys, whose cause was still pending. This is all that we learn from the "Perfect Diurnall,"—all, perhaps, that Birch wished to transpire in the House; but, if report might be trusted, the mischief was more serious, for Rushworth, in a letter to Ferdinando Lord Fairfax,[2] dated July 20, mentions among the news of the day, "that Colonel Birch's agitators do tread the steps of the Northern, and seized upon the Colonel and his brother the Major, and (to boot) the castle of Hereford and 2,000*l*. in it, besides clothes, shoes, and other provisions; upon this ground, that the Colonel and Major declared against permitting the soldiery to associate with this army. Upon the Colonel's fair language his soldiers gave him his liberty, upon his word not to engage against the army. The Major, castle, and money they keep." This circumstantial detail looks like the truth. Anyhow, the House saw that the affair was not to be trifled with, and accordingly the General was desired "to give order for the speedy sending away" those troops into Ireland, as they had engaged. The letter was sent to the General the next day, and Fairfax no doubt acted with decision. But such was the state of discipline among this greatly-vaunted soldiery that the regiment must have flatly disobeyed; for we find them in January, 1647-8, still at Hereford, annoying the country by their exactions, and refusing to disband except in the manner most agreeable to themselves. A letter read in the House of Commons, dated Jan. 24, from "an eminent person" who acted at Hereford as Parliamentary Commissioner, gives a curious insight into the state of the army in parts remote from head-quarters. It appears that in pursuance

[1] Rushworth, iv. I. 482. [2] Bell's Fairfax Correspondence, i. 370.

of instructions alike from the Parliament and the General, communicated through "Major Harlow" (afterwards better known as Sir Edward Harley), the new Colonel, Humphreys, had attempted on the 19th to disband the foot regiment by companies, but they had refused obedience on those terms, and still seemed likely to prove refractory. The letter contains a grievous as well as very instructive complaint of the exactions of the soldiery: "never more oppression when both Armies were on foot. As for example in *Radnor* shire they quartered three weeks some six hundred men, wher they have taken for every foote-man 3*s.* a day, in which place, before they came thither, they had paid their six moneths contribution. In this county they do the like wher they have paid their contribution to a penny, and now in the Treasury. And without your tender care for the preservation of this County they are utterly ruined: And we are fain both for here and *Gloster* not to leave any money in the Treasury, but convey it daily to private Houses for fear of miscariage by reason of the violence of the Souldiers. * * The sum of monies that will disband these two Regiaments will be 5,000*li.*" All mention of the Irish service seems to have been ignored; and in an order of the House of Commons of Oct. 18, 1648, it is not only admitted that those "forces went not," but specified that in consequence they only received the two months' arrears (due, as above, in March 1647): 750*l.* out of the balance being now appropriated to liquidate part of the claim of Col. Birch, and the rest being unaccounted for. The Colonel no doubt had a just right to his arrears; but under such a system of insubordination, mismanagement, and selfishness there is little room for surprise at the country's complaints of violence, rapine, and extortion.]¹

APPENDIX XXIII.

[The following brief chronological notices of some of Colonel Birch's proceedings subsequent to the taking of Hereford, drawn from the Journals of the Houses, the Harley correspondence, and other sources, do not pro-

---

¹ See also Cary's Memorials, i. 101, 138, 221, 277, 282.

APPENDIX.   235

fess to be complete, but contain some interesting facts not recorded in the preceding pages, and may throw additional light on parts of his personal history.

- 1645, Dec. 18.. Hereford surprised.
  - Dec. 22 . Birch appointed Governor. About this time 50*l*. per annum was granted to him out of Lingen's estate; but whether it was paid does not appear.
- 1645-6, Jan. 15.. Empowered with martial law.
  - Feb. ... Manœuvres against Astley with 220 foot and 200 horse, but owing to floods no engagement ensued.
  - Mar. 9... Burns the stable at Goodrich.
  - Mar. 13 or 14. Goes to confer with Morgan at Gloucester.
  - Mar. 21 . Defeats Astley at Stow.
- 1646, Mar. 26 . Faces Worcester with Morgan and Brereton.
  - Apr. 24 . Invests Ludlow.
  - May 20 . Returns to the surrender of Ludlow, where "expecting fair terms and performances, out of knowledge of the said Colonel and others there, they yeelded sooner than otherwayes they needed."
  - July 31 . Captures Goodrich Castle.
  - Aug. 1.. Purchases the Castle of Hereford of Edward Page. During his governorship he is stated to have borrowed 100*l*., possibly on this account.
  - Aug. 7... Writes from before Raglan Castle to the Speaker, referring to a petition he had addressed to the House.
  - Oct. 6 ... Insulted by Bromwich.
  - Oct. 23.. Petition against him presented to the House by Sir Robert Harley.
  - Dec. 9 .. Took the Covenant on entering the House as Burgess for Leominster in the room of Serjeant Eure, ejected as having been Speaker of the Oxford Parliament.
- 1646-7, Jan. 22 . Sends orders from Worcester to Hereford as to quartering his soldiers " on Delinquents and Newters."
  - Jan. 30 . At variance with Colonel Harley and the Hereford Committee about quarters for his horse.
- 1647, Mar. 26 . Engages for the sums of 6740*l*. and 857*l*. 4*s*. 8*d*. to send 1000 foot and 200 horse to Ireland. A few more (120?) horse were added June 18.
  - Apr. 12 . Sells the Castle of Hereford for 600*l*. to the Harleys and other Herefordshire members for the use of the county.
  - June 15, 16. Passes his account before the Committee

June 21. Having left London for Hereford by way of Bristol, where he was to receive part of the money for his regiment, he was arrested at Bagshot, in compliance with a general order, notwithstanding the Speaker's pass, by Rainsborough's soldiers, and escorted to head-quarters at St. Alban's, whence Fairfax sent him back to London.

July 19. Complains to the House of a mutinous spirit in his regiment.

Oct. 4... Serves on a committee respecting Ireland.

Oct. 26.. An order was sent to the Lords that the lead of the *Clochium* or Great Steeple attached to Worcester Cathedral should be sold for the repairs of certain churches and almshouses in that city. This noble building, 70 yards in height, constructed at an early period of great unsawed Irish timber for the purpose of holding the bells, was in consequence destroyed, and the materials, valued at 1200*l.*, purchased by Birch for 617*l.* 4*s.* 2*d.* But for his seat in Parliament, he would have been probably questioned for this at the Restoration.

Dec. 23. He serves on a committee to go to the Army at Windsor.

Dec. 24.. Obtains an order for payment of 2500*l.* with interest until paid.

1647-8, Jan. .. He and his brother Major Birch threaten the Hereford Committee with violence.

Feb. — June. With others as commissioner in Edinburgh, where they complain of bad accommodation.

1648, Oct. 18.. His troops having failed to go to Ireland, he is allowed 750*l.* towards his claim out of their intended pay, and 800*l.* from the sequestration of Sir Edward Morgan of the county of Monmouth.

Nov. 22. Begged the High Stewardship of Leominster.

Dec. 5... Serves on a committee for conferring with the General.

Dec. 6... Seized by the Army and excluded the House.

1649-50, Feb. 22. Purchased the Bishop's palace and manors for 2475*l.* 12*s.* 5*d.* (having previously bought Whitbourne).

1651, end of Aug. Attends King Charles II. at Worcester.

1655, Mar..... Arrested by Colonel Rogers.

Nov..... Released through Major-General Berry.

1656, Sept..... Signed the Remonstrance.

1657, June 26. Present, as Member for Leominster, at the inauguration of the Protector.

1658, Jan..... Returned for Leominster to Cromwell's Parliament.

1666............ Proposed a good method for the uniform rebuilding, under Trustees, of London after the Great Fire.

INDEX.

Abingdon, 13, 89, 90, 98, 168, 177, 208
Accounts passed, 152, 223
Adderton Moor, 171, 182
Alderne, Capt. 29 *n.* 118, 194, 218, 219, 220, 221, 222
Aldworth, R. xi
Alresford, 9, 79, 82, 84, 174, 177, 182
Alton, 4, 69, 70, 73, 78, 82
Andover, 83, 174
Antiquarian Repertory, quoted, 67
Appleyard, Sir M. 10, 80, 177
Ardwick, 159 *n.*
Armies, character of, 58, 63, 64 *n.* 77, 89, 233
Arrears, 151, 234
Artillery Garden, 51, 163 *n.*
Arundel, 5, 9, 69, 72, 76, 78, 168
Arundel, Col. 15, 95
Ashby-de-la-Zouch, 50, 109
Ashley, Major, 16
Astley, Lord (Sir Jacob), 26, 31, 33, 34, 35, 36 *n.* 65, 66, 92 *n.* 127, 129 *n.* 235
Aston, Sir A. 50
Auldborn Chase, 171
Aylesbury, 201, 202

Backhouse, Major, 190
Bacon, W. 201
Baillie, quoted, 98
Baines, Lieut.-Col. 64, 67, 87, 165, 166, 201, 212, 216
Balfour, Sir W. 9, 80, 91, 180, 181
Banbury, 12, 35 *n.* 86, 99, 202, 213
Barksdale, quoted, 154 *n.*
Barkstead, Col. 16, 97 *n.*

Barnard, Col. 108, 109, 111, 113
Barrow (Berow), Lieut. 26, 117
Barwick, Dr. 169, 171
Basing House, 64, 69, 78, 181
Basingstoke, 15, 16, 97
Bath, 21, 23, 100, 102, 104, 223
Baxter, quoted, 82, 158, 170, 178
Bedford, Earl of, 48, 162
Beeston Castle, 114 *n.*
Beggars, 76, 154 *n.*
Berry, Major-Gen. 95 *n.* 156, 157, 236
Biddeman, Lieut.-Col. 179
Birch, Col. John, *passim*
Birch, Col. Thomas, iv *n.* 199
Birch, Major Samuel, x *n.* 155 *n.* 233, 236
Birch, Rev. Thomas, x *n.*
Boles, Col. 70, 169, 207
Boucher, G. 2, 40, 42
Bowls, game of, 10
Bows and arrows, 92 *n.*
Boys, Col. 185, 216
Boys (merchant), 50
Brampton Bryan, 138, 175
Brecknock, 138 *n.*
Brecknocks, 165 *n.*
Brentford, 57, 99
Brereton, Sir W. 26, 34, 35, 127, 128, 235
Bribery, 117, 190
Bridgemen, 39
Bridgenorth, 102 *n.* 110 *n.* 128
Bridgwater, 21, 101
Bristol, 2, 21, 23, 38, 43, 44, 47, 51, 52, 60, 62, 82, 102, 104, 107, 162, 178, 236
—— bridge, 38
Bromley, H. 218
Bromwich, Col. 141, 142, 143, 144, 148, 150, 235

Brown, Sir R. 11, 80, 90, 168, 176, 191
—— Capt. 29
Browne, J. (of Harewood), 137 *n.*
Brudenell, Lord, 53 *n.* 115, 192
Brydges, Sir G. 115
—— Sir J. 23, 115, 116, 118, 194, 218, 219, 220, 221, 231
Buck, Capt. 39 *n.*
Burgess, 165
Burnet, quoted, iv. viii. 101, 156, 173 *n.*
Byron, Lord, 119 *n.*
Byster's Gate, 29, 193, 194

Calthorp, Lieut. 18, 187
Camden, 34
Canon Frome, 25, 28, 111, 112, 113, 114, 115, 221, 222
Cardiff, 168
Cardigan Castle, 92 *n.*
Carisbrooke, 10 *n.*
Carrier, Birch a, iv.
Carriers, robbery of, 49, 50
Cheriton, 79, 80, 81, 82, 99, 100
Cherwell, river, 86, 213
Chester, 26, 110 *n.* 127, 192, 233
Cheynell, F. 212
Chichester, 76, 78, 163, 202
—— wagon, 79, 212
Chillingworth, 76
Christchurch, 83
Christina, Queen of Sweden, 164
Clare, Earl of, 48
Clarendon, quoted, 53, 74, 76, 81, 177, 198
Cleveland, Earl of, 71 *n.* 87 *n.* 88, 214
Clochium, or Bell Tower (at Worcester), 236

238   INDEX.

Clubmen, 112, 116 n. 165, 190, 216
Coaches, 185
Colchester, 71
Committee of Safety, 84, 104, 114, 139, 143, 146
Congreve, Lieut.-Col. 179
Coningsby, F. 107
Corbet, quoted, 50 n. 179
Corfe Castle, 114 n.
Cornish troops, 44, 89
Cornwall, 14, 91, 94
Cotsforth, Major, 6
Coventry, 157
Craford, Earl of, 69, 70
Croes Owain, 139 n.
Croft, Bishop, 198
Cromwell, Oliver, v, 98, 101, 103, 104, 114, 129, 150, 156, 165, 166, 175, 179, 190, 197, 232.
Cromwell, Richard, 166, 189 n.
Cromwell, Henry, 166
Crondall, 4, 69
Cropredy, 13, 86, 87, 88, 89, 165, 178, 213
Croydon, 212
Cuirassiers, 174, 180, 183

Dacres, E. 42
Daventry, 50
Dean, Forest of, 123, 127 n. 195
Denbigh, Earl of, 86
Denbigh Castle, 168
Demoralization of Soldiery, 196
Denham, Sir J. 65
Devonshire Ditty, 77, 209
Digby, Lord, 168, 177, 191
———, Sir J. 179
Donnington Castle, 17, 100, 185, 187
Duelling, 191
Dunkirk, 188

Edgehill, 38, 57, 82, 99, 105, 107, 171 n, 175, 183, 201
Edinburgh, 236
Episcopal lands, 154, 158, 197, 236

Essex, Earl of, 12, 15, 51, 56 n. 58, 65, 77, 82, 85, 91, 93, 94, 97, 98, 101, 105, 107, 176, 178, 181, 191
———, Col. xi, xii, 41
Eure, Serjeant, 235
Evesham, 34, 86 n.
Exactions, military, 68 n. 149, 234

Fairfax, Lord, 233
——— Sir T. 15, 21, 47, 80 n. 90 n. 101, 102 n. 104, 114, 129, 149, 169, 171, 173 n. 176, 232, 236
——— Lady, 182
Fairs, 138
Farnham, 4, 5, 12, 64, 65, 66, 69, 72, 78, 84, 165, 166, 185
Farringdon, 165
Feilding, Col. 20
Fiennes, Col. xii, 38, 41, 42, 43, 44, 45, 46, 60, 65 n. 71 n. 178
Fire of London, 236
Five Members arrested, 53
Ford, Sir E. 65, 72, 212
Fords, on river Wye, 125
Forth, Earl of, 17, 19, 42, 99, 181, 185
——— Lady, 17, 100, 187
Fornova, battle of, 183

Garnstone, 158, 159 n.
Garrisons, 110, 111
Gloucester, 23, 26, 27, 33, 34, 43, 48, 50 n. 56, 92 n. 99, 104, 108, 115, 162, 234, 235
Goodrich Castle, 30, 31, 33, 36, 122, 123, 125, 127, 129, 130, 131, 132, 195, 226, 229, 235
Goodwin, Col. 152, 201
Goring, Lord, 91, 174, 205
Granadoes, 36, 211, 230
Grandison, Lord, 45
Green, Rev. J. 92 n.
Greenvile, Sir R. 95 n.
Gustavus Adolphus, 88, 99, 164, 172, 174

Hacket, Bp. quoted, 77

Hampden, J. viii, 49 n. 176, 195, 201
Harewood, 186
Harley, Sir R. 44 n. 107, 144, 146, 147, 148, 175, 235
———, Col. (Sir E.), 44 n. 154, 198, 216, 234
———, Lady, 44 n. 175
Hartlebury, 129
Harvey, Dr. 175
Hastings, Col. 50, 109
Herbert, Lord, 56
Hereford, *passim*
——— Castle, 31, 121, 126, 233, 235
Herefordshire, 105, 106, 159 n.
Hertford, Marquis of, 70, 107, 124
Hertfordshire, 77, 92 n.
Hesilrige, Sir A. 3, 9, 10, 14, 44, 50 n. 51, 52, 53, 54, 55, 66, 74, 80, 81, 86, 90, 163, 164, 180, 182, 203
Heywood, T. Esq. iii, 156
Hill, M. 149, 231
Hodges, Mr. 23, 118
Holland, Earl of, 48, 162
Holles, Denzil, 161, 180
Hom Lacy, 109, 186, 204
Hopton, Lord (Sir Ralph), 2, 4, 9, 23, 44, 65, 66, 68, 72, 73, 79, 80, 81, 82, 83, 100, 105, 180 n. 181, 203
———, Sir Richard, 107, 111, 231
———, Sir E. 111
——— Castle, 196
Hoskyns, Lady, 186
———, Serjeant, 186
———, B. 149
Howell, quoted, 41 n.
Howarth, Major, 118, 194, 218, 219, 220, 221, 222
Hudson, H. 96
Hull, 102 n.
Humphreys, Col. v n. 145, 146, 148, 149, 150, 233, 234
Hungerford, 16, 17, 185
Huntingdon, Earl of, 50
Hutchinson, Col. 171
Hyde, Capt. 145, 192

INDEX. 239

Intelligencers, 168
Irchinfield, 123, 125, 139
Ironsides, Bp. 199

Jenkins, Judge, 116
Jersey, 189
Johnson, H. 208

Kent, Earl of, 124
Kentish regiment, 14, 91, 94 n.
King Charles I. 12, 16, 42, 53, 60, 85, 86, 91, 92, 93, 97, 100, 108, 177, 213, 214, 215
—— Charles II. 156, 236
Kinnersley, 189
Kirke, Sir L. 128
Knolle, 14
Kyrle, Sir J. 107
——, Col. 33, 131, 194, 226
——, W. 149

Langdale, Sir M. 197
Langley, Jon. 218
Lansdown, 44, 65, 203
Latham House, 169, 188
Layton, Lieut.-Col. 10
Leather guns, 87, 88
Ledbury, 24, 26, 27, 28, 112, 114, 193, 216, 221
Leicester, 54, 178
——, Earl of, 172
Leicestershire, 53, 54 n.
Leominster, 37 n. 40, 157, 158, 235, 236
Lesley, Gen. 173
Letherhead, 212
Leven, Earl of, 113
Lichfield, 109
Lilly, 53
Lingen, Sir H. passim
Liskeard, 91
Lisle, Sir G. 71 n.
Little Dean, 179
London foot, 16
Lucas, Sir C. 188
Ludlow, 30, 31, 36, 88, 120, 126, 129, 170, 192, 194, 226, 235
——, Col. 53, 97 n. 170, 177, 183, 215
Lunsford, Sir T. 116, 191, 192

Luke, Sir S. 168, 190, 197, 216
Lyme, 91

Macaulay, quoted, iv n.
Madresfield, 23, 30, 126, 129
Manchester, Earl of, 15, 16, 17, 20, 68 n. 97, 98, 182
Marston Moor, 86, 98
Massey, Col. 50 n. 108, 112, 113, 114, 156, 190, 216
Maurice, Prince, 2, 22, 94
Mayerne, Sir Theod. 175, 176
Meldrum, Sir J. 180
Middleton, Col. Sir T. 87, 88, 214
Monk, Gen. 189
——, Bp. 198
Monmouth, 116, 126, 191, 195
Monmouthshire, 77 n. 195
Monro, quoted, 169, 171, 181, 183
Montgomery, 110 n. 171
Montrose, Marquis of, 168
Moore, Col. 149 n.
Moorfields, 51
Morehampton, 186
Morgan, Sir E. 236
Morgan, Col. Sir T. 23, 26, 30, 31, 33, 34, 36, 114, 116, 128, 187, 191, 192, 218, 235
Mortar-pieces, 36, 227, 229, 230
Myn, Col. 108, 109

Naseby, 108, 181
Neutrality, 190, 216, 217
New Inn, 139, 140
New Tricke to take Townes, 219
Newbury, 16, 17, 21, 82, 97, 98, 100, 174, 184, 185, 187, 215
Newcastle, Earl of, 102 n. 182
Newcome's Diary, iii
Newport Pagnell, 168, 190
Nicholas, Sir E. 49 n.
Nine Worthies, 107
Norfolk, Duke of, 186

Northampton, 13, 89, 98, 202
——, Earl of, 214
Norton, Col. 97 n. 215
Noseley, 54
Nottingham, 170, 171
——, Countess of, 53 n.
Nunington, 24

Oaths, 100, 178
Odiham, 78
Ogle, Sir W. 83
Old Gore, 33, 128, 130
Onslow, R. 213
Ottley, Sir F. ix, 171, 208, 218
Owain Glyndwr, 139
Oxenstiern, 164
Oxford, 12, 13, 31, 34, 35 n. 49, 65, 83, 84, 86, 89, 99, 111, 127, 167, 185, 227, 228

Parrett, H. 141, 142
Pengelly, Sir T. 166
Pengethly, 130, 232
Penrhyn, 158
Penruddock, 95 n.
Pikes, 171
Plymouth, 14, 15, 21, 91, 94, 95, 96, 97, 101
Portsmouth, 173
Potley, Sir A. 5, 12, 63, 73, 86, 164
Powell, Sir E. 130, 232
Powick, 38
Price, Col. 108
Prior's Hill Fort, 103
Priory of St. Guthlac, 24, 25, 29 n.
Prisoners, 170
Protections, 145, 232
Pye, Sir Walter, 107

Quarters, free, 77, 210
Queen's regiment, 20

Radnorshire, 178, 234
Raglan, 30, 33 n. 36 n. 109, 126, 168, 192, 235
Rainsborough, Colonel, 103, 230
Ralegh, Sir W. quoted, 159

INDEX.

Rapin, quoted, 48 *n.* 87
Raymond, Lieut.-Col. 29
Rea, Colonel, 11
Reading, 15, 16, 46, 50, 65, 83, 89, 97, 98, 166, 201
Recruiting, 51, 57, 89
Redmarley, 108
Regiment, pay of, 67
Remonstrance, The, 236
Roaring Meg, 36 *n.*
Roberts, Lord, 94
Roe, *passim*
Rogers, Col. 95 *n.* 157, 236
Romsey, 83
Roundway Down, 44, 50, 51 *n.* 81, 162, 181
Rupert, Prince, xiii, 2, 12, 21, 44, 46, 48 *n.* 71 *n.* 86, 103, 104 *n.* 107, 108, 111, 113, 114, 123, 178, 180, 192

St. Alban's, 45, 236
Salisbury, 83, 187
Scotch Nan, 168
Scots, 67, 74, 106, 113, 124, 132, 157, 172
Scroop, Sir G. 75 *n.*
Scudamore, Viscount, 107
————, Lady, 205
————, Sir B. 30, 108, 109 *n.* 110 *n.* 112, 113, 117, 119, 191, 192
————, Sir J. 192
————, W. 145
————, Jas. 146
Self-denying Ordinance, 101
Seneca, quoted, 42
Sequestration, 59
Sevenoaks, 94 *n.*
Seyer's Memoirs of Bristol, quoted, iv *n.* xii *n.* xiii *n.* 3 *n.*
Shrewsbury, ix, x, 43, 161
Skippon, Major-Gen. 21*n.* 22, 91, 93

Slanning, Sir N. 45
Slingsby, Sir H. quoted, 176
Smith, W. (Provost-Marshal), 170, 207
Smithfield, 51
Southampton, 94
Spies, 167, 205
Spiller, Sir H. 115
Sprigge, quoted, 121
Stamford, Earl of, xii *n.* 40, 105, 107, 111, 124, 191
Stanley, E. 172
Stow (in the Wold), 34, 35, 36 *n.* 129, 235
Stuart, Lord B. 88, 214
————, Lord J. 181
Sudeley Castle, 86
Surgeons, 75, 174
Sussex, 217
Swanley, 197
Swift, Vicar of Goodrich, 124
Symonds, quoted, 93

Taylor, Capt. 154 *n.*
————, Water-Poet, 77, 210
Thames, River, 49
Thorp, Lieut.-Col. 187
Throckmorton, Sir N. 191
Tombs, Rev. J. 40
Tower Hamlets, 13, 86, 87
Trenchard, J. 63
Tretire, 139
Trevanion, Sir J. 45
Trevor, A. quoted, 58 *n.*
Troop of Show, 175
Troy House, 186
Turenne, 188

Vaughan, Sir W. 25 *n.* 26, 30, 110 *n.*
Vavasour, Sir C. 177
Venn, Col. 197 *n.*
Volunteers, 38, 161

Walford Court, 195
Wallenstein, 227 *n.*
Waller, Sir W. *passim*
Wallingford, 65, 70, 120, 186
Walton, 83
Warminster, 47
Warwick, 51
————, Earl of, 49, 218
————, Sir P. 196 *n.*
Welsh loyalty, 105
Wemyss, 12, 87, 213
Weobley, 158, 159, 199
Weymouth, 14
Wharton, N. 58, 179
Whitbourne, 95 *n.* 154, 197, 236
Whitchurch (Dorsetshire), 83
———— (Shropshire), 110 *n.*
Whitelocke, 164
Whitham, N. 202
Wigmore, Capt. 179
William III. King, 186
Williamson, Rev. G. 40
Wilton Castle, 114, 115
Winchester, 11, 64, 65, 69, 70, 79, 83, 100, 163, 206
Windsor, 152, 236
Worcester, 12, 30, 31, 35, 43, 50 *n.* 58 *n.* 62, 86, 89, 105, 107, 120 *n.* 126, 129, 163, 192, 226, 235, 236
————, battle of, 88 *n.* 155, 157
————, Lady R. 186
Wright, Dr. 175
Wye, river, 30, 123, 194

Yeomans, R. iv *n.* 2, 39 *n.* 40, 42, 45
————, W. 42
York, 170
Ypres, 188

Westminster: Printed by Nichols and Sons, 25, Parliament Street.

June 5, 1873.

Camden  Society,

FOR THE   PUBLICATION OF

Early Historical and Literary Remains.

The Members marked (C.) *have compounded for their Subscriptions.*

President.
THE RIGHT HON. THE EARL OF VERULAM, F.R.G.S.

(C.) Right Hon. Lord Acton, Round Acton, Salop.
Dr. Edward Adamson, 4, West Street, Rye, Sussex.
George Edward Adams, Esq. F.S.A. Lancaster Herald, College of Arms, Doctors' Commons, E.C.
Edward Akroyd, Esq. M.P. F.S.A. Bank Field, Halifax.
William Aldam, Esq. Frickley Hall, Doncaster.
Richard Almack, Esq. F.S.A. Long Melford, Suffolk.
W. S. Appleton, Esq.
Lindsey M. Aspland, Esq. LL.D. Lamb Building, Temple.
Lieut. W. J. St.Aubyn, Sheffield Barracks, Sheffield.

J. E. Baer, Esq. Frankfort.
Right Hon. Lord Bagot, Blithfield House, near Rugeley, Staffordshire.
James William Baillie, Esq. Arundel Villa, Lansdowne Road, Croydon.
Mr. James Bain, 1, Haymarket.
William Proctor Baker, Esq. Bromwell House, Brislington, Bristol.
Rev. Edward Lowry Barnwell, M.A. Melksham House, Melksham, Wilts.
J. Sparvel Bayley, Esq. Knockholt Lodge, Greenhithe.

Executors of George Beaufoy, Esq. South Lambeth.
Thomas Bell, Esq. The Wakes, Selborne, near Alton, Hants.
Rev. Samuel Benson, M.A. Town Hall Chambers, High Street, Southwark.
Daniel Benham, Esq. 18, Regent's Square, Gray's Inn Road.
(c.) John Birkbeck, Esq. Anley House, Settle, Yorkshire.
Mr. Bishop, bookseller, Eye, Suffolk.
Rev. Beaver H. Blacker, M.A., Rokeby, Blackrock, Dublin.
(c.) James Bladon, Esq. Albion House, Pontypool.
(c.) Rev. Joseph William Blakesley, B.D. Ware, Herts.
Ven. George Bland, M.A. Archdeacon of Northumberland.
Charles Blandy, Esq. Reading.
William Blandy, Esq. Reading *(Local Secretary at Reading)*.
Robert Willis Blencowe, Esq. M.A. The Hook, Lewes.
Edward Blore, Esq. D.C.L. F.R.S. F.S.A. 4, Manchester Square.
Miss Bockett, Bradney, near Burghfield, Reading.
Henry G. Bohn, Esq. North End House, Twickenham.
John J. Bond, Esq. Public Record Office, Fetter Lane.
John Booth, Esq. Green Bank, Monton Eccles, near Manchester.
Rev. Wm. Borlase, M.A. Zennor Vicarage, St. Ives, Cornwall.
Mr. Thomas Bosworth, 198, High Holborn.
Rev. Joseph Bosworth, LL.D. F.R.S. F.S.A.
Sir George Bowyer, Bart. D.C.L. M.P. Radley Park, Abingdon.
Robert Greene Bradley, Esq. Slyne House, near Lancaster.
William Jerdone Braikenridge, Esq. Clevedon, Somerset.
Francis Capper Brooke, Esq. Ufford, Suffolk.
William Henry Browne, Esq. St. Martin's, Chester.
J. Brunskill, Esq. 13, Great James Street, Bedford Row.
W. G. Bulwer, Esq. Quebec House, East Dereham.
Decimus Burton, Esq. F.R.S. F.S.A. 1, Gloucester Houses, Bishop's Road.

Benjamin Bond Cabbell, Esq. F.R.S. F.S.A. 39, Chapel Street, Marylebone Road.
Frederick Caldwell, Esq. 4, Hanover Terrace, Regent's Park.
Colonel Carew, Crowcombe Court, Taunton.
W. Henry Pole Carew, Esq. Anthony, Torpoint, Devonport.
(c.) Sir Stafford Carey, M.A. Candie, Guernsey.
George Alfred Carthew, Esq. F.S.A. Milford, East Dereham, Norfolk.

Rev. William Henry Cartwright, M.A. Butcombe Rectory, Wigton, Somerset.
William Chapman, Esq. Richmond.
(c.) William Chappell, Esq. F.S.A. *(Treasurer)*, Heather-down, Ascot.
Georgiana Lady Chatterton, Baddesley Clinton, Knowle, Warwickshire.
Right Hon. Lord Chelmsford, D.C.L. 7, Eaton Square, S.W.
Right Rev. the Lord Bishop of Chester, Dee Side, Chester.
Very Rev. the Dean of Chichester, D.D.
(c.) John Walbanke Childers, Esq. Cantley, Doncaster.
Charles Clark, Esq. 5, Figtree Court, Temple.
Right Hon. Lord Clermont, 35, Hill Street, Berkeley Square.
Rev. Archer Clive, Whitfield, Hereford.
James Cobb, Esq. Yarmouth.
Right Hon. Sir John Duke Coleridge, H.M. Attorney-General, 1, Sussex Gardens, Bayswater.
John Payne Collier, Esq. F.S.A. Riverside, Maidenhead.
Col. Colomb, R.Art. Dalkey, Kingstown, Ireland.
John Coode, Esq. Polcarne, St. Austell, Cornwall.
William Hyde Cooke, Esq. The Green, Shellesley King's, Worcester.
Rev. James Cooper, M.A. 27, Woburn Square.
William Durrant Cooper, Esq. F.S.A. 81, Guilford Street, Russell Square.
Rev. George Elwes Corrie, D.D. Master of Jesus Coll. Camb. Jesus College, Cambridge.
Fred. Wm. Cosens, Esq. 27, Queen's Gate, Kensington.
(c.) John Ross Coulthart, Esq. Croft House, Ashton-under-Lyne.
Right Hon. the Countess Cowper.
J. C. Cox, Esq. Hazelwood, Belper.
(c.) James T. Gibson Craig, Esq. Edinburgh.
W. H. Crawford, Esq. Lakelands, Cork.
James Crossley, Esq. F.S.A. President of the Chetham Society, 2, Cavendish Place, All Saints, Manchester.
J. S. Crossley, Esq. Leicester.
(c.) George Cubitt, Esq. M.P. 121, St. George's Square, Pimlico.
Edward Cunliffe, Esq. 6, Princes Street, Mansion House.
Colonel Francis Cunningham, 18, Clarendon Road, South Kensington, W.
Hon. Edward Cecil Curzon, Scarsdale House, Kensington.

MEMBERS OF THE CAMDEN SOCIETY.

Edward Dalton, Esq, LL.D. F.S.A. Dunkirk House, near Nailsworth.
Thomas Dalton, Esq. Crockherbtown, Cardiff.
R. S. Longworth Dames, Esq. 32, Upper Mount Street, Dublin.
Louis Daniel, Esq. Valetta, Zion Road, Rathgar, Dublin.
James Bridge Davidson, Esq. 10, Old Square, Lincoln's Inn.
Francis Robert Davies, Esq. Hawthorn, Blackrock, Dublin.
Rev. James Davies, M.A. Moor Court, Kington, Herefordshire.
Rev. J. Silvester Davies, M.A. F.S.A. Woolstone, Southampton.
Robert Davies, Esq. F.S.A. The Mount, York.
(c.) Rt. Hon. the Earl of Derby, LL.D. 23, St. James's Square.
His Grace the Duke of Devonshire, K.G. D.C.L. 78, Piccadilly.
Francis Henry Dickinson, Esq. 119, St. George's Square.
Sir C. Wentworth Dilke, Bart. LL.B. M.P. 76, Sloane Sq.
(c.) Charles Downes, Esq. 29, Coleshill Street, Pimlico.
(c.) Sir William R. Drake, 12, Prince's Gardens, S.W.
Dr. Duckett, R.N. 5, Sefton Terrace, South Town Road, Great Yarmouth.
Sir George F. Duckett, Bart. F.S.A. The Manor House, Bampton, Oxon.
Rt. Hon. Sir David Dundas, M.A. 13, King's Bench Walk, Temple.

Samuel Edwards, Esq. Lewisham.
Sir Philip de Malpas Grey Egerton, Bart. M.P. F.R.S. V.P.G.S. Oulton Park, Tarporley.
Rev. Henry Thomas Ellacombe, M.A. F.S.A. The Rectory, Clyst St. George, Topsham.
(c.) Rt. Hon. T. H. Sotheron Estcourt, M.P. D.C.L. F.S.A. Tetbury, Gloucestershire.
John Evans, Esq. F.R.S. F.S.A. Nash Mills, Hemel Hempstead.
(c.) John Leman Ewen, Esq. Southwold, Wangford, Suffolk.
George Edward Eyre, Esq. M.A. F.S.A. 59, Lowndes Square.

MEMBERS OF THE CAMDEN SOCIETY. 5

(c.) Right Hon. Lord Viscount Falmouth, 2, St. James's Square.
(c.) Sir Walter R. Farquhar, Bart. 18, King Street, St. James's.
John Fetherston, Esq. Jun. F.S.A. High Street, Warwick.
Mrs. Fitzmaurice, Drayton Green, Ealing.
(c.) John Lewis Ffytche, Esq. Thorpe Hall, Louth.
Hamilton Field, Esq. Clapham Park.
Paul Hawkins Fisher, Esq. Stroud.
(c.) Rev. William Fletcher, D.D. Wimborne, Dorset.
(c.) Thomas William Fletcher, Esq. F.R.S. F.S.A. Lawneswood House, Stourbridge.
John Forster, Esq. LL.D. 19, Whitehall.
Hon. George Matthew Fortescue, 38, Grosvenor Square
Charles B. Fox, Esq. Malpas, Newport, Monmouthshire.
Francis F. Fox, Esq. Madeley House, 72, Pembroke Road, Clifton.
Charles Larkin Francis, Esq. 33, Gloucester Street, Pimlico.
(c.) Frederick J. Furnivall, Esq. M.A. 3, St. George's Square, Primrose Hill, N.W.

James Gairdner, Esq. Public Record Office, Fetter Lane.
S. Rawson Gardiner, Esq. M.A. *Director*, 22, Gordon Street, Gordon Square.
Henry H. Gibbs, Esq. 15, Bishopsgate Street, E.C.
William Gilbert, Esq. 14, Pembridge Gardens.
William Bulkeley Glasse, Esq. Q.C. 35, York Place, Portman Square.
Sir Stephen R. Glynne, Bart. F.S.A. Hawarden Castle, Flintshire.
(c.) Henry Gough, Esq. 10, Serjeants' Inn, Fleet Street.
Rev. S. Baring-Gould, East Mersea, Colchester.
Mrs. Everett Green, 100, Gower Street.
Benjamin Wyatt Greenfield, Esq. 4, Cranbury Terrace, Southampton.
Henry Gregory, Esq. Herne Hill, Dulwich.
J. Wyllie Guilde, Esq. 17, Park Terrace, Glasgow.
Rt. Hon. Russell Gurney, M.P. 1, Paper Buildings, Temple.
Frederick Gwatkin, Esq. 9, New Square, Lincoln's Inn.

MEMBERS OF THE CAMDEN SOCIETY.

Miss Hackett, 3, Manor Villas, Amhurst Road, Hackney.
Edward Hailstone, Esq. F.S.A. Lond. & Scot. Walton Hall, Wakefield.
(C.) Thomas Henry Hall, Esq. F.R.S. 16, Norfolk Crescent, Hyde Park.
William Douglas Hamilton, Esq. Public Record Office, Fetter Lane.
The Right Hon. Lord Hanmer.
Lady Frances Vernon-Harcourt, The Homme, Weobley.
(C.) Joseph Alfred Hardcastle, Esq. M.P. 54, Queen's Gate Terrace, S.W.
William Henry Hart, Esq. F.S.A. The Cedars, Overcliff, Rosherville, Kent.
Sir Joseph H. Hawley, Bart. Leybourne Grange, near Malling, Kent.
Frank Scott Haydon, Esq. Public Record Office, Fetter Lane.
R. W. Heslop, Esq. Ripon.
Henry Gay Hewlett, Esq. 24, Spring Gardens.
Wm. Oxenham Hewlett, Esq. 2, Raymond's Buildings, Gray's Inn.
G. F. Heywood, Esq. 25, Piccadilly, Manchester.
Henry Hill, Esq. F.S.A. 2, Curzon Street, May Fair.
(C.) Rev. Herbert Hill, M.A. King's School, Warwick.
(C.) Robert Holland, Esq. M.A. 64, Great Cumberland Place.
Miss Holt, 42, Gordon Square, S.W.
A. J. Beresford Hope, Esq. M.A. M.P. 1, Connaught Place, Edgware Road.
Charles Hopkinson, Esq. M.A. 74, Eccleston Square.
Rev. James Hughes, Dean, St. Patrick's College, Maynooth.
(C.) Richard Hussey, Esq. F.S.A. Harbledown, Canterbury.

(C.) Cosmo Innes, Esq. Inverleith, Edinburgh.

(C.) Rev. L. W. Jeffray, Wynlass Beck, Windermere.
Rev. Augustus Jessopp, M.A. School House, Norwich.
James Jones, Esq. The Oaklands, near Tarporley.
(C.) Joseph Jones, Esq. Abberley Hall, Stourport, Worcestershire.

Rt. Hon. Sir Richard T. Kindersley, M.A. Clyffe, Dorchester, Dorset.
Alfred Kingston, Esq. *(Secretary)*, Public Record Office, Fetter Lane.

David Laing, Esq. F.S.A. Scot. Edinburgh.
Philip Lang, Esq. Poltimore, Exeter.
J. Bailey Langhorne, Esq. Outwood Hall, Wakefield.
Charles Lawson, Esq. 35, George Square, Edinburgh.
J. D. Leader, Esq. Independent Office, Sheffield.
George Cornwall Legh, Esq. M.P. 6, St. James's Place.
Rev. Henry Richard Luard, M.A. 4, St. Peter's Terrace, Cambridge.

John Whitefoord Mackenzie, Esq. 16, Royal Circus, Edinburgh.
Rev. George R. Mackerness, M.A. Ilam Vicarage, Ashbourne.
(c.) David Mackinlay, Esq. 6, Great Western Terrace, Hillhead, Glasgow.
Robert Malcomson, Esq. Bennekerry Lodge, Carlow, Ireland.
Sir John Maclean, F.S.A. Pallingswick Lodge, Hammersmith.
Messrs. Macmillan and Co. Cambridge.
Robert Bullock Marsham, Esq. D.C.L. Merton College, Oxford.
Charles A. J. Mason, Esq. India Office, Whitehall.
His Excellency George Buckley Matthew.
W. G. Medlicott, Esq. Long Meadow, Massachusetts.
(c.) J. Miland, Esq. Clairville, Lansdown Road, Wimbledon.
Captain Mildmay, 19, Charles Street, Berkeley Square.
Right Hon. Lord Monson, 40, Belgrave Square.
Stuart A. Moore, Esq. 123, Chancery Lane.
Octavius S. Morgan, Esq. M.P. F.R.S. F.S.A. 10, Charles Street, St. James's.
Jerom Murch, Esq. Bath.
Charles Robert Scott-Murray, Esq. F.S.A. Danesfield, Great Marlow.

Richard Neave, Esq.
Mr. J. Newman, 235, High Holborn.
(c.) George Whitlock Nicholl, Esq. The Ham, Cowbridge, Glamorganshire.
John Gough Nichols, Esq. F.S.A. Treasurer of the Surtees Society, Holmwood Park, near Dorking.
Robert Cradock Nichols, Esq. F.S.A. F.R.G.S. 5, Sussex Place, Hyde Park.

MEMBERS OF THE CAMDEN SOCIETY.

Francis Morgan Nichols, Esq. M.A. F.S.A. Lawford Hall, Manningtree, Essex.
(c.) Rev. William L. Nichols, M.A. The Woodlands, Kilton, Bridgewater.
T. C. Noble, Esq. 79, Great Dover Street.
Most Hon. the Marquess of Northampton, M.A. Castle Ashby, near Northampton.

George Ormerod, Esq. D.C.L. F.R.S. F.S.A. Sedbury Park, Chepstow.
Rev. Sir Frederic A. Gore Ouseley, Bart. Mus.Doc. M.A. St. Michael's, Tenbury, Worcestershire.
Frederic Ouvry, Esq., Treas.S.A., 12, Queen Anne Street, Cavendish Square.

William Dunkeley Paine, Esq. Reigate.
Rev. Fielding Palmer, M.A. East Cliff, Chepstow.
W. M. Parker, Esq. Turk Street, Alton, Hants.
(c.) Anthony Parkin, Esq. Sharrow Bay, Penrith.
Rev. John P. Parkinson, D.C.L. F.S.A. Ravendale, Great Grimsby.
Lieut.-Colonel Pasley, R.E. H. M. Dockyard, Chatham.
George Peel, Esq. Brookfield, Cheadle, Cheshire.
Right Hon. Lord Penrhyn, Penrhyn Castle, Bangor, North Wales.
(c.) James Orchard Phillipps, Esq. F.R.S. F.S.A. 6, St. Mary's Place, West Brompton.
Lewis Pocock, Esq. F.S.A. 70, Gower Street.
Rev. William Poole, M.A. Hentlands, near Ross.
Right Hon. the Earl of Powis, LL.D. 45, Berkeley Square.
(c.) Osmond de Beauvoir Priaulx, Esq. 8, Cavendish Square.
S. E. Bouverie Pusey, Esq. Farringdon, Bucks.

Frederick John Reed, Esq. Hasness, Cockermouth.
Henry Reeve, Esq. F.S.A. Privy Council Office.
(c.) Ralph Richardson, Esq. M.D. Foley Cottage, Hampton Road, Redland, Bristol.
Edward Rimbault, Esq. Mus.Doc. 29, St. Mark's Crescent, Gloucester Road, Regent's Park.

The Most Hon. the Marquess of Ripon, K.G. D.C.L. F.R.S. 1, Carlton Gardens, S.W.
Messrs. Rivington and Co. Waterloo Place.
Rev. Charles John Robinson, M.A. Norton Canon Vicarage, Weobley.
(c.) Very Rev. the Dean of Rochester, The Deanery, Rochester.
Dr. Rogers, 34, Paul Street, Exeter.
Thomas E. Rogers, Esq. Yarlington, Wincanton.
Right Hon. Lord Romilly, M.A. 14, Hyde Park Terrace.
Walter Rye, Esq. 4, Craven Terrace, East Hill, Wandsworth.

Henry Sargant, Esq. 2, Stone Buildings, Lincoln's Inn.
Thomas Bush Saunders, Esq. M.A. Priory, Bradford-on-Avon, Wilts.
William Scott, Esq. Kington House, Northfleet, Kent.
Evelyn Philip Shirley, Esq. M.A. Lower Eatington Park, Stratford-on-Avon.
Rev. Thomas Short, B.D. Oxford.
Messrs. Simpkin and Co. 4, Stationers' Hall Court.
Mr. Skeet, 10, King William Street, Strand.
C. B. Slingluff, Esq. Baltimore.
Sydney Smirke, Esq. R.A. F.S.A. 7a, Whitehall Yard.
George Frederick Smith, Esq. 15, Golden Square.
H. Porter Smith, Esq. Sheen Mount, East Sheen.
Mr. W. J. Smith, North Street, Brighton.
William Wyke Smith, Esq. Metropolitan Board of Works.
William Smyth, Esq. Methven Castle, Perth.
Mr. H. Sotheran, 136, Strand.
(c.) Samuel Spalding, Esq. 147, Drury Lane.
James Spedding, Esq. 80, Westbourne Terrace.
Rev. George C. Stenning, M.A. Hobarton, Dover Street, Ryde, Isle of Wight.
Miss M. S. Stokes, Tyndale House, Cheltenham.
(c.) Right Rev. the Lord Bishop of St. David's, Abergwili, Carmarthen.
Hon. Sir John Stuart, 12, Old Square, Lincoln's Inn.
John Sykes, Esq. M.D. Doncaster.

MEMBERS OF THE CAMDEN SOCIETY.

Rev. Wm. Hepworth Thompson, D.D. F.S.A. Master of Trinity College, Cambridge, Trinity Lodge, Cambridge.
William John Thoms, Esq. F.S.A. 40, St. George's Square, Pimlico.
Joseph William Thrupp, Esq. 50, Upper Brook Street.
J. Tolhurst, Esq. 60, Tooley Street, S.E.
T. G. Tomkins, Esq. Great Ouseburn, Yorkshire.
Geo. Montgomery Traherne, Esq. St. Hilary, near Cowbridge, South Wales.
Sir John S. Trelawny, Bart. M.P. Trelawny, Liskeard, Cornwall.
Sir Charles E. Trevelyan, K.C.B. 8, Grosvenor Crescent, Belgrave Square.
Sir Walter Calverley Trevelyan, Bart. M.A. F.S.A. Wallington, Newcastle-on-Tyne.
Robert Samuel Turner, Esq. 1, Park Square, Regent's Park.
(c.) Edward Tyrrell, Esq. Birkin Manor, Horton, Slough.
(c.) J. Robert Daniel-Tyssen, Esq. F.S.A. Lower Rock Gardens, Brighton.

(u.) Sir Harry Verney, Bart. M.P. Claydon, Bucks.
Gabriel Vrignon, Esq. 119, Harley Street.

William Elyard Walmisley, Esq. 11, Cavendish Road, St. John's Wood.
Charles Walton, Esq. Manor House, East Acton.
(c.) Right Hon. the Earl of Warwick, Stable Yard, St. James's.
Very Rev. the Dean of Westminster, M.A. V.P.S.A. The Cloisters, Westminster.
Baron Van de Weyer, 21, Arlington Street.
John Weld, Esq.
James Whatman, Esq. M.A. F.R.S. F.S.A. M.P. 6, Carlton Gardens.
Ignatius Williams, Esq. The Grove, Bodfary, Denbigh.
(c.) Rev. John Wilson, D.D. F.S.A. Woodpery, Oxfordshire.
Joshua Wilson, Esq. Congregational Library, Bloomfield Street.
Charles Winn, Esq. Nostel Park, Wakefield.
Richard Henry Wood, Esq. F.S.A. Crumpsall, Manchester.
Sir Albert W. Woods, Garter King of Arms, F.S.A. 69, St. George's Road, Pimlico.

Rev. Adolphus F. A. Woodford, Swillington Rectory, Leeds.
Henry Workman, Esq. Manor House, Charlton, near Pershore, Worcester.
Francis Worship, Esq. Yarmouth.
Rev. John Reynell Wreford, D.D. F.S.A. 19, Richmond Terrace, Clifton.
William Battie Wrightson, Esq. 22, Upper Brook Street.
Messrs. D. Wyllie and Son, Aberdeen.

LIBRARIES.

Astor Library, New York.
Athenæum Club.
Bank of England Library.
Berlin Royal Library.
Birmingham Public Library.
Birmingham Free Library.
Bolton Public Free Library.
Boston Athenæum.
Bradford Subscription Library.
Bishop's College, Bristol.
Brown University, Providence, Rhode Island.
Canterbury Dean and Chapter Library.
Cheltenham Permanent Library.
Chetham Library, Manchester.
Christ College, Cambridge.
Congress Library, Washington.
Cornell University.
Devon and Exeter Institution.
Dover Proprietary Library.
Durham University.
Edinburgh Free College Library.
Edinburgh University Library.
Edinburgh, Library of the Writers to Signet.
Glasgow University Library.
Gottingen University Library.
The Hon. Society of Gray's Inn.
Hackney Reading Society.
Hamburg City Library.
Harvard College, Massachusets.
House of Commons' Library.
Hull Subscription Library.
Royal Irish Academy.
King's Inns Library, Dublin.
King's College Library, Cambridge.
Law Institution.
Leeds Library.
Leeds Public Libraries.
Leicester Literary and Philosophical Society.
Hon. Society of Lincoln's Inn.
City of London Library.
London Institution.
London Library.
Manchester Free Library.
Marburg University Library.
Munich Royal Library.
National Library, Paris.
Newcastle-on-Tyne Literary and Philosophical Society.
Norwich Dean and Chapter Library.
Norwich Literary Institution.
Oxford and Cambridge Club.
Oxford Union Society.
Owens College, Manchester.
Peabody Institute, Baltimore.
Library Company of Philadelphia.
Preston Library.
Providence Athenæum, Rhode Island.
Reform Club.
Royal Institution.
Royal Library.
Sacred Harmonic Society.
Science and Art Deparment, South Kensington.
Sheffield Library.
Sion College Library.
Stonyhurst College.
St. Andrew's University.
St. Catharine's College, Cambridge.
St. John's College, Cambridge.
Sydney Free Public Library.
The Hon. Society of the Inner Temple.
Trinity College, Cambridge.
Tubingen Library.
Vienna Imperial Library
Virginia State Library.
Warwickshire Natural History and Archæological Society.
Watkinson Library, Connecticut.

www.ingramcontent.com/pod-product-compliance
Lightning Source LLC
Chambersburg PA
CBHW031958230426
43672CB00010B/2191